My Main Obsession

My Main Obsession

by

Ricardo Guardia Vázquez

Safari Press

Guardia Vázquez, Ricardo

Second edition

Safari Press

2013, Long Beach, California

ISBN 978-1-57157-429-9

Library of Congress Catalog Card Number: 2012931140

10 9 8 7 6 5 4 3 2 1

Printed in China

This book is dedicated to the loving memory
of my maternal grandmother,
Amalia Dent,
who, after trying to dissuade me by every means
from making my first safari to Mozambique—
certainly I would get eaten, trampled, or gored by
some ferocious beast—contributed financially
to make it possible.

Table of Contents

Introduction: A Breed Apart

In a culture that places maximum value on comfort and convenience, it is strange to be a hunter. When I attend a party or social gathering and someone finds out about my inclinations, I am viewed as something different, something set apart. Inevitably, questions follow.

- "You mean you would rather go to British Columbia or Montana and pay more to freeze your butt off there than to go to New York City and dine in the best restaurants and attend the best plays?"

- "Are you saying you have guns and shoot animals for pleasure?"

I guess I was born with some instinct toward hunting and wild animals, for my vaguest memories are of my nanny taking me to the zoo. We went almost every single day; fortunately, it was under a half-mile from home. To this day when I revisit the old zoo, still in the same place, the smell immediately transports me back fifty years. I can visualize myself holding tightly to my nanny's hand, watching the lions, tigers, cougars, and jaguars in awe and admiration. They fascinated me then, and they still have the power to captivate me today.

I clearly remember my fifth birthday, for my grandmother gave me a large wooden box with a sliding glass door about a yard square to use for my collections. The pleasure it provided me as I slowly filled it with butterflies, moths, and beetles of all shapes, colors, and sizes was indescribable! To this day, the desire to be a collector remains as strong as ever, albeit for bigger animals.

As time went by, I also became fascinated by firearms. I nagged my father until he gave me a .22 Remington for my eleventh birthday, which I was supposed to load only with one round for safety reasons. And he never let me have a BB gun on the grounds that I would lose respect and become careless with firearms. That was the turning point in my life, and after that, I became an ardent, dedicated, and maybe even slightly obsessed hunter. Hunting became a way of being and has remained so to this day. I cannot imagine my life without the anticipation of my next trip, be it a morning pigeon shoot or a full-fledged safari to the Dark Continent.

I shot my first deer—a tropical whitetail—during my high-school years. I must confess that my enthusiasm was somewhat tinged by sadness at the

death of that beautiful animal. Fortunately, it was a one-shot kill, for I don't think I could have endured a wounded animal. The mixed feeling has never left me, and I still loath the hunter who shows no respect for his quarry and who inflicts unnecessary pain. I guess that is why I have never considered bow hunting. I suppose this is also why I have never hunted with dogs, not only because of the panic it must generate in the prey, but also because I cannot convince myself that it is sporting to shoot a helpless animal out of a tree. I know the reason is very subjective and other hunters may criticize me, but again, hunting is a lonely sport practiced for your own personal satisfaction.

If I shoot a big-game animal, it is because it deserves a place in my trophy room. This rationale has kept me from collecting many inferior specimens that would shame me. That first white-tailed buck wasn't very good, but it was my first one and it's still in my trophy room.

Being an attorney by trade and with a logical mind, I learned first to justify hunting to myself and then to those who oppose it. But as only the nonsmokers can blame the smokers, only the vegetarians can blame the hunters! But even the vegetarians probably never ask themselves if the tree feels the lumberjack's ax, the wheat the reaper, or the lettuce the knife. And yet, plants are as alive as we are.

I believe anyone who eats a steak or dines on fish and yet anathematizes the hunter is like a communist driving a Mercedes Benz. A code of ethics, however modest, does not permit us to remain on both sides of the fence. The fisherman is rarely questioned, although the sport represents the quintessence of cruelty. The fish is hooked through the lips or gills, battled to exhaustion for hours on end, and finally thrown onto a boat to slowly and relentlessly asphyxiate. Oh, but fish are not mammals like us, they're slimy and ugly and don't cry out. Because there is less anthropomorphism, fishermen are not as harassed as are hunters!

The fact is, man was created omnivorous. He was designed to eat flesh. That is why we have pointed canine teeth to tear the meat we eat—not unlike tigers and wolves—prehensile thumbs to grasp our prey, and predator eyes set on the front of our face to give us detailed vision. Our eyes are unlike those of deer and antelope that are set on the sides of their heads to give them peripheral vision that is so necessary to escape predators.

If hunting is morally wrong, Christianity is morally wrong too. After the flood, God said to Noah that every beast, every fowl, and every fish

would fear man and that all of them he delivered to man. "Every moving thing that liveth shall be meat for you; even as the green herb have I given you all things." (Genesis 9:2–3) Nimrod was praised as a mighty hunter. (Genesis 10:9). Esau was praised as a cunning hunter, a man of the field. (Genesis 25:27)

And then there are those among us who would eat one kind of meat but not another. These are the hypocrites who argue that it is more virtuous to kill and eat a beautiful innocent white calf than to kill a fat buck and eat it. Indeed, man must kill in order to eat. Sentiment cannot prevail over reason.

The fact is that man has always been a predator, born and bred with the physical build and natural instinct to kill and eat flesh. There is hardly a human being alive in this world today who is not, directly or indirectly, responsible for killing animals. I don't think Adolf Hitler killed anybody himself, yet it would be extremely difficult to argue that he is not responsible for the over twenty million deaths attributed directly to him.

It really makes no difference at all to an animal whether he is killed to feed somebody, to be mounted on the wall, or for the thrill of the chase. All are purely selfish motives. As selfish as the motives of an antihunter when he eats a steak or buys a new pair of shoes. It doesn't make much sense to be selfish about your belly and unselfish about the decorations on your trophy-room walls!

It was the great American president Theodore Roosevelt who put it more eloquently than I can ever expect to when he said: "There is no need to exercise much patience with men who protest against field sports unless, indeed, they are logical vegetarians. If it is morally right to kill an animal to eat its body, then it is morally right to kill it to preserve its head." (Roosevelt was, by the way, the founder of the first national park in history, Yellowstone National Park.) As far as I am concerned, I would much sooner become a vegetarian than relinquish my trophy collection or my firearms, for that matter.

To the really ardent hunter, hunting is an instinct. And as with all our instincts, they need to be controlled through discipline and education and wise game laws. And just as we loath and despise the criminal who satisfies his sexual desires by raping a school girl, we should also express our profound contempt for the game-hog who shoots a dozen white-lipped peccaries from the perch of a tree.

If animals and hunting are to survive, a high level of education is imperative. Closed seasons have to be strictly observed, laws strongly enforced, and bag limits closely controlled. This is why hunters have created game laws and game preserves throughout the world—to protect the game. It was Theodore Roosevelt in North America, Selous and Ionides in Africa, Jim Corbett in India, and King Alphonse XIII in Europe who helped educate others about conservation. And I contributed my drop in the ocean by drafting the game and gun laws that govern my country. And I don't remember getting any help from the antihunters!

Ni tan ignorante que no escribiera un cuento
ni tan desconsiderado que escribiese muchos.

Baltasar Gracián 1601–1658

(Not so ignorant that he could not write a story
or so inconsiderate as to write too much)

A Change of Game

Chapter 1

Had I known that Gerardo Gutiérrez was going to change my game plan, I wouldn't have gone deer hunting! Not only did I fail to get a buck, I nearly ended up in a hell of a mess. . . .

Mr. McAlpin had recently sold Chapernal Ranch in the province of Puntarenas in northern Costa Rica to a Cuban, who didn't care much about patrolling it, unlike the previous owner. Talk about the news reaching the poachers! After more than thirty years of working to build up the herd, suddenly the situation became a free-for-all. Poachers were having a permanent field day, and vultures gorged themselves on the remains of the deer, which were mainly shot at night. I pleaded before the Game Department but to no avail.

There were still a few guards and Gerardo was one of them, but there was little they could do against the onslaught. To make matters worse, the Cuban couldn't have cared less about the deer. Now it took me at least another half-hour to reach the ever-receding edge of the forest. It's amazing how much land can be cleared by two Caterpillars in a few short months.

It appeased me somewhat to have silence return to the jungle as the operators killed the engines of their noisy contraptions. It was now 4 PM and maybe, without the hideous racket, a big buck would step out to feed in the open. We would hunt until dark and then take the main road, which bisected the ranch, back to the house and my car. It was a hot and balmy afternoon with the ubiquitous mosquitoes droning monotonously around us. I ended up not shooting anything—the main reason being that, because I hated to compare myself to the scavengers who were depleting the land, I would probably have shot only a real trophy buck. I shuddered at the "empty forest" concept so vividly described and criticized by Teddy Roosevelt.

As the orange sun sank behind the western horizon, we stopped by an unpolluted stream to water the horses and wash the sweat from our faces and arms. We were both tired and disgusted.

It surprised me to see the lights of the ranchhouse in the distance—they had been invisible on other trips. Then I realized that all the intervening trees had been cut. . . .

As we rounded a bend in the road, Gerardo stopped his horse and stood in the stirrups. A couple of hundred yards away, two powerful lights danced in the gloom of the tropical night.

"Poachers," Gerardo whispered between clenched teeth. "Let's go get them."

I didn't have much time to think whether it was a good or bad idea—before I could say anything, Gerardo was on his way. All I could do was follow. We dismounted when we had cut the distance in half. I gave Gerardo a powerful four-battery flashlight and pulled my Sako .308 from my saddle scabbard. It had rained and the wet, tilled soil completely muffled our approach.

The two men were so immersed in their jacklighting that they were completely unaware of our presence. At ten yards Gerardo beamed the light on their faces while I yelled: "Rural Guards, you're under arrest!" The two poachers froze momentarily, paralyzed with fear.

I took advantage of the moment and ordered Gerardo in a gruff voice: "Lieutenant, confiscate their weapons." Briskly Gerardo covered the few feet that separated us and extricated a .22 rifle and a shotgun from the poachers' hands.

I was feeling as tough as Dirty Harry until I got a dose of my own medicine: The unmistakable sound of a round being fed into the chamber of a lever-action rifle caused my heart almost to stop as the night lit up behind me. I turned in panic to see the looming figure of what appeared to be a huge man with a beard. Mind you, I don't really know if he was huge or not, but he certainly looked that way behind his headlight. And besides, the ominous short barrel of a .30-30 pointed at my guts didn't do much for my self-confidence.

I somehow controlled the almost irresistible urge to get the hell out of there and the predicament I had gotten myself into. And to think they weren't even my deer!

I paused for a few seconds while my soul reentered my body and I regained my composure. I tried to swallow but for some reason found my mouth quite dry. Instead I cleared my throat and repeated the line about the rural guards and his being under arrest. I then ordered my newly

appointed lieutenant to confiscate his weapon. I guess it didn't sound very convincing, given that my subordinate didn't move.

"Mister," the man behind the light said as he took one menacing step forward, rifle at full cock, "you'll have to kill me if you want this gun."

It was a Mexican standoff as we faced each other for a few interminable seconds. I remember thinking that I should have shot Gerardo instead for getting me into this predicament. But then help came from where I least expected it.

"Carlos," said one of the two other poachers, "we're in enough trouble as it is. The captain is right. Give him your rifle."

He faltered for a few seconds but then said, "I will never turn in my rifle."

But I had noted his hesitation and took full advantage of the opportunity: "Then unload your weapon and give me the cartridges," I said. He hesitated.

"Now!" I ordered and stepped forward. He worked the lever five times and stepped back. "Lieutenant," I ordered, again sounding like Clint Eastwood, "recover the cartridges."

"Yes, captain," he acknowledged, and handed them over. We then marched single-file to the ranch headquarters, where the trespassers were picked up by the real rural guards, who arrived after a phone call from the ranch manager.

My only regret was that they didn't take my lieutenant with them. Permanently!

Pincer Tactic

Chapter 2

Tropical white-tailed deer hunting at Chapernal Ranch in northern Costa Rica could hardly have been any better! Its three or four thousand hectares (7,400 to 9,900 acres) of prime habitat were literally overrun with deer. More than once I had come to the ranch early and asked Gerardo Gutiérrez, my guide, to fetch the horses while I drove my Volkswagen station wagon along the ranch roads, only to return an hour later with a buck already in the back of my car.

Only my amigo Max Echandi and I were allowed on the premises. Over a dozen guards kept poachers off the ranch. We had a sweet deal and we kept our mouths shut. The deer season in Costa Rica ran from the first of July through the end of November, the first and third weekend of every month.

Thus we were allowed to hunt only two weekends per month. However, as most seasoned deer hunters know, hunting is lousy on the days of a full or a new moon. So we came to an agreement with the ranch owner allowing us to preselect the weekends we would hunt during that five-month period. We rationalized that hunting pressure would be exactly the same whatever weekends we chose, since we were the only hunters on the ranch.

Ah, but envy is a terrible thing! Someone informed the Game Department that we weren't hunting exactly by the book. Now, the game wardens never came to this ranch, because they knew it was properly managed, but it was different if a formal complaint was made.

One day Max, Gerardo, and I were riding our horses at a leisurely pace early in the afternoon, when we rounded a bend. Before we realized what was happening, we were surrounded by fully uniformed Rural Guards, .30 caliber M1 carbines firmly in their hands. I felt a knot tighten in my gut and remained speechless. Gerardo likewise froze in his tracks.

It was Max's voice that broke the deathly silence: "Who is in command?" he asked.

"I am," a heavily moustached guard answered as he stepped up.

"About time," Max answered in an unfaltering voice. "It's the first sign the government is doing something about the poaching going on at this ranch."

The man nodded. Max seized the opportunity: "We are going to employ a pincer movement and catch the poachers when they come in from the estuary. I have not had enough men for this until today."

"Lieutenant," he continued, "you and your men cover the left flank. My men and I will cover the right side of the estuary." To my utter amazement, the military training in the lieutenant kicked in and he followed instructions to the letter.

"Behind me," he ordered his men, who followed him without question.

So much for military intelligence!

Gerardo and I quickly followed our commander to the right, pushing our steeds as fast as we could.

But we had picked a good weekend for hunting. As luck would have it, we hadn't gone half a mile when a splendid six-pointer came boiling out of a patch of *zarza* bush (mulberry), startled by the trot of our horses. I leaned back to watch him run. Max piled off his horse in a flash and yanked his scoped .270 out of its scabbard. I couldn't believe he would dare shoot. But he did. Not once, but twice. The buck did a double somersault and disappeared in the *jaragua* grass (Hyparrhenia) as the shots reverberated in the distance. The reaction from the lieutenant was immediate. He was slow, but this time he caught what was going on. From his shouts in the distance, we surmised it had dawned on him that the two shots were not part of the pincer strategy.

We threw the deer carcass on Gerardo's horse and took off at a dead run. I kept hoping that the lieutenant's legs would be as slow as his brains!

We made it to Max's Range Rover and threw the ungutted buck inside, where we covered it with our raincoats. And we didn't stop until we got home.

And we made darned sure after that day to hunt only the right weekends!

Leopard at Dusk

Chapter 3

I couldn't believe my eyes as Peter and I looked over the partly eaten remains of the warthog I had shot the previous evening and which Danjero and John, two of the camp's staff, had managed to lodge in the crotch of a yellow fever tree. We had been hanging baits all over the place for the last thirteen days, but with no luck. Peter Faull, my professional hunter, had carefully selected the most promising places in wooded areas near water, but so far our efforts had been fruitless. To be sure, a couple of *chui*s had come to two of the baits, the last having carried away the live goat we had put there to draw him in, but both had failed to return. We had waited anxiously for long hours in complete silence, but only hyenas had looked hungrily at the hanging meat.

The warthog hanging there had been shot quite by accident. I had been left stranded in camp while Max Acosta, my hunting buddy from San José, Costa Rica, and Peter had gone to look for a buffalo. By 5 PM I had become restless and decided to go for a walk near camp with two of the camp boys. At dusk, which comes around seven, I had managed to flush a small band of warthogs and drop the smallest in the dim light. Disappointed with the poor trophy, I decided to hang it in the big tree so we could use it for bait in a suitable area the next day. For some reason, it had never occurred to us to bait a short mile from camp.

By closely examining the claw marks on the tree trunk, Peter was able to determine that it wasn't a very big leopard, probably a female, but I couldn't afford to get choosy on the seventeenth day of my twenty-one day safari in Kenya. After all, opportunity seldom knocks twice at the same door. Besides, it had been hard enough to get the necessary permit on the grounds that the cat was a stock killer.

The tree happened to be just perfect for the purpose of baiting: It was on the edge of a clearing in the forest, and after a little trimming, everything was set. Maybe *chui* would offer a perfect shoulder shot, silhouetted against the eastern sky.

Peter personally supervised the construction of the blind, located sixty long paces from the bait tree at the base of a large thornbush. In the process, he asked if I had any suggestions.

"I want no excuses when you miss the bastard," he said.

I took him literally and had the driver go back to camp for a folding armchair—"the one that squeaks the least," I advised him. I not only wanted to be comfortable so that I could be absolutely silent, which I found difficult in a standing position, but I also wanted a two-point hold for that all-important one-shot kill I had traveled more than twelve thousand miles to take. From experience, I had found out that there is no better cure for buck fever, a malady that sometimes haunts me, than a good solid rest.

Once the chair was in the blind, Guario, the head tracker, put the finishing touches on my peephole. I was able to leave my rifle resting on its base, pointing in almost the exact direction of the bait. Care was taken to remove every leaf from the floor of the structure, and every twig that stuck out from the sides was trimmed on the inside to prevent any unnecessary noise. The faint breeze was blowing from the bait to our faces, and the small blind entrance through which we would have to crawl to get in would be covered by a branch from a similar bush. We would be completely invisible from the outside, save for the protruding barrel of my .308 Sako rifle.

With our work finished by midmorning, we replenished the bait with a fat baboon to make it more attractive, scouted the area in the Jeep for other possible game, and were back in camp by noon. There I paced off sixty yards and fired a couple of my 180-grain Remington Core-Lokt bullets at a paper target; they struck a half-inch high at that range. When the time came, I would hold right on. A meticulous man, I kept wondering what else I could do to shorten the odds, but nothing else came to my mind.

During lunch Peter pointed out that leopards, although nocturnal, come to bait while there is still daylight. They do this to avoid hyenas, which are strictly night creatures and of which they are deathly afraid. He also mentioned that I should make every effort to kill the leopard dead under the tree—not only because tracking a wounded leopard can be hazardous to your health but also because, as he put it, "I wouldn't have enough skin to put around my hat" if the hyenas found the cat before we did.

After lunch everybody decided to take a nap, but I was too excited for that. Instead I shaved and took a good bath; I wanted to sort of dress up for the occasion!

By 5 PM we were on our way, and a few minutes later I was crawling into the blind with Peter right behind me carrying his .458 double, the kind of backup gun that every self-respecting professional owns. Guario took pains to close the small door completely. We were taking no chances on being seen by a bait-circling leopard.

I eased the rifle through the peephole and sat back on the chair, the sweet odor of the dry grass blowing gently against my face. Every few minutes I leaned slightly forward and checked the empty branch against the fading light. No way would I miss the trophy I had come so far to collect at sixty yards. No way . . . I hoped.

The silence was broken only by the barking of the ubiquitous baboons, a troop of which had decided to roost along the trees bordering the same river that flowed through camp. A herd of impala grazed so close to us we could hear the grass snap. Guario had done a good job, however, and they were invisible behind the wall of the blind. As the sun slid toward the west, myriad multicolored birds decided to spend the night on the small tree at whose base we had built the blind. As long as we kept motionless, they simply stared at us from a few feet away. I suppressed a burst of laughter when a dropping landed on the back of Peter's hand as he squatted on the ground.

Then the sun dropped behind the horizon and everything was silent: The birds ceased their singing while the night creatures had not yet begun their night greetings. A bright moon was clearly visible among the branches of the trees.

At seven I had about given up hope but nevertheless checked the warthog through the rifle's telescopic sight. Against the fading sky it was quite distinct, but only as a black form. Again I eased back in the chair and waited for those last few minutes to drift by so we could return to camp. I remember checking the bait twice during the next ten minutes—before I saw a rope dangling from the first crotch of the bait tree. Although we had used ropes to hoist the meat up the tree, wire had been used for the process of securing the bait. Through the riflescope I checked the spot and with a start discovered a leopard feeding on the offal we had left on the first crotch to arouse his appetite. In the fading light I could make out only a darker spot against the thinning branches of the other trees—the unorthodox critter was sitting on the "wrong" branch, and his body wasn't outlined against the eastern sky. The light was so poor that I couldn't distinguish one end from the other.

Gesturing and signaling—I don't think my voice would have come out anyway—I managed to convey to Peter that the leopard was there. After a long look through his light-gathering binocular, and seeming to read my mind, he finally said, "Take him in your own time, but don't wait for him to climb to the other branch—the light is fading fast and you may not be able to see him at all."

The posts of my German-made two-and-a-half-power Karl Kaps telescope were clearly visible, but I couldn't tell one end from the other on my intended fur piece. And I didn't have a loaf of bread in hand, like the blind man who fed it to the dog that had just bitten him in order to determine where his mouth was so he could kick him in the fanny. So I waited.

A few long seconds later *chui* raised his head to lick his chops and looked to one side. Against the light-colored trunk of the yellow fever tree, I could clearly see his outline. When he lowered his head again to resume feeding, I knew he was facing me. I centered the scope's pointed post just above the back of his neck and started the most careful trigger squeeze of my life. At the rifle's blast the leopard simply slid off the tree, dead before he hit the ground. I dimly remember frantically trying to get out of the blind and Peter patting me on the back and grinning broadly.

When I finally reached my fallen quarry I discovered that the bullet had hit exactly right, breaking the spine above the shoulders and exiting through the rump. He never heard the roar of the rifle.

Peter helped me position the spotted body across my back, and presently we walked triumphantly into camp.

After all the necessary photography, reconstructions, and congratulations, we handed the cat over for skinning and toasted with red wine to my luck. Thankfully, I didn't have to make any excuses for missing.

The Lazarus Buck

Chapter 4

Many years ago I read an article by noted author Warren Page in which he recounted the story of an elk he had shot in the Gros Ventre Range in Wyoming. Apparently, after the animal had been "dead" for five minutes, it had gotten up and walked away. The bullet had gone high through the withers without doing any permanent damage, only stunning the animal. I vaguely remember Page's frustration at having lost the animal he had worked so hard to collect—for he never caught up with it again. I never thought that a few years later I would go through a similar experience.

Early one Saturday morning my long-time hunting buddy Max Echandi and I had decided to go to a ranch named Poco Sol near the Nicaraguan border. I really wasn't too keen on going; the place was far away (by Costa Rican standards anyway), and I knew the locals hunted it heavily. Max finally convinced me to go on the grounds that a stock-killing jaguar was in the vicinity and we might just get a crack at him. Besides, we hadn't been in the area for quite some time, and we would hunt on a plateau where the weather would be nice and cool and there wouldn't be any mosquitoes. My only condition was that on the way back we would hunt for at least half a day at another ranch I knew just a two-hour drive from San José, and which at the time was crawling with deer.

As it turned out, Poco Sol was completely shot out and I managed to see only one doe during the entire hunt. The jaguar, of course, made himself scarce and all we could find were some old tracks. Max hadn't done much better.

Monday morning found us driving south along the Inter-American highway headed for home. Monday had already been lost as a working day, so I insisted that we stop at the ranch for which I had made plans initially. Max agreed but said it would have to be a short hunt—half an afternoon and we would head for home. We were dog-tired anyway!

By three o'clock our horses were saddled and ready and we departed on more or less parallel paths toward the lower and swampy side of the

ranch. Gerardo, the cowboy generally assigned to me as a guide, rode ahead, his skinny frame bouncing steadily to the trot of the horse.

It was a hot, clammy afternoon, and as we neared the patchy jungle, hordes of mosquitoes sank their red-hot needles into our naked arms and faces. I took the time to literally bathe in "Off," but some of the little bastards always managed to find a spot where I hadn't sprayed. Pretty soon I felt as if I had just been to a flea convention.

It was cooler under the canopy of trees through which we were riding, and it was one of those days when deer were moving. Apparently the mosquitoes were pestering them as much as they were us, and the whitetails were wagging their tails and kicking around, making them all that much more conspicuous. We saw does and fawns and spikes and white tails disappearing in the underbrush, but no big buck worth taking. We had to be especially careful on this ranch: Max and I were the only two hunters allowed there, on the promise that we would shoot only mature bucks—no spikes or forkhorns, which we didn't care for anyway.

We had agreed to each hunt a particular route and to meet at the horse shed when it was too dark to see. As it turned out, Gerardo and I finished our roundup a bit early, arriving at the starting point with a good half-hour to spare. About a mile away I saw Max in a bend of the trail, headed back.

That's when Gerardo mentioned that he had been seeing a big buck with what appeared to be an eight-point rack at the far end of the airstrip on the higher end of the ranch, and that we would have a better chance of collecting him if we went over there rather than sit here on our butts.

I was dead-tired by now but bought the idea that it would be better to wait for nightfall in a good hunting place rather than in a horse shed. Presently I found myself pushing my protesting steed toward the far end of the landing strip. Max would understand if I was a little late.

The brush and grass were about chest-high on three sides of the airstrip, and after going all around it, we had seen nothing. We exited the strip on the far side through a collapsing wooden gate and decided to head back using an abandoned gravel road that ran parallel to it. The sun had dipped behind the horizon a good half-hour before, a few crimson and golden cumulus clouds marking the place where it had disappeared. A few early whippoorwills were already beginning to whistle in the dark splotches of forest.

Gerardo and I were talking casually as the horse shed loomed ever closer. Suddenly I saw the head and horns of a buck pop up from the underbrush along the airstrip about a hundred yards away. I piled off the horse and yanked my .308 from its scabbard so fast the leather squeaked. Nobody had to tell me this was the buck we had been looking for. The bases of his horns were thick and black and grew somewhat backward, in a peculiar fashion; the main beams and the spikes were exceptionally long for a Costa Rican deer. As the center post of my German-made telescope began to settle on the neck, the buck decided his curiosity had been satisfied and ducked his head. I tried to follow his progress through the swaying grass, but could catch only glimpses of the sliding form. To make matters worse, two smaller deer, which looked like does, had joined the buck and were in the way. The animals were away from the trees and thick jungle and were not yet spooked, so I decided to try to get closer, hoping to get a clear shot where the brush thinned out in places. Besides, there was a sandy, dry stream bed that would muffle my approach. The air was dead calm.

As I tiptoed through the dry creek bed, my view was completely obliterated by the high grass on both sides. When I estimated I had cut the distance to my quarry in half, I carefully started to climb the bank, hoping to see the buck at any moment.

I held my rifle as you would a shotgun when the flush of a covey of quail is imminent. My mouth went dry, and I could feel my heart thumping with anticipation. As I topped the small rise I took four or five careful stops and stopped. Nothing! Another six or eight quicker paces and nothing yet.

Then it dawned on me that the buck had probably winded or heard me and was hightailing it to the next county. That's when I panicked and started running in the buck's general direction, tearing through the brush like a wounded buffalo. As I rounded a fallen tree covered with creepers, there stood my buck not more than thirty yards away, staring at me in amazement. I don't know which of us was more surprised, but he laid his ears back and took off like a turpentined tomcat, his bounds taking him high over the tall grass. I counted one, two, three bounds as the buck quartered away from me and on the third jump touched off a 180-grain Core-Lokt just ahead of him. I could see the orange tongue of fire spitting out the barrel of my Sako.

I cannot say I heard the bullet strike, but I did see my intended trophy go down. I took my eyes off the spot for only an instant as I bolted another shell into the chamber. I checked the surrounding area for movement, but nothing stirred. Shortly, I watched the two does scurry across the landing strip. Behind me I heard Gerardo bringing in the horses and commending me on a good shot—he had seen it all!

I walked triumphantly to the spot where my buck had fallen, ready to start counting points, but nothing—my buck was gone! With a knot in my guts, I advanced a little through the high grass, expecting to see my deer at any moment, but still nothing. Two hours later, with flashlights in hand, the three of us—Max had joined us—had to admit that we were licked. Though the place looked like the favorite pawing grounds of a herd of bull elk, my buck—like Lazarus in the Bible and Page's bull in his story—had risen from the dead.

We couldn't find any blood, much less tracks, in that thick stuff. Reluctantly I finally left the spot, but not before extracting from Gerardo a solemn promise to check the area in the morning and, if unsuccessful, every day after that until he located the buck by the presence of vultures. That way, I could at least save the antlers. A generous tip was offered to motivate the lad. Immediately upon finding the carcass, he was to inform me by telephone.

"They call it buck fever," Max commented on the way home, and I had to fight the urge to shoot him!

All day Tuesday I waited for Gerardo's call in desperation. Every time my phone rang I snatched it up without waiting for my secretary to do it, but alas, they were all business calls. Someone always wanted to know how his legal case was going or if his deed was ready. I didn't get much work done that day. My mind kept going back to the "dead" buck that had been swallowed by the earth. And I couldn't even call Gerardo myself. The only telephone in the area was a good hour's ride from his house. So, impatient, I had to wait.

When Friday finally came, I was as anxious as a lass awaiting a pregnancy report. I still hadn't received the call and I couldn't bear it any longer.

When I informed my wife that I would be leaving that weekend again, she howled like a soul in torment. Sunday was my birthday and she had arranged a small party with family and friends. I had better not leave to

look for another no-good, moth-eaten deer when I didn't have enough room to hang it on the wall anyway. Besides, I had missed the buck and I might as well face it. She usually wins such contests and she had good, solid arguments this time, but I just couldn't stay home. We finally agreed that I would leave early the next morning (Saturday), hunt until dark, and return home on the same day. That way I would be around on Sunday for my birthday party. Having left everything ready in my station wagon the night before, I found myself driving the Inter-American highway long before dawn on Saturday.

"I can't figure it out," Gerardo said as he greeted me with a cup of steaming coffee in the predawn. "I saw that bugger go down like a sack of bricks when you shot him. And yesterday, when I checked the spot for about the tenth time, there he was with his two does, healthier than a prizefighter. Now I really believe that he rose from the dead after the third day!"

The jungle around us was just beginning to wake up, flocks of parrots noisily greeting the rising sun, as we rode into it. Howler monkeys roared hoarsely in the swinging branches, occasionally silhouetted against the eastern sky. A few whippoorwills were still whistling in the darker spots. But beautiful as it was, my senses were concentrated on finding that buck again, a picture of him vividly fixed in my mind's eye.

Up and down the hills around the airstrip we went, without so much as a glimpse of a deer. They weren't moving this day. We went through the area where I had fired the week before and found the grass and bush still lying flat in some places. An empty pack of cigarettes told me Gerardo had checked the area as promised.

The thought flashed through my mind that if I didn't find "my" buck, Max just might decide to try for him the next weekend—and maybe succeed. After all, he was too lucky for my comfort, especially given that he knew the buck's haunts.

Noon found me trying to take a "siesta" under a mango tree to escape the hot sun, but the parrots perching on it insisted on keeping me awake. Mosquitoes, although less plentiful at midday, were doing their part too.

Shortly after three we were off again, the great Pacific Ocean shining bright blue in the distance. The plan was to ride around the ranch for a while and be in the area where I had shot the buck around five, when I knew I would have the best chance of seeing him.

When we again entered the territorial buck's domain and the faint breeze blew the sweet smell of grass into my nostrils, I again began to feel

the knot tighten in my guts. We rode into a small valley and there, about two hundred yards away, was my buck, his glossy coat shining bright in the slanting sun. He was off before I touched the ground and made it over the crest of the nearest hill before I could get a bead on him. I turned to Gerardo in despair, but he didn't seem too concerned.

"He wasn't really spooked," he said. "If we give him a little time, we may just find him in another little valley where I've seen him before and where the grass grows lush and green. But you will have to be quicker this time."

Knowing the buck would be watching his backtrail, we made a large circle and slowly entered the valley Gerardo had mentioned.

"Get ready," he said as the horses silently picked their way across the side of the hill. I slipped my rifle out of the scabbard and as noiselessly as possible fed a round into the chamber.

As we came around a clump of trees, there stood my buck about a hundred and fifty yards away. I jumped off the horse as the deer lowered his head like a dog and began to sneak behind a small hill. I took a few steps to one side, my arm tight in the rifle's sling and the safety catch in the off position. First I saw the antlers and then his back as the animal trotted briskly, still partially concealed by the rise. I remember holding high for fear of hitting the ground before me and saying a quick prayer.

As I recovered from the recoil, I could see nothing because of the lay of the land. Without even bothering to bolt in another cartridge, I ran like a madman toward where the buck had last been, and there he was, dead in his tracks, his back broken slightly behind the shoulders.

Although Gerardo and I checked him thoroughly after counting the nine points on his rack, we found no sign of the first shot. I guess I will have to live without an explanation of what happened on that first shot, which is much better than having a good explanation but no buck.

*Costa Rican deer are classified as *Odocoileus virginianus truei* but look very similar bodywise to a Coues deer, a mature buck averaging about 125 pounds on the hoof. They seldom grow more than eight points (eastern count), and such a set of antlers will be about ten inches in length.

The Singer, Not the Song

Chapter 5

I have always been leery about hunting on preserves, especially when the animals are fenced in. The only thing that gives full meaning to hunting, I have always held, is the possibility of failure. The moment the hunt loses its aleatory nature—its uncertainty—it becomes an execution. And I have never longed to work in a butcher shop!

But I wanted at least one sheep in my trophy room, and at the time, a Corsican ram didn't seem like a bad placebo. After all, they are supposed to be wild sheep from the island of Corsica in the Mediterranean Sea, and a true challenge to the most discriminating sportsman. And besides, I couldn't afford a Dall sheep hunt in the Yukon Territory. Another factor was that I could hunt these highly elusive beasts in the state of Florida, with Miami being the closest point of entry to the United States from Costa Rica.

Still, though, I wouldn't hunt if the animals were fenced in—that is, until I found a hunting preserve surrounded not by a cyclone fence but by water. Thus I could hunt on an island, in exactly the same habitat in which Corsican sheep are hunted in their native Corsica. Or so I convinced myself!

I rented a car in Miami and drove straight north on U.S. 95 for eight or nine hours, arriving at dusk at a roadside motel where I would spend the night. As arranged, my guide retrieved me at dawn and we proceeded to cross to the island. It sort of surprised me to find a working cattle ranch there, flat as a table and with few trees.

After a quick breakfast, I climbed up on the high seat placed on the bed of a pickup truck to start my hunt. My guide whispered in my ear as we rode around the featureless island that we should be absolutely silent or we would spook our wary quarry all the way back to their native island.

There is nothing easier in this world than to convince someone of something he is already predisposed to believe! And that balmy morning I desperately wanted to be convinced that I was on a real sheep hunt. Besides, the fresh morning air caressing my face felt much like the

African breeze I'd experienced on my first safari to Mozambique a few years back.

At least the island was big—it took us a good hour to arrive at the pasture where our intended quarry was calmly chewing its cud. To be sure, there were two Corsicans of similar size and color. When we were about two hundred and fifty yards away, my guide tapped the roof of the cab and the vehicle came to an abrupt stop.

"I dare not get any closer," my host informed me, "or they will bolt and we will never find them again. Do you think you can hit one from here?" I nodded as he checked the rams through his binocular.

"Take the one lying down," my guide ordered. "The horns look heavier." I leaned on the crossbar and took careful aim with my trusted Sako .308. At the report of the rifle, the ram rolled over and remained still. The next instant my guide was patting me on the back and congratulating me on the most remarkable shot he had witnessed during his entire guiding career. I nodded in agreement as the truck headed toward my prize. As we jumped out of the pickup, my guide with a steel tape in hand, I noticed three things:

- It was the first time during the entire hunt that I had gotten off the truck.
- There wasn't a speck of mud on my boots.
- The surviving ram kept chewing his cud from about ten yards away.

The guide noticed the look in my eye and was quick to say the sheep was undoubtedly very sick and unable to move. Again, I nodded in "agreement."

It was a lousy song throughout, but I'll tell you—the singer never lost a beat!

British Columbia or Bust

Chapter 6

When I finally gathered enough courage to inform my wife that I had booked a two-week hunt in northern British Columbia with outfitter Don Peck during the first half of September 1978, she screamed like a Sandinista just caught by Tacho Somoza's National Guard. After all, it hadn't been much more than a year since my Kenya safari, and it was now her turn to go shopping and to Disney World with the kids.

Everybody was against me! My little daughter looked at me with watery eyes, and my five-year-old boy promised to flunk kindergarten if he wasn't taken to see Mickey Mouse. A great aunt of mine went into a trance and predicted in Urdu that nothing good would come of my trip. My miniature Doberman bared her teeth and growled gutturally every time I walked into the house. But the deposit had been sent and the hunt was on, although I did manage to ease the tension by promising the Disney trip for the Christmas holidays.

As September drew ever closer, I increased my weekend trips to my dad's farm to check the zero on my new Sako 7mm Remington Magnum, topped by a 2½–8X Bushnell scope. After I adjusted the trigger to a two-pound pull, it printed consistent one-inch groups, three and a half inches high at one hundred meters with 175-grain Remington Core-Lokts. At least every other evening I took the time to run a good half-mile around my neighborhood.

The amigo with whom I was making the trip, Dr. Sergio Bonilla, a dentist by trade, was as anxious as I was. This was his first hunting trip abroad, and he never stopped asking questions about what to take along.

Finally, on the last day of August, we boarded the Lacsa plane in Costa Rica that would take us to Miami. From there we would continue through Denver to Seattle, where we would get the rest of our hunting equipment. (Insulated underwear, down jackets, and warm sleeping bags are as scarce in Costa Rica as pork chops in a Jewish restaurant.)

Eddie Bauer taken care of, we continued on to Vancouver, Fort St. John, and finally Fort Nelson, which looked exactly like a frontier town of the Old West. Next afternoon found us skirting the snow-clad peaks of the Rocky

Mountains, en route to what was to be our first camp: the Horse Range, as it was called. On a couple of silver lakes surrounded by purple timber we saw our first two moose; on both occasions I slammed my forehead against the window trying to get a better view of them.

Half an hour later we were met by Ross Peck, a tough-looking red-haired hombre with long hair and whiskers, who would be responsible for us two dudes during the next couple of weeks. Four Indians helped to unload our gear and sized us up with casual glances. Would we be able to take the hard hunt that lay ahead and prove our worth when the opportunity presented itself?

Shortly after, we were comfortably installed in a spacious log cabin with a cheerful fire burning in the fireplace. Next stop was an improvised range, and one round was all I needed to feel sure the zero of my rifle hadn't changed. It printed exactly three inches above the center of the paper target I had brought all the way from home. A few minutes later, a bull elk started bugling on a hill directly in front of us, and we were eventually able to locate him about a mile away with a spotting scope, his golden horns gleaming majestically in the last rays of the northern sun. A chill went down my spine again as he sent another shrill whistle echoing through the wilderness before he disappeared into the black pines.

Early next morning, after a hearty breakfast of pancakes and moose meat (which was to be our main diet during the duration of the hunt), I was assigned a Cree Indian named Lorne Letendre (I understand there was some French in him) as a guide. An Indian, he spoke very little.

When we finished saddling the horses, he ambled up to me, sized me up, and asked, "Can you ride?" His attitude bothered me a little, and I answered that this was the way I always hunted deer in Costa Rica and that I could ride as long as he could. When we got off the horses at about seven that night, I felt as though I had been through a meat grinder (quarterhorses definitely don't have the softest trot in the world), but I had earned new respect from Lorne.

In the meantime we had been checking an elk carcass a previous hunter had shot to see if a grizzly might have come to it. One had indeed, but we caught only a glimpse as it vanished into the willows as we approached. We decided to wait a while to see if the bear might return, and of course the only animals we saw were those for which I hadn't bought a license: timber wolves. As I looked through the scope at a huge black male casually sniffing

around about two hundred yards away, I cursed myself for not having spent the seventy-five bucks for the wolf license.

At dinner we were informed that we would be moving camp next day. Early next morning we set out with our two guides, Ross, a camp helper and his friendly wife, who was to be our cook, and a long string of packhorses through the most spectacular country I had ever seen. We would be following the path of the Tuchodi River, around which rose immense, snow-clad mountains, their foliage beginning to turn red and yellow in the early northern autumn. I cannot express the anticipation and excitement I felt at that moment as I stood in the stirrups and filled my lungs with the cool mountain air that blew gently on my face.

It was a long ride, a good twenty-five miles, and nightfall found us making camp by Greater Tuchodi Lake. The horses were hobbled, and soon I found myself being lulled to sleep by the tinkling of the bells tied to their necks.

Next morning broke clear and sunny, and on my suggestion, Ross sent Sergio and me ahead of the packstring with Lorne to scout for game. At about one o'clock we stopped by a small stream to have a bite. Somewhat concerned about how far away the next camp was, I asked Lorne. I should have known better!

"You'll know when we get there," he said, got on his horse, and rode off at a quick pace without so much as a backward glance. Sergio and I got on our horses and dug in our heels to keep up.

By midafternoon, as we were carefully negotiating a precarious trail on the side of a mountain, I happened to look up at the mountain opposite us and noticed half a dozen specks of white against a grassy bench far above timberline. I called to Lorne and pointed at the objects. He dug his field glasses from under his jacket and grunted.

"Them goats. We get one."

Down this mountain we went, our sure-footed horses negotiating the terrain like the game we were after, across the river, and up the face of the other mountain. After a good hour, we tied our steeds to a clump of willows and continued our climb on foot, using a small draw to keep out of sight on the steep slope. Since we had only one guide, we had tossed a coin for first shot and Sergio won. However, knowing that goats don't panic easily, I went along in the hope of also getting a shot. Lorne scampered ahead of us with great ease as we panted along behind on hands and knees, gasping in the thin mountain air. Every now and then he would look down on us, shake his

head, and say something like, "You gotta eat more moose meat—get tough like grizzly bear."

After another hour we had progressed as far as we could go—still a good four hundred yards from the goats, which had left the bench and bedded down for the night on a shale slide. A ten-minute rest brought our breathing back to normal.

Sergio decided on the goat farthest to the right. I decided on an animal in front of that one which appeared to have a good set of horns and looked somewhat stockier that the others. I took a good solid rest and waited for Sergio to fire. As his shot echoed across the mountain, my goat jumped up and looked nervously in our direction. With my scope at full power, I held on its back and touched one off. Shale flew between the goat's legs, and it started making its way up the treacherous mountain. Realizing that my intended trophy was farther away than I had estimated, I held a full body's depth above it, held my breath, and squeezed off another round. The animal fell and slowly slipped behind a rise in the ground.

"I got myself a goat!" I yelled in triumph. Sergio told me to shut up and jacked another shell into his chamber. His goat was trying to get up as he kept spraying it with lead. When I finally convinced him that his trophy wasn't going anywhere, he stopped the fusillade and we started across the steep mountainside. Lorne went with Sergio to help him finish off his goat.

It took me a good hour to navigate the four-hundred-plus yards to my billy. As I pulled myself up over a ledge, my goat got up and began to walk slowly away. The angle was so steep that I just eased down on my belly and whacked him on the shoulder. The animal hit the ground as if poleaxed and began rolling down the steep incline, creating a small avalanche in the process. I took a detour to reach him, praying that his horns had not broken in the two-hundred-yard fall. They hadn't, but as I stood there in a clump of willows admiring my hard-earned trophy, I raised my eyes in panic at a rumbling sound, just in time to see a boulder the size of my favorite couch back home headed straight for me. I jumped back, landing on my fanny, just in time to watch it go sailing by. The goat had almost had its revenge!

I still had the shakes when Lorne walked up to me to cape out the eight-inch billy. He informed me that Sergio was on his way down with a similar-size nanny.

We arrived in camp at about 9 PM under a steady drizzle, dog-tired but with a proud new concept of what a hard-earned trophy really means.

Two days later I connected on a really nice 52-inch, 19-point Canada moose, dropping him with two shots to the shoulder from 250 yards. It was over so fast and the animal was so huge that I had to keep touching the antlers to believe it.

We weren't very far from camp, so Lorne decided to go back to fetch a packhorse to carry out the meat and horns. He wasn't gone long, and soon I found myself helping him tie the hulking rack securely on top of the meat load on the horse's back.

The moose had been shot on a steep slope, and as we trotted downhill leading the packhorse by the halter rope, the horns jarred loose and one of the points dug into the steed's ribs. To say the results were spectacular is an understatement. The nag shot straight up into the air, bucking and kicking like a banshee. Meanwhile, my own palomino, after giving some serious thought to his buddy's predicament, decided that I must be responsible for not tying the moose rack properly. Snorting his disapproval, he likewise went into the bucking antic. The next thing I knew, I was sailing high over the dwarf willow, landing with a resounding thud in a shallow mud hole. The air was knocked completely out of my lungs and I couldn't get up. That's when Lorne walked his horse up to me and asked, "What's the matter, partner, lost a quarter?" and then trotted away. I cursed myself again for not having a redskin license!

Later in camp I casually asked Ross what would happen if someone broke a leg while hunting. His answer: "They shoot horses, don't they?"

During dinner he also mentioned that the palomino which had thrown me was a one-man horse. "Only problem," he added, "is we haven't been able to find the right man for him."

The very next day I was lucky enough to collect a beautiful silvertip grizzly sow with one shot through the shoulder at about one hundred yards.

The ninth of September found us high above timberline looking for a mountain caribou. For some reason I was extremely anxious to get one. The terrain soon got so rough that we had to dismount and lead our horses. Eventually we came to a wash of loose shale and large boulders. I thought there was no way we could cross with the horses. Lorne thought otherwise, and after considerable coaxing and cursing, he got his across. There was no way I could get my noble beast to risk it across the loose shale. His patience exhausted, Lorne got behind the animal and beat him with a stick while I pulled on the halter rope and coaxed him on. Finally the horse decided to

guts it and started across. When his feet slipped out from under him, I tried to stabilize him with the halter rope, but he was too heavy for me. He rolled about fifty yards down the draw, taking half the shale with him, and eventually stopped against a jack pine, all four feet in the air.

After quite some work, we managed to cut the jack pine and get the horse to stand up. He was quite bruised and bleeding profusely from a deep gash in the rump. Lorne tore off one of his shirtsleeves to try to stop the bleeding. It was, of course, out of the question to ride him, and three or four hours later we arrived in camp, me soaked to my thighs because I had to wade the horse across the Upper Tuchodi River.

In the meantime Sergio had also scored on a moose, so we decided to move camp to another area that was supposed to be more productive for caribou. It was a ten-hour ride, and we spent most of the next day getting there. The area consisted of rolling mountains covered with alpine fir and willows, which later gave way to the moss and lichens that are the caribou's main food. I never ceased to marvel at the vastness of this land—it just seemed never to end.

As things turned out, on our second day there Sergio made a spectacular 300-yard running shot on a smallish caribou, but all I was able to find were females and their young. Apparently the caribou hadn't yet started their migration and were making themselves scarce.

After another fruitless day, we decided to move camp again and split up. Because Sergio already had his caribou, he would go back to the Horse Range whereas I would give it one more try in an area called the Caribou Range. I was assigned Sergio's Indian guide, Amos Achla, because he apparently knew the area better. Amos and I departed with just one packhorse, loaded with our gear and food. This area, of course, proved to be only a few light years away, and after a thirteen-hour stroll (I later learned the distance was fifty miles), I welcomed the sight of a cozy log cabin built beside a swift-running river whose clear water sparkled in the last rays of the sun. After a hasty meal, my sleeping bag had never felt so good.

Early next morning we were up and away at dawn. We had only two days left—caribou season would close the next day (15 September). Not far from the cabin we began seeing caribou cows and calves; they would stare at us curiously, or move away with their peculiar springy trot, their little white tails held straight up. But again, no bulls. Apparently the cows and young begin their migration first and there wasn't a bull in sight. Nightfall found

us sitting gloomily by the cabin stove, with nothing to show for our efforts. But I wasn't licked yet. Tomorrow would be another day, and there had to be a bull somewhere in the crowd. I kept reminding myself that caribou are supposed to be pretty dumb and that I just had to outsmart one.

The next morning dawned dark and cold, with a fierce wind whistling among the tall jack pines. A native of the tropics, I shuddered at the thought of crawling out of my sleeping bag and into the half- frozen saddle, but there seemed to be no other way to collect a good representative specimen of *Rangifer tarandus.*

An hour's ride from our cabin found us emerging from a patch of forest into some bare hills. Amos reigned in his steed as a bull caribou raised his head to glance at us before resuming his breakfast. I piled off my horse and scampered to a small saddle, where I got prone and steadied the cross hairs on the bull's shoulder. My hold was rock-steady and the bull was standing broadside, but something was wrong.

"Is it smaller than Sergio's?" I asked Amos. At his nod, I slowly lowered my rifle and eased away.

A couple of hours and fifty to a hundred caribou cows later, we stopped for a sandwich and Amos began to shake his head. "I don't think we get caribou. You should have taken the small bull. Better that than no trophy."

The sandwich was tasting terrible in my mouth when I saw Amos tense and dig out his binocular from under his jacket. After gazing through the glass for a few moments, he said, "I think I see two bulls. I can't see their antlers, but their necks look white. Must intercept them before they go into them trees."

We got on our horses and were off immediately, half-trotting and half-galloping while dodging low branches. The weather had gotten worse and a howling wind lashed our faces with a freezing drizzle. As the trees thinned out, Amos signaled me to dismount and follow him. As I hurried behind him, I fed a round into the chamber of my rifle, trying to keep water off the scope.

Topping a rise, we saw the two caribou headed in our general direction at a determined trot. Both were good bulls, one with a narrow spread, the other with a wider one. I decided on the second one. I positioned myself behind a large jack pine and waited for them to cross a small glade about a hundred yards away. I was winded from the hard run, and to make matters worse, when I rested the rifle on the side of the tree, it swayed back and forth in the gale.

For some reason Amos kept whispering, "You're too winded and excited; you're going to miss him!"

Daintily, the first caribou crossed the glade. As his big brother came through, I tried to hold on his shoulder, but the cross hairs danced onto and then away from his body. During those agonizing moments I held my breath while the bull neared the edge of the clearing. Then Amos yelled "Hey!" and the bull froze in his tracks. It was now or never! I tightened my grip on the trigger and saw the antlers go down at the crash of the rifle. There were a few thrashing sounds and then only the wind broke the silence of the north country. I had mixed feelings about the magnificent trophy lying at my feet. I felt sad for killing it, but elated at having scored at the last moment. Suddenly the wind didn't seem as cold and the rain eased a little. I was happy with myself and the world.

That same day we headed back for the Horse Range. Sergio was pleased at having taken a large black bear while I had been hunting my caribou. Now all we were missing was the elk.

Dawn found Amos and me crossing the river's swift, glacier-fed waters. I raised my feet as high as I could to minimize water in the boots. After crossing a few open glades sparkling with frost in the first rays of the sun, we entered dark evergreen forest. A few minutes later a bull elk's shrill challenge sent my heart into high gear. We dismounted and advanced carefully.

Apparently, the bull had confused the progress of our horses with other elk, for he sent another bold challenge, which reverberated in the still mountain air. Amos coaxed him closer by rubbing a dead shrub with his mittened hand. The bull crashed closer for the showdown, but stopped short so that only the magnificent head and a small part of his neck showed. I raised my rifle and took just one side step to get a better view of my quarry. But fate decreed that this was not to be my bull. My right foot landed on a dry twig that cracked like a rifle shot. Before I could steady myself, the bull was gone. Amos mentioned something about what I should do with my big feet, which I will not repeat here for the sake of good taste. I felt as low as a toad's posterior as we walked gloomily to our horses.

After heading in the bull's general flight direction for a good half-hour, we again heard a shrill challenge resounding among the mountains. We dismounted, and Amos pointedly told me to take off my nylon jacket to keep it from brushing against leaves, and to watch where I put my big feet. We didn't have to walk long before the bull gave away his position by telling

everyone that he was the toughest dude in the neighborhood. I was looking down to make sure I didn't step on another twig when Amos squeezed my arm. There, no more than sixty yards away, his head emerging from a clump of small pines and his horns skylined, was my elk.

"Shoot him!" Amos hissed as I raised my rifle. Because the bull was facing me and only his head was visible, I held just under his chin and touched one off. The animal staggered backward a few yards and went down. When I reached him, I noticed that he had six points on one side and five on the other. Somewhat upset, I demanded to know why Amos had let me shoot it—I had set a minimum of six points to the side.

"The one you spook had six points," he answered. Then I realized that he was making me pay for my mistake—I had blown my chance on the bigger elk and now I had to suffer the consequences. I wasn't too pleased at having to settle for second best, but after all, we always have to pay for our mistakes, even though we may dislike the price.

And besides, this was a nice bull and I had a full bag—not to mention a good excuse to return to this harsh but beautiful land to look for the big one that got away.

Second-Place Winner

Chapter 7

Someone should have told me that bucks and does are such vastly different creatures. I had to learn the hard way!

And to make matters worse, I was just finding out that *Odocoileus virginianus texanus* had the highest I.Q. of all the whitetail subspecies. Despite all my efforts, it was becoming clear that collecting a doe, let alone a buck of trophy proportions, was simply impossible. It didn't help that I was hunting North American whitetails for the first time, and without the help of a guide. It is difficult to accept the fact that the senses of white-tailed deer are so much keener than those of a human that we cannot even see them, let alone shoot one! So far I had succeeded only in making a fool of myself.

I had been pondering these imponderables for three days now at Jim Lacey's ranch in south Texas, about sixty miles southwest of San Angelo. I had been invited here by Charles Lacey, Jim's brother, who is an ex-cattleman now working in Costa Rica.

Jimbo had been nice enough to pick me up at the airport and take me to the ranch, but was too busy to lead me by the hand to a good buck. I was assigned a comfortable trailer, which was to be my home for one week, but was on my own as far as the hunting went.

After three days, I was desperate for help. I convinced Jimbo that he needed a break and that he could relax by helping me score on a nice buck (he soon demonstrated that such creatures actually existed on the ranch).

The morning of 11 December 1981 broke cold and calm, and dawn found me huddled against the trunk of an oak while Jimbo tried to rattle a buck out of the surrounding mesquite. At least partly because I had not experienced this hunting method before, I nearly jumped out of my boots when a beautiful eight-pointer materialized out of the bush. But Jimbo wouldn't let me shoot because the buck was on the other side of a fence that separated the ranch from the neighbor's land. That was, of course, the only buck we saw during the rest of the morning.

I couldn't refuse an invitation to ride Mr. Lacey's favorite horse early that same afternoon, but by four o'clock I was ready for another stint of horn rattling. We crossed the main highway in Jimbo's pickup truck and began a slow descent along a twisty, mesquite-bordered road. I was riding next to Jimbo, and as we crossed a sendero, there appeared the most majestic twelve-point buck I have ever laid eyes on. He stood there statuelike while Jimbo let the truck coast to a stop. He would later tell me that he couldn't stop immediately or the buck would have bolted. As the vehicle came to a full stop, I eased out of the already-open door, took a rest on the side of the roll-bar, and frantically looked for horns. The only problem was that the dry mesquite branches sticking straight up looked just like horns. I glanced frantically at Jimbo and tried to read his lips, which were saying: "Monster, next to the big cedar."

I glared in desperation through the telescope until I picked up the enormous antlers. Lowering the cross hairs, I looked frantically for an opening in the mesquite. Finally I thought I could make out the base of the neck in the infernal tangle. I had a solid rest, and the buck had already stood there for too long. I squeezed one off.

In a jump the buck vanished. I couldn't have missed—not at sixty yards! I rushed to where the animal had been, only to find deep tracks where he had jumped. I followed easily in the sandy soil, expecting to find blood at any moment. But not only did I fail to find a blood trail, I soon lost the tracks on rocky ground.

I simply could not explain what had happened, and could not accept it. I retraced my steps back to the cedar under which the buck had stood and gazed at the red pickup. Through an opening in the maze I spied two broken branches the size of my thumb—almost certainly, they had deflected the bullet. It was of little consolation to know that my aim had been true but that luck had played a dirty trick. I really couldn't kick myself, since it wasn't my fault, but shooting myself didn't seem like a bad alternative.

I got back in the pickup with Jimbo, who had the courtesy to keep his mouth shut.

It was already dark when we headed out of that section of the ranch and came upon the gate at the main highway. As Jimbo pulled the truck to a stop, he pointed out, suspended in the night sky, a round object that emitted an incandescent light in various tones of yellow, red, and green.

Jimbo asked what I thought it was, and I answered that it looked like some kind of beacon on an antenna.

"Do you remember what the land looks like over here?" he asked.

"Flat as a table," I answered, acknowledging that no tower could be that high.

He then ordered me to open the gate, and remained silent for the next few minutes, even though I peppered him with questions about the strange object suspended in the sky.

Upon reaching the ranchhouse, Jimbo began blowing the horn, urging his mother and father to come out. As they did, and to my utter amazement, he yelled, "Hey, Mom, Dad, bring the binoculars—it's another of them UFOs."

I looked at all of them in disbelief as they passed the field glasses from hand to hand. Presently they all tired of looking, giving me the glasses and saying that we should all go into the house as dinner was getting cold. As I put the binocular to my eyes, the object seemed to glow more intensely and suddenly disappeared in the immensity of the heavens.

Over dinner I queried my hosts silly. I was sure they were pulling my leg, but they stuck to their story about the UFO. To this day I have no explanation for what I saw.

Thirteen December broke dark and cold with a merciless drizzle. Jimbo agreed to guide me again—I think on Mr. Lacey's orders, given the fact that guests, like fish, begin to smell after the third day. I needed to score fast and get out of there.

Jimbo drove the pickup to a well-known deer crossing at the far limit of the ranch. There we disembarked and walked some fifteen minutes to a wooded area. I found a snug little spot among three ancient oaks where I could hide while Jimbo rattled. I had good views to my front and to my left, from which I estimated any deer attracted to the rattling would come. Jimbo was hiding about twenty yards away.

At the first clashes of the antlers, I was tense as a bowstring, but when nothing happened for twenty minutes, I began to relax—until I caught the first glimpse of a set of huge antlers closing in from the right. As I tried to maneuver into position, the buck caught the movement and froze. Before I could bring the rifle to bear, the deer satisfied his curiosity and took off. I had time only to raise to my knees and get off a hasty shot as he bounded across and behind a drop in the land. I followed frantically,

with Jimbo in hot pursuit. We topped the hill simultaneously as the buck broke cover at full speed about two hundred and fifty yards away.

It has always been my belief that a fleeing deer has more to lose than I do if I fire—it can cost me only about a dollar, but it can cost the buck his life! In desperation I threw the rifle to my shoulder and found the buck's tail as it waved me farewell. Holding right between the basketlike antlers, I touched one off. At the blast of the .308 I was amazed to see the buck go down in a cloud of dust, shot through the spine. Jimbo insisted that it was the most spectacular shot he had seen in his life. I of course insisted that I could shoot like that all the time! After all, I had to redeem myself for the fiasco of the day before.

When we drove triumphantly to the ranch headquarters with my ten-point, eighteen-inch-spread buck, Mr. Lacey was elated at the termination of my hunt. What I'm not too sure about was whether his happiness was due to my success or to my departure.

General Quarters

Chapter 8

My buddy Max Echandi and I had the best deer-hunting deal in Costa Rica. We had discovered that the prison island of San Lucas, located in the Gulf of Nicoya on the Pacific Ocean, was overpopulated with tropical white-tailed deer. They were beginning to die of starvation during the dry summer months, however, and a cull was in order to thin the herd, estimated at around five hundred animals, on an island of about three times that many acres.

We established a three-way program between the game department, the ministry of justice (which oversaw all prisons), and ourselves. The game department would provide biologists to conduct the needed study; the ministry of justice would pony up the room and board as well as guards, guides, and horses for the culling; and Max and I, of course, would perform the shooting. My uncle would provide the yacht for the fifty-minute ride to the island.

That first year a program was established to cull thirty bucks and forty does. Forty young deer were to be captured for relocation on the mainland. All meat was to be donated to the prison administration to supplement the inmates' diet. The entrails, skins, and lower jaws of the animals would go to the game biologists for scientific research on food habits, disease, and parasites. For our pain and suffering, we would be allowed to keep the useless antlers and, if we insisted, an occasional cape if the buck was worth mounting. It was a marriage made in heaven!

Although San Lucas Island was also known as Devil's Island, to us it was Deer-Heaven Island. We had been there before to determine whether it was overpopulated with deer, only to find it was overrun with them. As a matter of fact, we had seen the first ones from the yacht, and when we made our first tour of the island itself, we were practically never out of sight of deer. As usual, there were more does and young deer than bucks, but among the last were some trophies to behold!

This was to be our first time on the island with rifles, and we had to pinch ourselves to make sure we were awake. Upon arrival we presented

the warden with a letter from the minister of justice herself (she was a lady and a good friend of my older brother—they had been classmates in law school). We were to be provided full cooperation for our pro-bono work!

We quickly discovered that the human fauna inhabiting the island was far more diverse than the game we were after. Aside from the murderers, rapists, bank robbers, and swindlers of all kinds and colors, there were the "special" inmates. Like the two toothless murderers who, of all things, had bitten their victim to death! Then, upon learning that they were to be examined by a forensic dentist to determine whether the wounds had been inflicted by the suspects' teeth, they had somehow managed to pull them out. And there was Mr. Ortiz, well educated and fluent in English, who was responsible for holding up a bank half a block from my office in San José and who had stashed the money away. And the crack-shot hitman from the town of Miramar who had been hired by an American to kill his next-door neighbor on account of his having "salted" a gold mine he had bought from him and which, of course, proved worthless.

And then there was *Mata-Suegras* or the "Mother-in-Law Killer." This man, after finding his wife two-timing him in his mother-in-law's house, had blocked all the exits and set fire to the house, thereby ending the lives of everybody inside, including his children, the family dog, and a parrot. And he freely talked about the deed and claimed that he had unlimited requests to eliminate mothers-in-law upon his release . . . and, no, I don't have his current address!

Max and I also soon learned not to let anything out of our sight or it would disappear in a manner that would put Houdini himself to shame. We even devised a padlock for our saddlebags to keep our belongings safe. And, at the top of the list, we never lost contact with our rifles.

We also learned how a society of violent paupers views the different values of things—especially commodities. Inmates would kill for drugs, of course, but also for a pack of cigarettes or an unreturned Playboy magazine, no matter how crumpled.

And I will never forget my first visit to the "Disc," a maximum-security facility where the inmates were kept in solitary confinement for serious offenses like aggression or trying to escape to the mainland by swimming across the shark-infested waters. When the swimmers were found by the coast guard, usually exhausted and clinging to a piece of driftwood, they

were brought back in shackles and lowered into an underground dungeon; there they would spend the next thirty days in complete darkness, not knowing whether it was day or night and surviving only on bread and water. But what impacted me the most on that first visit was the ominous poem written on a wall, undoubtedly the inspiration of a desperate man. In Spanish it read:

En este sitio maldito,
donde reina la tristeza,
no se castiga el delito,
se castiga la pobreza.

Roughly translated to English, it goes like this:

In this God-forsaken place,
governed by sadness and greed,
it's not the crime that is punished,
but the poverty and the need. *

After a few trips to the island, Max and I began to discover more about the inmates. One truth: Assassins are usually the prisoners who give the least problems, for they will sometimes kill an enemy in a rage but are otherwise honest citizens. Because I am an attorney myself, although I hardly practice criminal law, I had all the requests for legal assistance one can imagine; all the prisoners were, of course, innocent and unjustly deprived of their freedom.

For reasons unknown, *Mata-Suegras* became our servant on every trip and would eagerly await our arrival on the dock, which was off-limits to all other prisoners. A man of enormous strength, he would load himself up with our two saddles, two saddlebags filled with food, water, ammunition, binoculars, skinning knives, and other paraphernalia, and carry everything in one trip to the stables, where the horses waited to be saddled.

*For my Spanish-speaking readers who may not agree with my English version, let me remind them that translations are like women: If they are faithful, they are not beautiful; and if they are beautiful, they are not faithful!

Thanks to the tips and gifts with which we expressed our gratitude for his efforts, *Mata-Suegras*—I never knew his real name—became one of the most prominent prisoners, mainly as the sole distributor of Playboy centerfolds.

Having gained his trust after a few trips, I ventured to ask him why his arms and chest were covered with scars. He confided that he had never relinquished hope of escaping from Devil's Island; in fact, he had tried to swim to the mainland on several instances. However, he had failed every time (due mainly to the treacherous currents around the island), and was captured and confined to the Disc. Being claustrophobic, he would use the granite walls of his dungeon to sharpen a spoon or a cup, which he would use to inflict upon himself terrible cuts and other wounds. These would force his jailers to take him to the infirmary to save his life. And I never doubted his dexterity with a knife: Always waiting for us upon our return from the hunt, he would skin and quarter the deer with the ability of a professional butcher.

But I digress. I was assigned the warden's white mare, named Blondie, and soon found myself trotting briskly behind an elderly guard who had been assigned as my personal guide. As we ascended the rounded hills behind the compound, the morning sun glinted on the dew-covered grass with an indescribable iridescence. The island was covered with huge and ancient trees that gave it a parklike appearance, maintained by the inmates, who were required to keep the ground free of brush. Brilliant green parrots and parakeets with yellow heads and crimson wing feathers were noisily going about their business, and troops of howler monkeys eyed us suspiciously from the safety of their perches. Occasionally they would let out a low, rumbling roar that reminded me of a time when I was a kid on my first trip to Guanacaste province with my father. He had stopped at dusk so that I could answer a call of nature. I walked a few feet away behind his 1949 Nash Ambassador and behind some bushes. Just as I was answering the call, a howler monkey roared his displeasure at our intrusion.

"You better get back in the car, son, or that tiger is going to get you," my father called. And they teased me all the way back to the hotel because I had wet my pants in my hurry to get back in the car.

As I trotted up the emerald island surrounded by the sparkling sapphire-blue Pacific Ocean, anticipating the beginning of a virgin hunt,

I thought about how incredibly lucky we were. We had our own private shooting preserve bursting at the seams with deer. It was patrolled every hour of every day of the year by armed guards ready to shoot anybody who dared enter—or leave, for that matter. What's more, it wasn't costing us a cent to hunt there and we didn't even need a hunting license!

But I digress again.

As we advanced along the animal trails that crisscrossed the island, deer scampered ahead of us like rabbits. I must have gotten on and off my horse a hundred times to check out the bucks, but even with this population density, the big boys were scarce.

I, of course, wanted the biggest buck on the island. The thought that this deal was too good to last kept haunting me, and I just had to make the best of each hunt, even the first one. I saw at least a dozen bucks I would have taken in a heartbeat elsewhere, but not in deer paradise. I had all of Saturday and Sunday to hunt and could afford to be choosy. To be sure, shootable bucks were in evidence, but as is often the case with *Odocoileus virginianus,* they weren't prone to stick around to be harvested.

Shortly after midday, with the tropical sun beating mercilessly upon us in the 90-degree temperatures, we stopped at an abandoned shack next to a sparkling stream of crystal-clear water. After eating a couple of stale sandwiches, I took my hat and shirt off and began splashing water on my head and chest.

In the middle of my ablutions, my guide surprised me by grabbing my arm and handing me my rifle, motioning for me to follow him. He went straight to a huge boulder and urged me to kneel next to it and take a peek. At about one hundred and fifty yards stood the two most magnificent tropical whitetail bucks I have ever laid eyes on. The one nearest me had a set of antlers so heavy that I thought he was in velvet. I got into a shooting position as the guard urged me to fire. The bigger buck turned and began to slowly walk away. I'm a firm believer in the well-placed shot, but I believe even more firmly in taking any reasonable shot that is offered, especially at an outstanding trophy. In fact, if I'm armed with a proper caliber and bullet, there is nothing wrong with a properly directed "Texas heart shot."

At the report of my rifle, the buck lurched forward and stepped sideways, trembling. I worked the bolt and fired again into its shoulder. It took two steps and fell over.

As I held up the impressive eight-point antlers, I realized that their thickness and dark coloration were what had led me to believe the buck was in velvet. The guide and I were still admiring the fine animal when Max walked up, undoubtedly attracted by the gunfire. I asked him what he thought. He just stood there nodding his head. Finally he said, "Never in your wasted life will you shoot a bigger buck."

And this was only the first half day of hunting on deer-heaven island!

We quickly gutted the deer and headed back to the prison headquarters so it wouldn't spoil in the searing heat. And I did make sure to tuck the head and attached cape into my Igloo ice chest.

It was going on three when we remounted our protesting steeds and again headed out into the hills, fully aware that the late afternoon would bring another peak of deer activity. As we meandered, I began to familiarize myself with the different locations. There was Cannon Point, a sharp peninsula jutting into the ocean, so named because in days gone by a cannon was placed there to defend the island from pirates. And there was Tumbabote Beach and Lemon Beach and Cirial and Admiralty Hills—from which I would glass and see deer in groups of five and ten at a time.

Aside from having one more full day to hunt, I guess I had been somewhat spoiled by the morning's success. Now I wanted to find a buck at least similar to the one I had collected. And that was a pretty tall order.

Dusk of that very long day found us riding out of Cirial, on the main road leading to the prison compound, deerless. We were only about a half-mile from the "barn," softly talking to each other without paying much attention to our surroundings, the hunt over for the day. There was hardly light enough to shoot.

As we rounded a bend, I heard a loud snort and saw a huge buck explode from thick brush to our left and streak across the road. Nobody had to tell me this was my first buck's older brother. I piled off my horse and yanked the rifle from my scabbard.

Startled whitetails rarely stop for a second look, especially at close quarters. I led the bounding form as it appeared and disappeared in the tall grass and fading light. It was now or never: I fired once, twice, three times—and the bounding stopped. I stepped through a barbed-wire fence in a hurry and lost part of my shirt and skin in the process. But my buck was there, shot through the neck, dead as a doornail.

As we were loading the buck onto my guide's uncooperative steed, all hell broke loose at the prison compound. Sirens wailed and shots were fired into the air. As we neared the prison grounds, armed guards, flashlights in hand, streamed out of every door.

"Runaway prisoners . . . prisoner breakout!" was all I could make out in the noisy pandemonium.

Then it dawned on me!

"What is the alarm signal when an inmate escapes?" I asked my guide.

"Three shots fired into the air in quick succession," he answered.

Talk about falling on your face during your wedding ceremony! I prayed for sudden death, but it wouldn't come. . . .

As we trotted into the stables, the prison warden confronted me. "You're late returning from your hunt," he said in a gruff voice.

"Yes," I answered, regaining my composure. "I made a one-shot kill on this big buck at about four o'clock and couldn't find him in the tall grass until dusk. We almost lost him.

"But what's the reason for all the commotion?" I asked innocently.

"Some idiot fired three rapid shots, which is the signal for general quarters when a prisoner escapes," he replied. "Apparently, it was a false alarm."

"Glad to hear that," I said, eyeballing my guide to keep his mouth shut.

"If I find the fool who caused this, I'll lower him into the Disc," he said as he walked away.

"You should feed him to the sharks," I urged.

As it turned out, my second buck was smaller than the first one. But they are still the two largest tropical whitetails of the seventy-plus bucks I have taken, ranking No. 2 and No. 3 in the *Safari Club International's Record Book of Trophy Animals.*

And no, I never again fired three shots at a deer on San Lucas Island!

Nez Perce Buck

Chapter 9

My left boot was killing me from all the mountain hiking, the mule deer weren't cooperating, and I needed a change of terrain. White-tailed deer haunts are supposed to be generally less steep than mule deer country. I figured we should use the ATV more along the logging roads bordered by forested ridges and brushy draws full of elk, deer, and black bear. And besides, I was having a hell of a time driving my new toy in this spectacular country. The vastness of this land is exceeded only by its beauty and solitude!

Although I love to hunt in a variety of different places, I had struck up an immediate friendship with guide Don Vogel on my first elk hunt with him a couple of years back and decided to book a second hunt with him in November of 1992. I contacted outfitter Dave Bream in Lewiston, Idaho, and was soon making plans for my second trip there.

I had a brand-new 7mm Remington Magnum custom rifle just finished by Sam Johnson, the famed riflemaker out of Davison, Michigan, which I just had to put to the test. Quarter-inch groups aren't supposed to make much of a difference when hunting, but they work miracles on your confidence.

Our plan of attack for the crafty whitetails would be similar to the one we'd tried unsuccessfully on the mulies, with one variation: In addition to the endless glassing, and after convincing ourselves that there were no visible bucks, we would roll rocks down the nearly vertical canyons to see if we could flush out the invisible ones.

First light on 2 November found Don and me huddled together on a windswept ridge in a freezing drizzle. I was having trouble keeping the rain off my binocular lenses and eyeglasses and even more trouble reminding myself that I was having fun.

As usual, it was Don's keen eyes that spotted the splash of light brown color against the dark trunk of a Ponderosa pine. The big buck was watching a doe as she browsed near a draw. Even at that long distance, the antlers looked huge and I drooled over them. But to no avail: He was

on the mountain opposite us, with the Snake River in between. After a few minutes, head lowered like a hound, he followed his hot date into the all-concealing pines.

"He was humongous," Don said, "but I guess that's the last we'll see of him."

And he was right. Turned out the buck wasn't even on the ranch we were hunting.

Plan B—the Boulder Roll—then went into effect. Don would loosen big boulders and send them down the steep canyon walls while I waited, rifle in hand. On the third day a band of chukars exploded so close they nearly gave me a heart attack, but no deer were flushed. As the saying goes, the repetition of a stimulus results in the elimination of the response. After a dozen tries, I found myself seriously doubting the rolling-stone technique.

One morning a little after ten, I was battling the cold drizzle that was severely restricting my view through a fogged-over scope and dripping-wet eyeglasses. After the third or fourth fruitless rock went bounding downhill, I slung the rifle on my shoulder and removed my eyeglasses to wipe them dry.

Don had a baseball-size rock in his hand. He spat in pitcherlike manner, took aim, and sent it toward a patch of particularly dense cover. The next moment there was a clattering of stones as three deer exploded from a patch of dwarf pines about a hundred fifty yards away. Frantically I tried to hook my eyeglasses to my ears but got them only halfway seated when my cap got in the way. I took the rifle from my shoulder, flipping off the lens covers in the process.

In the meantime, Don was telling me what I already knew:

"Take the buck, the last one—he's good, and it's your only chance."

Hunting rarely offers shots with benchrest steadiness, which is why it's so important to practice shooting from different positions before you take to the field. If I have learned anything in my many years of hunting, it's to take the shot when it's offered. It will probably be your only chance. There was an opening in the bushes that the deer would have to cross. . . .

"Watch him," I whispered to myself, sucking in a breath of air and letting half of it out.

It would not have been an easy shot, even with good visibility and a steady rest. To make matters worse, if I missed, I couldn't blame the rifle.

These circumstances really challenged my ability. I am accustomed to the diminutive tropical whitetails of my country—this hulking animal looked like a mule through my scope. As it bounced up the slope, I held the cross hairs slightly ahead of its neck and touched the bullet off. When the shot bellowed across the canyon, the buck swapped ends and headed straight back where he had come from.

Don said he had heard the bullet hit, and I wholeheartedly agreed, maybe more to convince myself than anything else.

Since Don is color-blind, especially to red, it was decided that I would go down the draw to look for blood while he circled with his four-wheeler. Though others may say otherwise, I don't believe in waiting after the shot, so now I immediately began climbing down the draw. Thorns poked through several layers of clothing as I slid and tripped to the bottom. I then hiked to the little glade that the deer had crossed. There I found deep-gouged tracks where the buck had turned in the rain-soaked earth. They were easy to follow downhill. Where the buck had jumped a fallen tree, I found blood splashed as if spilled from a bucket. From there on, it had tumbled and slid down the steep slope for over sixty yards, finally stopping on a grassy saddle.

As I bent down to raise the head of the fallen monarch, Don's voice rang out: "Did you find any blood?"

"No," I lied. "But I found the deer."

Lightning Strikes Twice

Chapter 10

José Calderón may have been old, but he was tough as nails. We had been riding steadily for about five hours and he showed no signs of fatigue, even though he was in his early seventies. We were headed toward a huge plain surrounded on three sides by mountains overhung with vines and tropical foliage. The sparkling blue of the Pacific Ocean bordered the fourth side.

It was just the beginning of the rainy season, so the lush green vegetation would not yet be high enough to hide the tropical whitetail I hoped to find. As we approached this deer haven, accessible only by horseback during the rainy season, sign was everywhere. Big rounded and splayed tracks pockmarked the soft ground, and I expected to find the buck of a lifetime at every turn.

As we reached the huge plain, which itself held patches of deciduous forest, the sea of foot-high *jaragua* grass waved gently in the afternoon breeze. The pounding of the waves in the distance and the calls of the *pava*s, or tropical turkeys, gave the place a magic sense of peace and solitude that I experience only in truly wild and isolated places.

We stopped by a crystal-clear stream flowing from the nearby hills, ate our sandwiches, and could not resist the temptation to remove our shirts and wash up a bit before continuing our hunt in this special place. But in spite of the remoteness of the place, deer were not as plentiful as we had hoped—fishermen had been poaching them, as revealed by the bones bleaching under the tropical sun.

After unsuccessfully fringing the huge basin, we cut straight across the plain. I was fascinated by the massive flights of wild parrots, busily talking to one another and flashing green, red, and yellow in the westering sun. Given the fact that there was very little cover in the emerald ocean of grass, we weren't hunting anymore. No self-respecting deer would be in a place devoid of cover.

I awoke from my meditations when José reared his mule to an abrupt stop. As usual, he had located the game first: He pointed to a

low, thorny *zarza* bush about a hundred yards away. I knew better than to ask questions and lose precious moments of a shooting opportunity. I jumped off my steed, yanked my rifle from its scabbard, and made a beeline for the lonely bush in the otherwise featureless plain. I had seen nothing yet, but from previous trips had learned to trust José's eyes. As I cut the distance, a tawny, rounded head popped up for an instant behind the shrub. *A darn coyote,* I said to myself, which I wasn't going to shoot for fear of scaring the deer.

For reasons attributable only to severe brain damage, I swung the rifle on its sling over my shoulder (where it did about as much good as if it were in my gun cabinet) and continued to close the distance. I hadn't gone another ten yards when the head of the "coyote" materialized again behind the brush. Only this time it came up higher and I was near enough to identify it as that of a cougar. Problem was the cat simultaneously identified me as hostile, no matter how stupid I looked. As our eyes met, the big cat sensed impending danger and made a dash to his right as I frantically struggled to unsling and shoulder the rifle. As I flicked the safety off, the lion was bounding away in the fading light with graceful leaps, head held high, body crouching low to take advantage of the foot-high grass covering the savannah. I held in front of its head and slapped the trigger as if I were shooting quail, only to realize that my bullet had gone over its back. As I frantically worked the bolt, the puma switched to overdrive and started to really make good time. I lost my composure and sent two more projectiles behind him but to no avail. I stood there trembling as José walked up to me.

"Had he been hungry, he would have eaten us both," he said jokingly.

I considered shooting him but instead asked him to retrieve a flashlight to look for blood in the fading light. We searched for over an hour on all fours, accomplishing nothing besides our own ridicule.

In the weeks that followed, I would wake up in the middle of the night to a terrible anguish, caused by missing an easy shot at an incredible trophy—for I knew perfectly well that I would never again have such an opportunity.

Incredible as it may seem, however, lightning does sometimes strike twice in the same place!

In mid-October, peak of the rainy season, hunting in the lowlands was out. Not only would the grass be too high, but the lower areas would

be impassable. So I headed for the Guanacaste mountain range, where I again hoped to clobber an unsuspecting whitetail.

I went with a friend, and when we reached the corrals at the base of the rounded mountain where we were to hunt, we decided to climb it on opposite sides, meet at the top, and descend where the other had climbed. This was about a ten-hour deal, and we figured that by the time we started down, any animal startled during our climb up would have had more than enough time to settle down. Besides, we would stop at the summit for a rest and a snack, giving the animals even more time.

I was assigned a guide dubbed Gato (which means cat eyes in Spanish), a sinewy cowboy with a dark complexion and green eyes that sparkled brightly under a wide-brimmed hat. We were given riding mules, which can climb better in the rocky terrain and are more sure-footed than a horse. Now, I don't particularly like mules, but one does not look a gift horse—or a loaned mule, for that matter—in the mouth. Anyway, my friend and I saddled up, wished each other luck, and trotted off briskly in opposite directions.

I remember seeing a few deer, but nothing that made me even get off my gentle riding mule. Four or five hours later we met at the top and stopped to chat under a grove of huge mango trees. The place was as noisy as a women's tea party because of the bands of yellow-naped parrots feeding on the ripe fruit.

My buddy had fared similarly, having seen no big deer. As we relaxed in the cool afternoon shade, he did mention a tawny animal streaking across the path near the "old wooden gate." I didn't pay much attention to his story, and after a short nap, we again wished each other luck and started on our way down, on opposite sides of the mountain.

Upon reaching the old wooden gate, Gato opened it and waved me through. I waited for him, scanning the countryside as he slammed it shut. At the crack of wood hitting wood, a rounded head popped up behind a low thornbush not fifty yards away. As if to prove that foolishness is not always a permanent condition, I piled off my mount and silently pulled my Sako .308 from its scabbard. But even before I touched the ground, the head had disappeared behind the concealing scrub.

I surveyed the situation and noticed that the bush was in the middle of a small clearing with sparse and stunted grass. With raised rifle, I froze. It was the cougar's move. I don't think he had yet realized that he had

been discovered. I knew, however, that curiosity would get the best of him and I would have my chance. After all, it's curiosity that kills the cat, they say, and this was not going to be the exception. Slowly the rounded head came up again. As I leveled the rifle, our eyes met. But before I could find the neck, it disappeared again. The tension mounted. I knew the puma would lose his nerve and make a dash for it. If he were cunning enough, he would run straight away, keeping the cover between us. Fortunately for me, he apparently wasn't all that experienced: He began to slink away to my left, and I didn't give him time to gather speed. The moment he broke from cover, the cross hairs settled on the muscular neck. The two-and-a-half-pound trigger broke smoothly and I lost the sight picture to recoil. As I recovered, the first thing I saw was the long tail twitching spasmodically.

As I reconstructed the events, I realized they had been almost a repeat performance of what I had experienced only a few months back.

As I sat there admiring my trophy and the incredible stroke of luck, I realized that lightning sometimes does indeed strike twice in the same place!

And then . . .

After the picture session, Gato brought up my mule and began to load the precious trophy. We had put it in a large cotton bag to prevent any damage to its hair on the long ride home. The wind was blowing on the mule's face when we loaded the cougar on its back, which was probably why it didn't protest. But when we finished the loading process and retightened the cinch, the mule looked back and caught a whiff of lion scent. Its eyes rolled in panic, its ears snapped back, and with an angry squeal it let fly with both hind legs, one of which caught me on the right thigh. I landed heavily on my butt as my otherwise gentle mount bucked in a manner that would shame the star bronco of a rodeo. And it continued bucking until it threw not only my pacified lion but my saddlebags as well. Then it stood at the edge of the clearing snorting and shaking violently as if with ague.

I picked myself up, still dazed from the blow, trying to figure out how we would carry my prize to where we had left the car. Gato walked to the bundled-up lion and opened the bag. He stuck his right hand in and came out with it smeared in blood. Then he walked over to the mule and rubbed his hand on its mouth and nostrils. The mule snorted and

protested mildly. Then he walked over to the bagged puma, literally picked it up, and swung it over the mule's back without a protest.

"Climb up," Gato said with a wry smile. "It's through bucking."

As we rode down the mountain, Gato looked back at me and advised: "And if a skunk ever sprays you, bathe with ketchup."

I haven't tried that one yet, but after what I saw that day, I'm sure it works!

The World's Greatest Game Animal

Chapter 11

My eyes snapped open instantly at the sudden hysterical, nerve-wracking calls of a band of chachalacas *(Ortalis garrula)* perched high in the canopy of trees under which Manuel had decided to make our camp. As I came fully awake, I remembered I was on the first day of a week-long hunt with Manuel Queb-Novelo, the only outfitter in the world who could consistently produce jaguars over bait.

I lazed in my comfortable cot for a few more minutes as the first golden streaks of sunlight filtered through the leafy tangle, reminiscing about the twenty-year quest that had brought me to Campeche, México, after jaguars, which I consider the world's greatest game animal. And I was lucky enough to make that hunt shortly before the permanent ban on jaguar hunting was imposed in March of 1987. Maybe the Bengal tiger should top the game-animal list, but today it is fully protected and surely out of my reach—except maybe in the kingdom of Bhutan, where it may be hunted only by special invitation of H. R. H. Jigme Singye Wangchuck. So I tend to classify the Bengal tiger right next to the tyrannosaurus.

Jaguars had been no strangers to me in Costa Rica. Several times I had heard their deep, rumbling roars as I trekked wearily back to camp after a day's deer hunting. Numerous times I had come upon the rounded tracks of large males, tracks as big as a small plate. On occasion I had come upon a fresh kill, usually a domestic cow, and had never ceased to marvel at the strength of a jaguar's powerful jaws, which almost never failed to snap the spine of its prey where the neck joined the skull. I had tried every legal method to collect one but never succeeded, though on several occasions I had come very close.

Jaguars are mainly nocturnal, but I figured that if I hunted them long enough, I would eventually bump into one. Right? Wrong! I didn't keep exact track of the times I hunted at night, but it must have been close to a hundred. And only once did I come upon *el tigre*—in Guanacaste province near the Nicaraguan border. It was just getting dark when he walked out of a patch of jungle into a small clearing. I distinctly remember how the

fiery, reddish-white orbs of the big cat's eyes reflected the powerful beam of my headlamp. But before I could dismount from my steed and yank the rifle from the scabbard, he was back in the jungle in two graceful leaps. I followed frantically, of course, but although I searched the heavy underbrush insistently, the quarry eluded me.*

The next obvious tactic was to use dogs. All I had to do, I figured, was find a fresh track, set the mutts on it, and shoot the jaguar out of a tree half an hour later. Right? Wrong! I soon found out that there are three kinds of jaguar dogs: those that chase jaguars but never catch up with them, those that catch up with them but never live to tell about it, and those that are supposed to chase jaguars but always end up chasing something else. These last, I quickly found out, are the most common.

Once, I got a call from an acquaintance who owned a large ranch in northern Costa Rica. He wanted my help in eliminating a notorious cattle-lifting cat that had accounted for almost three dozen head. Apparently it had just taken its thirty-third milk cow and should be a "cinch" to obtain.

I managed to collect five hounds of dubious origin and reached the ranch the next day. We did not come upon the dead cow until early on the morning of the third day. The carcass was surrounded by the fresh pug marks of a big cat. The dogs went into a frenzy and we immediately released them. The trail led into the thickest, nastiest swamp one can imagine, a nightmare of sawgrass. Eight hours later—wet from perspiration and from falling into the murky water, exhausted from following the dogs, our arms bleeding from the sawgrass—we came upon two of the dogs. Or, rather, they came back to us, all the fight and bravado knocked out of them, their tails tucked between their legs, uttering soft whimpering sounds. The three others, including a hound-and-German-shepherd crossbreed, had apparently caught up with the jaguar but never had a chance to inform us for they were never found.

On another occasion, we set two smallish hounds on the trail of a large jaguar on the slopes of the Turrialba Volcano at an elevation of nearly twelve thousand feet. This tigre had also killed a cow but had failed to return to the

*Some of these were considered "harmful animals" because they were depredating cattle. I hunted those with special permits issued by the game department for cattle killers.

kill, which suggested that it might be nearby and hungry. The hounds took off in a cacophony of barks and howls and caught up with the jaguar in no time. Or, rather, the jaguar caught up with them. That day we couldn't find the dogs, but early next morning we found—literally—their heads and tails. The jaguar had been nearby, sure enough, but it sure wasn't hungry anymore!

Outside of poison, only the tactic of sitting over a kill, natural or provided, remained. This should be rather easy. After all, having gained some expertise from collecting two African lions and a leopard over dead baits—not to mention a cougar that was bumped off while I was looking for a deer—potting *el tigre* from a distance of thirty feet shouldn't pose a problem. Right? Wrong again!

For one thing, jaguars don't seem to readily come to bait, either dead or alive. When one finds a natural kill, which occurs as often as winning the lottery, a machan or tree platform has to be built. This is not always possible. I once came to a ranch that I normally hunted for whitetails, and the foreman announced that a heifer had been killed by *el tigre* the previous night. He was expecting me for a deer hunt, and horses were saddled and ready to go. We made it to the kill in about an hour but found that the jaguar had not dragged its victim, as is this cat's custom, but had eaten his fill in an open pasture. Only a few runty trees, typical of poor soils and not over twelve feet high, grew in the immediate vicinity. I had no choice but to climb the only tree overlooking the dead steer.

Sure enough, as the late-afternoon sun sent its last crimson rays into the orange sky, a covey of quail that had already settled for the night flushed in panic to my right. I was almost sure they had been spooked by the tigre. As the night wore on, a slit of moon became visible in the otherwise inky sky, and I presently heard a low *A-oogh! Aungh-ha! Oum! Oum!* as the jaguar circled his kill, fully aware of my most unwelcome intrusion. I never saw that animal.

Many years later, as a result of having offered a generous tip for information leading to the object of my obsessive feline desire, I received a call from Agapito Campos, a half-Indian from Limon province. He told me he had already built a machan to sit over a young bull killed by an enterprising cat that had previously accounted for several of his cows. I immediately took off, arriving at the site at about 5:30 in the afternoon after a long walk through thick jungle.

The machan was set about twenty feet high in the fork of a smooth and branchless tree. Earlier I had asked Agapito how I was supposed to climb to

my platform. His reply: "The same way I did—take your boots off and use your toes to shinny up there!"

My shinnier wasn't working, so I had to quickly find an alternative course of action—erecting a ground blind. Sure enough, the wily jaguar returned around 2 AM and gave the kill a sharp tug. I slowly rose from my blind, rifle in hand, as the jaguar dragged the heavy body another few feet. When I turned on my light, all I could see was the dead bull, but I heard a faint rustle as the jaguar took off under the protection of the screening jungle.

About three weeks later, a doctor friend of mine shot the very same jaguar from a machan that had been constructed over another kill. I was sick about that for over a week!

I seemed to be pretty much out of options, every method for taking a jaguar having failed me. In desperation, I considered the possibilities offered by one close friend and one distant cousin. The friend had thoroughly impressed me with his gruesome tale of the huge jaguar he had wounded with a .22 magnum revolver from a machan he had built overlooking a kill in the dry tropical forest of the northern province of Guanacaste. As the story went, he had then proceeded to brave the impenetrable jungle, razor-sharp machete in one hand and trusted six-gun in the other. There was a confrontation: As the flailing form of fang and claw sailed through the air with vengeance in its heart, my friend had sent three perfectly directed bullets straight into the spotted devil's heart, and the creature landed at his feet, claws reaching out in vain for his executioner.

Well, the story seemed to change from listener to listener, and eventually the truth broke out: I had hunted deer in that same area and was trying to find a good guide in the little town nearby. Everyone knows what everyone else does in a small town, so I was soon introduced to a man known as the best hunter in the area—he had even collected a large jaguar the previous year. Upon meeting him I asked to see the skin. He told me how, being very poor, he had followed a neighbor's advice to call this rich hunter from San José who would pay handsomely for the cat, so long as it hadn't been skinned. It seems my friend had arrived at this hunter's place in record time and proceeded to take countless pictures of himself with the quarry, .22 magnum pistol in hand, leaving no doubt about his prowess as a hunter and his courage as a man! Well, my newly found hunter and guide received a handsome tip and a directional antenna for his TV set.

As for the distant cousin, I had by chance encountered him in a government office, where he tried to impress me with the story of the last trophy animal he had taken. I asked how many points it had, thinking it was a deer. His reply was that I should ask how many spots it had, since he had changed his pursuits to worthier animals. He went on to inform me—in a rather hurried way because he had extremely important business to attend to—that he had received a call from his deceased grandfather's ranch in the nearby province of Cartago (where jaguars are extremely scarce) informing him that a huge cat had just taken one of the prized Jersey milk cows. He had climbed high into the upper branches of a tree—with great risk to life and limb—to avoid being smelled by the jaguar (forgetting that a cat's smell is its poorest sense) and had clobbered the tigre upon its return.

I will withhold certain details about how the news reached me (to avoid getting clobbered myself), but it seems the rancher who had really killed the jaguar, in the province of Alajuela, called a person in San José to sell the skin and was given exactly the same advice about not touching the deceased cat. The interested party missed work that day to keep the jaguar from spoiling, and took countless pictures of himself dressed in full camouflage (with nary a speck of mud on his impeccable attire) and with high-powered rifle in hand. Vanity and honor are not meant to live together!

Do you recall my strident chachalaca wakeup at the beginning of this chapter? Well, my daydreaming finally ended and I hastened to dress. The magic of the first full day of hunting in a different and strange place lay ahead.

When going after medium-size game, I prefer my own Sako .308, topped by a Scope Chief VI telescopic sight. As it turned out, my apprehensions about getting the rifle into México had been unjustified. I obtained the importation permit for the rifle in a record time of three weeks. First, I had to obtain a good-conduct letter from the Costa Rican Firearms Registration office, then pay a temporary import fee of $50. Upon my arrival in Cancún after a pleasant two-and-a-half-hour flight, I showed my permit to the officer in charge and got whisked through customs without a question being asked. As I walked out of the airport, my hunting buddy, Eugene M. Bishop from Atlanta, Georgia, was waiting for me along with our guide Manuel, who wore a big Texas hat—undoubtedly the gift of an American client—which made him look shorter than he actually was. Gene had had no problem with his rifle, another .308, either.

I once remarked to a friend how difficult it was to find a good hunting companion. He looked back at me and said there was something much more

difficult, and that was *being* a good hunting companion. This was my first hunting trip with Gene outside of Costa Rica, and I was about to realize how true those words were.

I had asked Manuel to meet us in Cancún in case there was any problem with the rifles. He had driven all the way from Campeche in an old and battered Volkswagen Brazilia, which, with all due respect, belonged in a junkyard. I was extremely surprised when we made it to Campeche at dawn after a nine-hour drive with only one minor breakdown. If only I had known Mexicana Airlines had daily forty-minute flights for $47!

We slept through the morning, and Raúl Reyes, Manuel's assistant, picked us up at 2 PM for a tour of some nearby Maya ruins, plus a look at the walled city and its ancient castle. We returned to the city for dinner and stayed overnight at a beautiful beach-front hotel.

Morning found us again heading northwest over an excellent road, loaded to the maximum in Manuel's "limousine," as we had come to call his little station wagon. Four hours later we left the paved road and switched to a Jeep, which was in no better shape than the "limo," and continued over a rudimentary logging road. The camp crew, composed of Manuel's son Javier, Luis Fernando, and Lorenzo, the cook, completed our group. They followed our Jeep in an old Chevrolet Power Wagon loaded with other paraphernalia and two goats, which in no uncertain manner voiced their protests about their mode of transportation. In two more hours we stopped in the middle of nowhere, where we would camp.

In no time at all camp was ready, and Lorenzo fixed us a truly gourmet dinner along with chocolate mousse. I later learned that in the off-season he was a chef in one of the better restaurants in Campeche.

We were in a dry tropical forest with very thick vegetation. It was practically impossible to hunt except on the logging roads. It came as a surprise to me that there were no rivers or creeks in the area, the only water coming from a few widely scattered natural water holes. Shooting would have to be at close range, and I pondered again my decision to bring a scoped rifle instead of a shotgun, as Manuel had advised.

Manuel carried a single-barrel 16-gauge shotgun of ancient vintage that had seen better days. For reasons unknown, its barrel had been sawed off short and a front bead crudely soldered onto it. It was hardly the Rigby Express rifle of an African professional. But professional Manuel was! Besides having an uncanny ability to find his way around in the jungle, he could vocally call any

creature that lived in the area. He demonstrated this ability the very first day by calling three peccaries right out to the road.

Later in the day Manuel left camp, returning at dusk with a dead horse that he had bought for bait. That same evening he went out by himself in the Jeep to set baits at likely places. He informed us that he would place them "at the jaguar's table" and that we should have one eating within three days. His confidence was most reassuring.

Manuel returned at about 9 PM with the bad news that the Jeep had broken down. He had managed to set only two of the baits. His normal practice was not to set baits randomly but rather to place them within the boundaries of each jaguar's territory, an area of at least ten square miles. We would have to check the baits on foot as the pickup had been returned to town.

On 5 March Manuel left camp before dawn to check for sign, informing us upon his return that neither of the two baits had been touched. After a late breakfast, he asked me to accompany him on a walk to check the area and maybe luck into a gray brocket deer or an oscellated turkey.

As it was, we didn't see much game except for a few partridges, and in about an hour's walk we came upon the first bait, consisting of the head and neck of the dead horse, securely tied to the base of a tree. My heart did a double somersault when Manuel announced that *el tigre* had been on the meat and that we should return immediately to camp, then return to the bait before 3 PM to build the machan and prepare for a long vigil. I never saw the pug marks of my intended quarry, because the laterite ground was hard and covered with leaves, but Manuel, with his uncanny ability, took the time to find a couple of short golden hairs to prove his assertion.

We reached camp at noon and I excitedly briefed Gene on the situation, suggesting that we flip a coin to determine who should sit up for the cat. If my house had depended on that toss, I wouldn't have been any more anxious to win, and here is where Gene taught me a lesson in generosity I will never forget. He conceded that I had been looking for a jaguar much longer than he had and that I should have first crack at this one. I remember insisting feebly that we should let luck decide, but he answered that he had made his decision before the hunt began. Friendship, like any other important element in life, is tested when the chips are down and the odds are high, and that day Gene proved to me what the word really meant.

My grandfather always said that to really know a man, one should observe him while drinking, gambling, and eating. From the first

observation, one would be able to determine his real personality; from the second, his nature and his greed; and from the third, his education and social position. Since my grandfather was not a hunter, he omitted mentioning going with a hunter friend on an important big-game hunt. To paraphrase George Bernard Shaw, men will play with their business and their money, but never with their games. One may know a person for thirty years before he goes on a big-game hunt with him. Then, when you shoot the bigger elk, watch Dr. Jekyll become Mr. Hyde! Anybody can share a friend's grief. To sympathize with his success requires an extremely delicate and sensitive nature.

After a quick lunch and shower, I checked my rifle, spotlight, and canteen and, along with Manuel and two of his helpers, made it back to the bait shortly after three. Manuel instructed Lorenzo and Javier to build a machan on the biggest tree overlooking the bait, and they took to the task with alacrity. By cutting five-foot poles and tying them securely with rope, they formed a ladder. At an elevation of some twenty feet, they tied a couple of green nylon hammocks. After climbing to my improvised perch, I insisted on an additional pole in front of my chest for added stability, and for that all-important rest for my rifle—even for a shot at a distance of about thirty feet.

When the two men walked away, my watch showed it was only a little after four. Manuel and I settled in for the long wait.

I have often been told how boring it must be to sit for long hours awaiting the return of game. But for me, the waiting itself is a pleasure that words cannot describe. Such rare occasions touch some inner chord in me. I feel myself in close contact with the infinite, far closer than I feel in any church, where the preacher automatically repeats words for the uplift of my erring and sinful self. There is so much to see and so much to listen to if one remains watchful and alert. I can only feel sorry for those who cannot appreciate this wondrous feeling.

About half an hour later, a band of spider monkeys came near the perch where we were sitting and, after eying us suspiciously, scornfully rejected our return to the abode of our ancestors by literally breaking branches and casting them at us. We remained passive, completely still, and the monkeys finally tired of us and swung indignantly away.

Manuel had told me that only about one out of three jaguars comes to feed in daylight, and as dusk rapidly followed the vanquished day, I realized my cat would not be the exception. The jungle before me assumed a purplish,

hazy hue, and I could hardly distinguish the dark splotch formed by the head and neck of the horse.

Softly Manuel broke the silence to whisper that he would touch my knee to let me know the jaguar was coming, again when it was on the bait, and a third time to announce that he would shine the light from his powerful six-cell flashlight. He refused to let me use my own spotlight for fear I might shine it before the jaguar began eating, in which case the coveted creature would disappear in one leap before I could fire.

The luminous dial on my watch marked a quarter to seven when the raucous chatter of a startled agouti (a rabbit-size tropical rodent) rent the silence of the jungle. This cry announced to every living creature in the forest that the spotted terror, the bringer of violent death, was near.

As the agouti's cries faded into the distance, Manuel's warning whisper was quite unnecessary to make me fully aware of the drama that would play out in the next few minutes and in which we were to be the main actors.

The minutes dragged slowly by, and the jungle seemed empty of any form of life. The silence was deep and complete; the stars twinkled down on me in eerie silence. Then the unmistakably heavy but softly muffled tread of a jaguar on the carpet of fallen leaves caused Manuel's cold and clammy hand to clench my right knee. The hair at the back of my neck seemed of its own volition to stand on end. Involuntarily, instinctively, my sweaty hand closed on the stock of my rifle as my thumb pushed the safety off. I lowered the muzzle with infinite caution in the direction of the bait. No matter how hard I strained my eyes, however, I was unable to penetrate the Stygian darkness.

For the second time Manuel's hand closed on my knee to indicate that the jaguar was on the bait. He would later tell me that he had been afraid the pounding of my heart would scare the jaguar away. The pressure on me during the seconds that followed was almost unbearable. I realized that this was it: The next few minutes would determine the fate of my twenty-year quest. I suppressed the torturous thought of missing, and again pushed the safety, which was already in the off position.

The distinctive cracking of bone and tearing of flesh again put Manuel's cold hand on my knee. I took a deep breath and prepared for this once-in-a-lifetime opportunity. As the beam from Manuel's powerful flashlight parted the inky darkness, the jaguar dropped the horse's head that it was holding up with its mouth but failed to look up. *El tigre* remained petrified, except for the nervous twitching of the tip of his tail.

I had been looking over the top of my telescope in the darkness, with the rifle pointed in the general direction of the bait. Now I lowered my eye and peered through the scope. The dual cross hairs showed sharp and clear against that wonderfully muscular, golden body. In a second I picked the point of the shoulder and touched the shot off. I was dimly aware of seeing the jaguar leap in the air, take off like greased lightning, and disappear into the all-concealing fastness of the surrounding forest. Then deathly silence reigned again.

I had an acrid taste in my mouth when I announced to Manuel that I was sure the jaguar was dead. He had crashed through the undergrowth as only a wounded animal would in his death run. Manuel seemed convinced. Now all I had to do was convince the jaguar!

I assembled my headlamp and we climbed down from the tree. I walked to the bait and found a large splotch of bright red blood. A distinctive blood trail led into a maze of vines and shrubs almost impossible to negotiate. As I began to follow the spoor, Manuel stopped me, announcing that it was the strict policy of his camp never to follow a wounded jaguar at night. Certain that I would never be able to survive through the night without knowing whether I had finally succeeded in collecting the world's greatest game animal, I explained to Manuel that the bright red blood indicated a heart or lung shot and that we shouldn't have any problem. After considerable arm-twisting, he agreed to the search.

The animal had bled freely, and the trail was easy to follow. After some twenty yards, we came upon a tangle of vines where a big *nauyaca* or fer-de-lance snake was coiled in perfect camouflage. Manuel dispatched it with his machete. I trebled my vigilance and we pushed warily on, rifle in hand, senses at full alert. Another thirty yards revealed the white underbelly of the jaguar—my jaguar—lying on its side. I let out a whoop of joy and embraced Manuel in triumph. My twenty-year quest was at last over!

We hung the jaguar by a leg from a tree and trekked back to camp. We awoke everybody upon our return and toasted my trophy with wine. Gene heartily congratulated me. But my mind would not slow down. Now that the jinx was broken, I was already looking forward to the time when I could collect another specimen of the world's greatest game animal on my own. I only hope it won't take me another twenty years!

The World's Wildest Game Animal

Chapter 12

I must confess I was concerned about the abundance of Coues deer on the ranch of Santiago Elías in northern Sonora, Mexico. After leaving the paved road at the colorful town of Arizpe—which would have made the perfect setting for a Clint Eastwood movie—we followed a miserable excuse for a road that led us ever deeper into the Sierra Madre Mountains. I was awed by the Sonoran Desert with its blue, oak-clad mountains in the distance, the lower slopes thinly clad in typical desert growth—saguaro, *pitahaya, cholla, palo verde, siviri,* and different varieties of *ocotillo,* all covered with formidable thorns ready to claw your clothes and flesh.

As dusk gave way to night, I expected the headlights of the old Ram station wagon to catch the furtive eyes of at least one deer, but it was not to be. All we saw were the ubiquitous hares typical of the desert, their huge ears sticking straight up. A lone coyote was slinking among the bushes as we neared the ranchhouse, probably trying to steal one of the scrawny chickens that would awaken us every morning.

"Don't worry," Jorge Camou León, my outfitter and part-time guide, assured me, "I'll show you dozens of deer tomorrow."

I was pleasantly surprised by the tidiness of the refurbished ranch house that Jorge had prepared for us, along with hot and cold running water, spring beds, and solar electricity. Presently Yaqui, the camp cook, had a fire going, red beans heating, potatoes boiling, and huge steaks browning in an oversize frying pan. We washed everything down with frigid Coke and were soon pounding our ears.

Dawn found Jorge, guide Arturo Munguía, and me huddled in the truck as it wound its way up the immense, rolling hills of the Sierra Madre. It was a special time to anticipate the first day of a fabulous hunt in a different place. To me, those moments are the highlights of a lifetime, wherever you find them!

I had hunted the smart, beautiful, and alert Coues deer before and knew what I was up against. The deer here had been obviously submitted to heavy

hunting pressure and were incredibly wild—or maybe that's the way they always are. In the following days I would be outsmarted and humiliated time and again, to the point that I would turn and toss in my bed, unable to sleep, assuring myself that eventually a big buck would have to make a mistake. Apparently I had disregarded the possibility of my intended prey being smarter than I.

As the sun tinted the eastern horizon with the desert's special combination of red, yellow, and magenta, Jorge killed the engine.

I had hunted Rocky Mountain mule deer and whitetails before in Montana and Idaho, where the former live in the mountains and the latter on the flats. South of the U.S. border, however, mule deer live in the low deserts in searing summer heat and whitetails in the mountain ranges that rise from the desert floor.

Jorge told me to leave my jacket in the truck or I would be soon sweating from exertion, even though the air was as dry as a socialist economy. I checked the bore of my custom 7mm magnum and silently chambered a 160-grain Federal Nosler Partition cartridge. We set out in single-file with Jorge leading the way and Arturo bringing up the rear. I hadn't realized the mountains were so steep until we started climbing, and as usual it was all uphill, going in and coming out!

We hadn't hoofed it half an hour when two deer, one a buck, exploded from some scant cover on the huge hill stretching into infinity in front of us. Though the range was a good three hundred yards and we were trying to be as silent as possible in the volcanic rock, those deer were spooked and running and not stopping for a second look. Jorge brought up his binocular and immediately ordered me to shoot. When I sat down to rest my elbows on my knees, both the jagged rocks and the vegetation partly screened the fleeing deer. I vainly attempted to fold the edge of my hat to block the blinding sun glaring into my rifle scope as I tried to follow the diminutive buck while it dodged the scrub bushes. As the animal topped the mountain, I touched the shot off, but nobody had to tell me it was a clean miss.

I really didn't feel bad—it was an impossible shot on the first morning of the hunt. I didn't start feeling bad until the days to come forced me to accept the fact that all I was getting were impossible shots!

My concern about a scarcity of deer on the ranch was completely unjustified, but seeing them and collecting one proved to be two completely different endeavors. Three hours into that very same morning, four more

deer materialized out of the scrub oak at a similar distance, trotting briskly up a sidehill. The lead buck carried a good rack, and again Jorge directed me to shoot. The performance was a rerun of the first, only this time I fired twice into air—and didn't feel so good about it.

During the next two days I repeated the performance several times, anxiety slowly giving way to anguish. And for readers who may have trouble understanding just how I felt, I must say that I agree with the anonymous wit who defined anxiety as the first time you can't perform a second time, and anguish as the second time you can't perform the first time!

On the fourth day Jorge decided we should hunt the other side of the Elías ranch, which was less accessible by vehicle—even though we were seeing fifty to sixty deer daily on this side. Perhaps our luck would change and we would find the big dumb one I so badly needed.

We drove as high as we could in the Dodge truck, parking on a crest so as to partly avoid the strenuous climb. Ever so carefully, Jorge, Arturo, and I tiptoed the side hills, never skylining ourselves. As I tried to figure out a better way to hunt these paranoid creatures, a big buck erupted from under an ancient saguaro some four hundred yards off and bounded away. I almost dreaded Jorge's order to shoot because I could visualize the outcome. It came as I dropped into a sitting position, hoping the buck would stop but knowing he wouldn't. I fired and again scored a clean miss, the bullet kicking up dust behind the invulnerable deer.

I couldn't believe that, as careful as we were trying to be, we just could not sneak up on an unsuspecting buck. It was almost uncanny.

I got up, slipped another round into the chamber, shook the dust off my torn pants, and, with lowered head, gloomily followed in Jorge's footsteps. We topped the next ridge and stopped under some oak trees, where I used a small stick to pry a cholla ball off the leg of my pants. Suddenly the characteristic clinking of dislodged rocks brought my senses to maximum alert. Not one but five deer were slinking away—not on the next hill but on the one beyond it, a good four hundred yards distant. The lead buck was excellent, his high and heavy rack gleaming majestically in the clear mountain air. I dropped on my butt and followed him with the cross hairs, praying for him to stop. He did, at the very top of the ridge. I held about six inches above his back and touched off a Nosler Partition. The deer leaped straight up and landed running, disappearing in two bounds over the mountain. Success at last—about time after seven straight misses!

Mostly to assure myself, I expressed to Jorge that it had been a perfect heart shot. He didn't seem too sure, but of course that was due to his lack of experience. Down the huge hill we went and up the other side, then down and up again; all the while I prayed that my buck was dead. I arrived first at the ocotillo next to which my buck had been standing when I fired. Inspection of the ground revealed deep footprints where he had landed after the shot but, strangely, no blood. Obviously the thick hair had absorbed it during the first few bounds!

Tracking was easy in the sparse cover, and I expected to see the white belly behind every bush. Jorge and Arturo joined me, and it would be only a matter of minutes before we found my buck. Half an hour later, hands tucked in pockets and shaking his head, Jorge announced that the buck's reaction was probably due to pebbles pelting him on his belly when the high-speed bullet struck the ground between his legs.

Unbelieving, I gazed at him in silence. Arturo avoided meeting my gaze. I was disgusted with myself and with hunting in general. After all, what's wrong with tennis? I sat down as despair set in, the sort that makes a man want to shoot himself rather than the deer.

Jorge instructed Arturo and me to intercept the nearest road and he would meet us there after going back for the truck. I was too whipped to make it back—morally if not physically.

I dragged along behind Arturo, my eyes fixed on his skinny frame, my spirits as torn as my pants. The hunt was over. I had lost. I didn't dare look at the hills—I might spot another deer and didn't want to miss again! The bushes became denser and we had to spread them apart to advance. It was close to 11 AM and the sun beat mercilessly down on us. We were going down the second biggest mountain in the Sierra Madre, and then had to climb the biggest one, where we were to meet Jorge. I knew he was hoping his next client would know how to shoot.

Halfway down the mountain, the two-man funeral procession stopped for a rest. When Arturo turned and looked my way, I avoided his gaze, pretending to dig out a thorn. He kept staring until I couldn't stand it anymore. As I looked up, I caught a flicker of movement and looked beyond Arturo. He sensed my anticipation and turned around. We saw the big buck just as it stood up. For some arcane reason—maybe because we didn't look like enemies in our dejected stances—the fine animal stared fixedly at us from some two hundred and twenty-five yards without bolting.

Instinctively, I dropped to a sitting position and rested my elbows on my knees. I could see only the head and neck of the petrified deer as the cross hairs wavered on and off the exposed neck. I started to squeeze the trigger, set at exactly two and a half pounds, but stopped the final pressure as the cross hairs moved beyond the target. When the cross hairs again bisected the neck, I applied the final ounce of pressure, releasing the firing pin. As I recovered from the recoil, I could detect no movement. Yet I knew my deer was dead. I sat there trembling as Arturo congratulated me.

It took us more than twenty minutes to reach my fallen trophy. It had a wide and heavy, if not terribly high, eight-point rack. The bullet had entered high in the neck, exiting the left hindquarter for an instantaneous kill.

Physically and mentally drained, I knelt beside my fallen quarry and caressed the knurled antlers. It dawned on me that the only thing that gives meaning to hunting is the imminent risk of failure, even if success is only the result of the quarry making the mistake of waiting too long.

A Lesson in Conservation

Chapter 13

I knew I shouldn't go to Argentina . . . but I was going anyway! Common sense dictated that it was crazy to travel halfway around the world in the same year that I was sending my kid to Georgia Tech and my daughter was getting married. But I just couldn't resist a handout. So when my good friend Hershel Neal called for the second time to ask why I hadn't called his friend Ronnie Foster in Buenos Aires to determine an arrival date, my resistance broke. The headquarters of Ladeco Airlines happened to be next door to my office, and after being tempted—just out of curiosity, of course—to ask about the price of a round-trip ticket, I was as hooked as an alcoholic with his first drink after a long dry spell.

Upon checking at the Argentinian embassy, I was informed that as a Costa Rican I didn't even need an entry visa and that the only reason my rifle permit couldn't be granted that very afternoon was because I didn't have the serial number!

I did find out that Argentina was a long way off: I boarded my plane on Saturday and, following a quick layover in Chile, got off Sunday evening. As I walked through the airport, Ronnie Foster walked right up to me—I guess it was easy to spot the guy with the dumb look and the silver rifle case in his hand. He introduced me to Alberto Severo, who had graciously agreed to guide me for the next few days, and we struck up an immediate friendship. Without further formalities, we boarded his Peugeot station wagon for the long haul to the Estancia La Corona, about two hundred fifty miles southwest of Buenos Aires.

The first thing that struck me was the flatness of the country; I mean table-flat! As we got farther away from civilization, I was awed by the huge flocks of waterfowl. Three hours later we left the highway to follow a gravel road leading to the estancia of Manuel Anchorena, whose grandfather was responsible for the introduction of the blackbuck antelope to Argentina.

To say I was impressed would be an understatement! The farmhouse and gardens were graced by huge trees dating from the beginning of

the previous century, and I was told that much of Argentina's history was written within its walls. Don Manuel greeted us in full gaucho dress, and his graceful wife assigned me the guest room, where I quickly shed my city clothing and jet lag in preparation to go hunting.

The warm fall clothing I had brought proved unnecessary—I found myself hunting in 60-degree weather, needing only a light jacket. As we entered a huge pasture near the estate, we caught the first glimpse of a blackbuck antelope as it disappeared in the high grass. I was drinking in my surroundings in the bouncing station wagon when we came upon more herds of skittish antelope, which raced off the instant they saw us. Presently we came to the house of Jesús Godoy, game warden for the ranch, who would be our guide for the next few days.

Although we saw a lot of game—including South American ostriches or rheas, hares, partridge, ducks, and stunning South American swans with white bodies, black heads and necks, and red beaks and feet—we never closed in on our elusive quarry. Darkness chased us back to the ranch house for a formal candlelight dinner of grilled steak and our choice of red or white wine. I rejoiced in the company of new friends and old wines.

After turning off the bedroom lights, I was lulled to sleep by the patter of rain and the occasional clap of thunder, thinking how much more comfortable it is to sleep in a house than a tent.

Next day broke foggy and rainy, and as I looked out the window I realized the whole countryside was flooded. A large storm had come in and the rain was unlikely to subside for at least a few days. Using the Peugeot to go to the hunting area was out of the question. However, Mr. Anchorena solved the problem by providing us with a four-wheel-drive Ford pickup truck.

Overnight the pampas had become a huge flood plain, and it almost seemed we were hunting sitatunga in the Bangweulu Swamps of Zambia.

We picked up Jesús Godoy and headed across the endless plain, covered by a good foot of water. We would try to spot a herd from the vehicle and hope to close in on foot, much like the way pronghorn antelope are hunted in the American West. Unfortunately, due to the poor visibility caused by the rain, by the time we saw each herd, the animals were running all out, and, no, they didn't stop for that last look.

By 10:30 we were thoroughly soaked and disgusted, but as we came upon a clump of pampas grass (like the plants used back home in fancy

gardens), a buck and doe antelope took off from beneath it at supersonic speed. Jesús slammed on the brakes and yelled at me to take the shot. I jumped out of the vehicle and used the side of the door as a rest while the speedy antelope stretched the distance between us. The buck was going straight away at about a hundred and seventy-five yards, and I decided to give it a try. After all, I was using a 7mm magnum custom rifle made by Sam Johnson's Answer Products Company and figured I couldn't miss. However, when the antelope zigged, the rifle zagged (misses are always the rifle's fault), and I saw the bullet strike water ahead of it.

However, the noise or the nearby bullet strike caused the blackbuck to stop for a moment to reconsider its route of escape, presenting me with a broadside standing shot. This allowed me to work the magic for which Sam's rifles are famous, making the animal disappear in a cloud of spray. In fact, it disappeared for a full twenty minutes, until we discovered one horn sticking out of the water. It was a beautiful specimen in its prime, with horns measuring twenty-two inches, and it qualified for *Safari Club International's Record Book of Introduced Animals of South America.*

The minutes—or hours—one spends in making a good shot at a magnificent game animal and then finally finding it after considerable effort are the highlights of a lifetime. I cannot think of another thing I'd rather do in public!

That night we savored the taste of antelope tenderloin in the estancia's own wine-sauce recipe, completing the flavor of the hunt in a particularly satisfying manner.

The rest of that day and the following morning proved fruitless. We were searching for a trophy axis deer, also introduced in Argentina around the turn of the century and considered by many the most beautiful deer in the world. The rain never ceased, however, and although we saw several does and small bucks, we never came upon the trophy I was looking for. In our quest for an axis buck, however, we did come twice upon a beautiful black fallow deer with magnificent yellow, palmated antlers, which gave him a striking appearance. I decided against taking him, though, having already collected a good specimen in the Hill Country of Texas many years earlier.

Toward evening of the third day the rain still had not subsided, and I realized that I would either settle for the fallow buck or return home deerless to Buenos Aires. As luck would have it, we returned to the same general area where we had seen most of the fallow deer and presently came

upon a small herd bunched under a stand of oaks in the driving rain. *Cervus dama* isn't the wariest deer in the world, but this old yellow-horns hadn't gotten big by being stupid! As the herd stampeded to the right and I frantically tried to find the big buck in my scope, Jesús nudged me and signaled to the left. In the fading light I saw the unmistakable wide yellow palms and decided to take the one-hundred-yard running shot. The rifle came up almost unbidden, and I remember holding slightly in front of the animal's nose. At the rifle's roar (not its recoil, which is practically eliminated by Mr. Johnson's trim-line muzzle brake), the big buck, hit in the neck, dropped immediately.

Next morning the rain continued in a steady downpour, and though we ventured out, we ended up having to hire a tractor to pull us out of the muck. With transportation so seriously impaired, the hunt for red stag—which in Argentina grow to tremendous size—was unfortunately ruled out.

We returned to Buenos Aires, where I enjoyed the city for a few days before returning to the southern part of this same province for a bird shoot. We left on a Thursday evening and drove half the night to the town of Azul, where we spent the night.

Early next morning found Alberto and me about three hundred miles from Buenos Aires and working two kinds of partridge over trained pointers. After a quick lunch, we decided to slightly diminish the population of Turkish pigeons, a big bird the size of a domestic pigeon, which inhabited the countryside there in pest proportions. There is no closed season and no bag limit, but after about a dozen birds, Alberto dragged me away to chase more partridge. I really didn't want to go, but he was running the show.

Later on we headed to the house of the estancia's manager, where we would spend the night. At dinner Alberto announced that we would undertake an early morning duck shoot and then leave. The reason for our departure, he said, was that the ranch owner was an "ecologist" and was against hunting. Then it dawned on me that I had seen no antelope, no deer or rheas, and very few hares. In fact, I had seen absolutely no game that didn't fly. A discussion with the manager provided the answer: There was no game warden—the man they had hired for the job was unproductive and expensive. Consequently, poaching was rampant, and even the manager confided that he shot hares for export to Germany, rheas

for their feathers (leaving the meat to rot), and deer for no apparent reason (he had no use for their meat, hides, or horns). Since game animals were "unproductive," except maybe to watch, nobody cared. The owner denied hunting access to his friends on the grounds that he was an "ecologist" and against hunting, while people he didn't even know exterminated every living thing!

As I reminisced about my hunt on the long trip back to Buenos Aires, I couldn't help comparing the anti-hunting sentiment with communism. Just as there isn't a single country in recorded history that has bettered the living conditions of its people by socializing its economy, there isn't one country in the world that has increased its game populations by banning hunting. Examples are legion, but suffice it to say that Kenya had about 166,000 elephants and 10,000 black rhinos when sport hunting was closed in 1977. Today, more than three decades after the "total protection" granted to Kenya's animals, there are less than 27,000 elephants and about 400 black rhinos, watched by armed guards night and day. And all the rest of Kenya's wildlife has met a similar fate.

Hunting, properly managed, provides a dramatic incentive to the local people to preserve big game. Most conservationists who know what they are talking about agree that sport hunting is the only long-term solution for the conservation of wildlife. Ecologically, tourists are more destructive than hunters; economically, they are less valuable. According to Tanzania's wildlife department, one hunter is worth one hundred tourists to the local economy.

It took half the world about three-quarters of a century to realize communism was wrong. I pray to God it will not take "ecologists" that long to see their mistakes. Our invaluable natural resources cannot wait that long!

Storm Jaguar

Chapter 14

I was immersed in my thoughts, pondering what the hell I was doing on a pitch-black night somewhere in the Nicaraguan or Costa Rican tropical jungle—I didn't even know which—when Manuel Queb's imitation of the challenge call of a male jaguar sent waves of goose-flesh through my body. Again he placed his hand inside the empty gourd called a *pujadera*, grasped the braided horsehair cord running down the center of the drum-head, and pulled hard several times in quick succession, allowing the braid to slip between his fingers. The result, a sullen, coughing roar, was reminiscent of a coarse-toothed saw cutting into a coffin.

I felt rather than heard the sound, and it rattled my very soul!

As the last grunt died down, an ominous silence pervaded the jungle. Even the crickets and whippoorwills held their breath in silent respect for the undisputed lord of the tropics.

Although it was April and the mating season was long past—which meant the jaguar wouldn't answer the call—I nervously fingered the safety catch on my Sako .308 rifle with one hand and the switch of my headlamp with the other.

Early that day we had stumbled upon the three- or four-day-old tracks of a big tom and had tied the carcass of a goat to a tree about six feet off the ground so that a jaguar would be able to reach it only with difficulty. That way, it could devour only some of the bait, leaving enough meat to entice him back the following night. The challenge was to make him stalk this neck of his twenty-square-mile territory for intruders, blunder into one of our baits, and hopefully wind up in my trophy room. But jaguars seldom follow the script.

We advanced slowly, Manuel calling out intermittently, until we reached the banks of the San Juan River where the outboard-powered dugout canoe was waiting.

This was the eighth day of one of the most grueling jungle hunts I had ever undertaken. Long treks in sweltering heat had already caused me to lose about fifteen pounds. The rains had begun, although not in earnest,

and each day we were pelted by sudden showers, which, fortunately, didn't last long. At first I wore a raincoat, but then realized I was getting just as wet from my own sweat as from the cool rains, which I finally learned to ignore and even welcome as a relief from the sticky dampness.

≈ ≈ ≈

In fact, after eight days in the jungle, I had learned to ignore everything: the heat, the rain, the mud, the swamps, the thorns, the ants, and the ubiquitous mosquitoes that always managed to find an unsprayed part of my sorry anatomy.

But all this only heightened my obsession to bag that mysterious and fascinating, beautiful, black-rosetted creature that seemed to exist only in my imagination. The only evidence of its presence were the large, round pug marks it left on the muddy trails used occasionally by the local hunters in their quest for white-lipped peccaries.

This was not a sport but an act of dedication! Nothing mattered but the unrelenting search, which had taken on the significance of a crusade. My world had narrowed to a compulsion to obtain the unattainable, for I was beginning to believe that jaguars are not real flesh-and-blood animals but phantoms living only in the minds of obsessed hunters. They have been declared endangered, for they are shy, jungle-dwelling creatures of the night. My brother even bet me $65 against $650 that I would come up empty-handed. My home, my family, my entire way of life in the city had faded into fantasy. The jaguar—the non-existent jaguar—had become my sole reality!

The hunt had not been completely fruitless. On the fifth day one of our many baits had been partially eaten. Exploration of the surrounding area revealed the tracks of a big ocelot, which, thanks to his appetite, fell to a perfectly placed neck shot from my .22 rifle at 7:15 PM.

I estimated his weight at over forty pounds and felt as proud as a fisherman who had landed a ninety-pound tarpon on twenty-pound-test line.

The next day was Sunday, and a pending law case transported me back home. But Manuel was not leaving: He would stay in the jungle with the two Nicaraguans I had hired to check the baits and, I hoped, would call me when one of them was taken. I held onto his passport and airline tickets so they wouldn't get lost!

By the following Friday I still had not received a call. Hope, expectation, and desire had given way to restlessness. The urge to return was irresistible and dawn found me driving northeast from Costa Rica's capital city of San José to keep an appointment with the cat whose unseen presence had possessed me to the point of sleeplessness.

The rainy season had advanced during my week-long absence, and the road to the river was impassable. Fortunately, Segundo Gaytán was waiting at the foot of a bridge spanning a small stream marking the end of the passable road. When we reached the "Rain Goddess," a luxurious sixty-five-foot houseboat that Dr. Alfredo López had generously provided as our headquarters for the hunt during the low tourist season, Santos, one of the hired Nicaraguans, announced that the jaguar had eaten.

"It hit our farthest bait, where we saw the biggest tracks," he said, "and Manuel says it must be a big male. What took you so long to get here?"

It struck me that this cat might actually be real; he might materialize after all. And if there was anyone in the world who could bring him to me, it was Manuel Queb. After all, Manuel was a magician who had already produced a female jaguar for me in Campeche, Mexico, a few years back and an ocelot a few days earlier.

I retrieved my rifle, headlamp, and hunting clothes from the houseboat and, for once, was ready in minutes. Santos opened the throttle of the outboard, and the dugout headed across the delta of the Colorado River to where it joined the San Juan. We halted for a few minutes at the Costa Rican border and again on the Nicaraguan side, where we unloaded the bottles of rum and provisions that were hindering our progress. After a half-hour of steady motoring, we reached the house of El Gordo—"Fatso"—the former guerrilla leader who had been so helpful and at whose house Manuel had been staying the last few days so he could call the jaguar every night.

Wet, haggard, and bearded but eager as a bird dog, Manuel jumped into the boat for the forty-minute trip to the site of the bait. He was in too much of a hurry even to greet us, but he did manage to tell me that, judging from the tracks, it was the biggest of the three jaguars that had taken baits and that the machan with braided hammocks was ready.

We arrived at the bait site shortly after 4 PM after a brisk fifteen-minute walk over firm ground. Manuel untied the peccary carcass from the tree and laid it on the ground to allow for a shot at a standing animal

instead of one straining to reach hanging meat. He then proceeded to tie the remains of the peccary lengthwise between two sturdy trees, to keep the jaguar from dragging it away, as they invariably try to do. Because of the thick vegetation enveloping us, any shot I would have would be at very short range.

It was going on five when we climbed up the near-horizontal poles to our hammocks and settled down for a long vigil. As we sat motionless, clouds of mosquitoes hummed and buzzed around us. I sprayed myself with repellent and prayed I wouldn't get malaria. Although we were perched about twenty feet high, where the jaguar would not likely sense our presence, the tops of the trees seemed far away and light intruded in rare, oblique rays, printing a delicate pattern of gold on the ground. The prospect of the jaguar appearing at any moment was agonizing and madly exciting at the same time.

For a while, all was serene. Birds fluttered in the trees above us, completely unaware of our presence. An opossum walked clumsily under our perch and suddenly reared up to test the air, its pink nose crinkling. Convinced that all was well, it tiptoed away on business of his own.

It was wild and beautiful and primitive. To me, this was the quintessence of the most magnificent of hunts.

Dusk fell rapidly, as it always does in the jungle. Suddenly we were engulfed by darkness, the stars completely obscured by clouds, a perfect setting for the *cocuyos (Pyrophorus noctilucus)*, giant beetles with a permanent glow above their eyes, which filed past us like a procession of miniature comets, leaving behind the all-pervading darkness of the night.

The jungle was as silent as a grave. No animal or bird uttered the faintest sound, nor did a frog croak or a cricket chirp. The hot, muggy air became tangibly close and stifling.

The reason for these unusual conditions was that a storm was brewing. Shortly after 8 PM its first drops touched my face, carried by a cool breeze. This was followed by a deafening crescendo, which I at first mistook for the sound of a jet engine overhead. I barely had time to slip into my Gore-Tex jacket before a sheet of water enveloped us.

Vivid flashes of lightning streaked through the blackness, followed by the ominous roars of thunder. Rain fell for the rest of the night with unabated fury, whipping off palm branches here and there and hurling them to the jungle floor. The blackness was so absolute that I couldn't see

Manuel, who was no more than an arm's length away. We sat motionless, staring into the darkness with our ears.

At 9:45 I heard a faint snap, as of a thin bone being broken. Frozen like a statue, I strained my ears but couldn't make out any further sounds amid the downpour's continuous roar. Minutes dragged on, and then suddenly I felt Manuel's hand grip my arm, a signal that he was going to shine the light. The moment of truth had come, and I realized how important that first shot was going to be, for one shot was all I was going to get.

I slowly and carefully brought the rifle to bear and waited for a few seconds, covering the telescopic sight with my body to protect it from the lashing rain. The powerful beam parted the crushing blackness, revealing in a split second only the reeking carcass of the partially eaten peccary. All remained calm, except for my wildly beating heart, which I hoped the jaguar couldn't hear.

During the next five or ten minutes, tension built up in me stealthily and insidiously before Manuel's cold, clammy hand again clutched my arm. When he again beamed his light, an apparition appeared that momentarily left me paralyzed.

There, not more than forty feet away in the tiny glade that we had cleared, was the jaguar. In the eerie light he seemed very light-colored, his head blocky and wide as he squatted by the bait. I had the presence of mind to aim quickly but carefully at the base of his neck and between the massive shoulders before I put the last ounce of pressure on the trigger to release the firing pin.

Although I believe death was instantaneous, Manuel urged me to shoot again for good measure. Then I just sat there in silence for a few minutes, savoring the moment like champagne, one small sip at a time.

I then slowly and cautiously climbed down the makeshift ladder to kneel beside my jaguar in contemplative admiration. It will have its place in my trophy room, and I will dream about this hunt until the inevitable happens and the crab hidden in my gut or the wolf hidden in my heart takes the final bite.

Nightmare

Chapter 15

I had met Gene Bishop on a dove shoot in Costa Rica several years before. He is a natural southern gentleman and a friend of mine. The last fact doesn't make him a bad person. Nobody's perfect!

Like me, he had hunted Africa, Canada, and the United States, but wanted a jaguar really badly. Now, Costa Rica has quite a few jaguars, but finding one of these shy and nocturnal creatures in the impenetrable rain forest they inhabit is another story. I should know, for I had been trying unsuccessfully to get one for the previous twenty years or so. But then Manuel Queb had appeared in my life and the opportunity had presented itself. At last I had my cat.

On that memorable night in the jungles of Campeche, Mexico, Manuel, Gene, his lovely wife Sherry, and I downed at least four bottles of vintage Chardonnay to my good luck. I had to pinch myself to make sure I wasn't dreaming. It had been a long day and was close to midnight when we decided to turn in. Sherry had warned me about imbibing with Gene: "He'll drink you under the table," she had warned.

He stood up fresh as a daisy, while I staggered to my tent and passed out on my cot. That's the last I remember before regaining consciousness the next day to the raucous call of the chachalacas. What happened next I know only because Gene told me the next morning.

The fire had been out and the Coleman lanterns extinguished for at least a couple of hours. Nothing disturbed the silence of the tropical jungle besides the soft whistling of the whippoorwills and the occasional hooting of an owl. As Gene explained the next morning, he suddenly regained full consciousness at a blood-curdling scream in English from my tent saying: "I am going to kill you!"

Now, Gene figured that if I was yelling in English and not in Spanish—my native language—it was because I was trying to warn him of "clear and present danger."

His military training as a ranger during the Korean War came into play and he switched to autopilot: He picked up his lever-action .308, fed

a cartridge into the chamber, and tore out of his tent in his underwear, ready to shoot the first thing that moved. Fortunately, nothing stirred.

Then Sherry's voice came to calm Gene down: "That's only another one of Ricardo's nightmares. He does that all the time."

Gene slowly turned around, the rifle still quivering in his hands, and asked: "And how do *you* know that?"

As it turned out, I'd had the foresight to warn Sherry of my occasional nightmares as we rode together in the back of the Volkswagen station wagon that had taken us from Cancún to Campeche.

Next morning it was my turn to be fresh as a daisy over breakfast—though Gene seemed a bit haggard from lack of sleep.

Never Trust a Mule

Chapter 16

Sam Johnson, the custom rifle maker out of Davison, Michigan (Answer Products Co.), had just sent me a sweet little .308 rifle built on a Remington action topped by a Swarovski 2.5X4.5 scope. I had to try it out. Given that I lived in San José, Costa Rica, tropical whitetail deer hunting meant pretty much going to Guanacaste province in the northern part of the country. It had been raining like hell the last few days, but I figured that would only make the hunting better. Besides, I wasn't made of sugar and the rifle had a Nylite finish so it wouldn't rust.

It took me the better part of an hour on Friday evening to load rifles, saddles, scabbards, cooler boxes, cots, hunting clothes, and other paraphernalia into my Nissan Pathfinder and to convince my twenty-year-old son to accompany me. I didn't want to make the five-hour drive alone. We would hunt Saturday afternoon and Sunday morning, returning home that second day. Certainly he could miss two days of his vacation from Georgia Tech!

It rained on and off all the way to the little fishing town of Cuajiniquil, nestled in a valley surrounded by big, rounded hills not far from the Nicaraguan border. From here it would be only about a fifteen-minute drive to the house of Manuel Mata, the local guide who was always as keen as a bird dog to guide me. Besides, he had good horses on his hundred acres of land. To reach his house we would have to ford the Murcielago River, which was no big deal thanks to its rocky bed. When we reached the river's edge, it looked much wider than I remembered and had an ominous roar I didn't like. Its otherwise clear waters were a dark chocolate, churning and tumbling downstream. I seriously considered crossing until my son pointed out that Pathfinders are not ideal for white-water rafting. At the last moment, I chickened out.

Crossing the river was out, but the hunt was still on. All I needed were three horses and another guide. I knew a backup guide, and all I had to do was convince the foreman of a ranch owned by an airline pilot—who was never there anyway—to rent me three nags. Besides, they wouldn't

be using the horses on the weekend and he could probably use a little cash. It turned out one horse had been bitten by a tarantula, another one was sick, and the third had been sold! But still I figured there was no problem: I was welcome to use the three ranch mules for approximately thirty bucks. It was getting late, so I instructed Chago, the backup guide, to round up the three animals and meet us at the house of Manuel Mata's brother, located at the edge of the ranch we were going to hunt.

We drove like hell to our meeting place, unloaded, changed into hunting garb, and grabbed a quick bite. I was getting ready to go back and look for Chago when he rode in, pulling two more mules by the halter ropes. He was cussing over the three animals.

I was in too much of a hurry to be mad at him for being late and went on with the business at hand. Both unsaddled mules were tied to sturdy trees, but the moment I approached either one with a saddle, it would lay its ears back, roll its eyes, and get in position to kick out. I was raised around horses and can pretty much predict what they are going to do, and now my better judgment told me to stay away from their hind legs. I remembered Winston Churchill's comment about horses being uncomfortable in the center and dangerous at both ends. And I guess he never rode a mule!

But a'hunting we were going, and no stubborn mule would keep us from doing so. We tied both equines really short between a fork in a tree and then used a jacket to cover their eyes. If they couldn't see, they couldn't kick me! I saddled both mules and cinched them tight, ignoring their little squeals of protest. Now it was time to ride them, and my son, who so far had been a bystander, would go first. He immediately reminded me of the great delay that a broken leg would mean in his becoming an industrial engineer, but to no avail.

Ever so carefully, he mounted the just-christened "Bucky." I guess he didn't think the name was funny, because he didn't laugh! For some reason, his face resembled the pale gray color of his steed. Then I slowly and carefully untied the halter rope and removed the jacket. Bucky gave a couple of half-hearted jumps and broke into a brisk trot. After circling the corral a couple of times, it pricked up its ears and came to a stop. We all sighed in relief!

My son smiled and informed me that now it was my turn to ride "Widowmaker." I replied nonchalantly that it would be no problem—all

three mules were well broken in. A bit apprehensive, I mounted my steed and had Chago repeat the procedure with the halter rope and the jacket. Widowmaker just stood there trembling while I expected the worse, holding on with tooth and nail for dear life. Then I nudged the noble beast with my heels and it took off at a quick trot.

"You see," I patronized my son, "if you don't show fear to an animal, it will respect you."

I had Chago put my rifle in the saddle scabbard, and we all trotted briskly away.

Deer weren't very active that balmy afternoon and we only saw two or three before the onset of night. All disappeared before I could even take a good look. The hunt being over for the day, we turned around and headed calmly back to the truck, following an old dirt road. I was leading the way slowly, at peace with the world, when suddenly the devil himself possessed Widowmaker. If I remember accurately, it passed gas twice, laid its long ears back, kicked out, and took off at a dead run. I held on for dear life like a monkey on a branch in a tornado, pulling at the reins with all my strength while dodging low branches that I could hardly see. I let out a couple of yells that would have impressed Pavarotti himself. Either my yells stopped the wretched creature or my sudden French exclamations exorcised its evil spirit: Widowmaker suddenly stopped dead in its tracks, momentum almost thrusting me between her long ears.

I quickly dismounted and tied my hybrid host to the nearest tree before it became repossessed. Presently, Chago and my son caught up with me.

"It's sure a good thing that mule respects you, Dad," my son said, giggling spasmodically. "I guess it stopped when you let out that battle cry and it realized you weren't afraid."

I made some comment relative to how much I respected my own father!

Figuring something was wrong with the way I had saddled her, I went through the tight halter rope and jacket procedure again, removing the saddle and blankets and carefully resaddling the noble beast. The truck being pretty far away, and reluctant to show any weakness, I held my breath and climbed aboard.

Again Widowmaker trotted along without batting an eye.

As the minutes dragged by, I became less apprehensive and slowly relaxed, the fresh night breeze blowing the sweet smell of wet grass into

my nostrils. It must have been a hitch in the saddle blankets or the cinch that had made the gentle beast buck and run.

But apparently I wasn't the only one enjoying the smell of nature. Widowmaker must somehow have sensed my reacquired calmness, increased by the fatigue of the long ride. Like the man overdue in his payments to his exorcist, my otherwise gentle steed was suddenly repossessed! She stopped dead in her tracks. Then she shuddered all over, violently, as if with ague. I braced myself as she let out a loud snort and attained top speed in about one and a half seconds flat. Try as I might, I couldn't stop my galloping mount until it plunged into the Canelo River and calmly lay down in the deepest part. I quickly dismounted and yanked my rifle out of the saddle scabbard to keep it from getting wet. I was drenched to my belt, of course, but somehow refrained from shooting the damned mule. I swear this last is true: At that moment she gave out a sound that can only be described as an equine giggle.

Being much more intelligent than a dumb mule, and determined not to give in and walk all the way back to the car, I found a way to solve the problem. I gave Chago the halter rope, which he tied to his saddle horn. That way we would ride abreast of each other, and if my mule again decided to play games, Chago's mule would hold it.

I drained my boots and remounted, apprehensive but proud of my ingenuity.

After a mile or so of steady trotting, the problem seemingly solved, I again relaxed and entertained myself by watching the fireflies weaving singly and in twos and threes among the branches of the trees. There seemed to be thousands of them as they flashed, faded away, then broke out again, sometimes in bunches and at other times in myriads. For brief moments they would outline and illuminate the towering trees and their boughs, which otherwise were indistinguishable in the gloom. This rural spectacle of ethereal charm can seldom be seen in inhabited areas and is slowly disappearing due to the uncontrolled use of pesticides. It brings, at least to me, an ineffable sense of beauty and wonder.

Unfortunately, Widowmaker wasn't impressed and decided to give it one more try before we made it to the truck. This time there was no warning of the evil spirit reentering—the sudden lunge took us all by surprise, including Chago's mule keeping abreast of mine.

Either Chago was stronger than I was or his mule was weaker than mine—or perhaps she wasn't in default to his exorcist—because Chago

was able to stop it in its tracks. Now, I always use an extra-long halter rope (to allow my horse to feed when I still-hunt)—which meant that my mule kept right on running when Chago's stopped. But not for long: The end of the rope brought my animal to an abrupt stop, twisting its neck and pitching both of us head-over-heels into a ditch on the side of the track. I remember kicking the blasted animal away from me in the darkness and trying to avoid the flailing hoofs as I stepped up and away from it. The synchronized flashes of a thousand fireflies revealed the rapidly disappearing hind end of the devilish creature, with Chago in hot pursuit.

In complete darkness my son and I sat on a rotting tree trunk and prayed for Chago to find my mule. I was so mad I would have shot the damned animal, except I didn't even have my new rifle to shoot it with.

After what seemed an eternity of feeding the mosquitoes and no-see-ums, we concluded that Widowmaker should be able to find its way home. A sliver of moon had appeared in the horizon, and I started to follow my son and his mount. There was, of course, another stream to cross before we reached my truck, and I had to wade it. Since I was already soaked to the waist, it didn't matter much, except that I completed the process by stepping on a slippery rock.

I think it was the Romanian philosopher Emil Cioran who said: "The secret of men is the secret of their sufferings, those that they have chosen." I should have listened to my mother when she told me to play tennis!

We were both surprised to meet Chago when we reached my truck. Apparently he had gone back home to see if Widowmaker had done likewise. Unfortunately, such was not the case. It was about 3 AM and I was too tired and cold to go back out to search some more. I changed to some dry clothes and passed out with a last thought for the whereabouts of my custom rifle.

Three hours later I woke up to a pale dawn and the songs of a myriad of birds, among which I was able to identify the tropical wild turkey *(Crax rubra).* I looked for Chago but he was gone. I prayed he would find my rifle. Unable to stand it anymore, I jumped in my truck and went looking for him. After fording the stream, whose water had subsided, and driving for about a mile, I stopped in the middle of a huge field to see what I could see. It surprised me to hear three shots fired in quick succession from a high-powered rifle. Either Chago had found my rifle and was signaling, or

he was executing the mule, either of which was fine with me. As it turned out, he had found my sturdy steed placidly feeding on the lush greenery with my rifle hanging precariously from the scabbard. He was able to sneak up on the unsuspecting beast of burden and yank the rifle from its scabbard, whereupon Widowmaker had again disappeared in chlorophyll. My problem was nine-tenths solved: I could have kissed Chago!

We decided to return to the house where I had slept and leave the rifle there. I wanted to avoid temptation when I found Widowmaker.

We returned immediately to her previous location, but try as we might, Widowmaker had disappeared, along with the spirit that had possessed her. Upon our return in defeat to the little house, Chago's sister-in-law informed us that a saddled mule had just raced down the road, faster than a soul on its way to hell. We all gave quick chase, coming upon my mule inside a police training camp about a mile away, duly tied to a sturdy palm tree. Two armed guards with stern faces were guarding her.

I explained to the policemen how the mule had thrown me while I was inspecting some cattle I was planning to buy, and that I was ready to unsaddle and return her home. I guess I looked honest, for they untied her and handed her over by the halter rope. I lost no time unsaddling and threw everything into my Pathfinder. Upon unpacking back home, I realized I hadn't looked honest but rather stupid to the policemen: They had pilfered my saddlebags!

Ah, but life has its compensations: The very next week, Widowmaker was bitten by a rattlesnake and became permanently repossessed.

Always Go First Class

Chapter 17

Being a slow learner, it took me some time to discover that if you can't afford an expensive elk hunt, book a first-class deer or antelope hunt. And it took me even longer to figure out that it is very hard to combine a hunt for two species, at least in the continental United States.

Now, I'm not particularly turned on by mediocre trophies and I had been burned before, so I finally decided on Mick Chapel of New Mexico Professional Big Game Hunting, Inc. Mick couldn't have come more highly recommended, and I was not to be disappointed.

Unable to afford the elk hunt, I lowered my standards to his two-day trophy antelope hunt on private land. Not having fully learned the second lesson cited above, I also booked a five-day try for black bear, the hunts to be taken back to back.

One lesson I did learn long ago was to hunt one-on-one, not only to maximize opportunity but also to avoid the competition that sometimes arises and has the potential to turn the best of friends into bitter enemies. Two good friends from Costa Rica, Mauricio Vargas and Randall Gazel, would join me on this trip. It would be Mauricio's first international hunt.

The flight to Albuquerque was uneventful except for our high expectations—especially Mauricio, who could hardly restrain his enthusiasm.

Dawn of 30 September 1995 found Dale Kalberg—my guide and friend-to-be—and me huddled in the cabin of a pickup truck waiting for the glorious sunrise that would mark the beginning of a hunt for a great game animal in a fascinating place. We were to try for a particular "goat" that had been located previously by Mick. This creature had managed to grow trophy-class horns by living among the oaks and cedars that dotted the area's higher elevations. But try as we might on opening day, the buck had disappeared.

≈ ≈ ≈

After several hours of unsuccessful scouting and glassing, we moved to the immense plain extending endlessly below us, to see if "Old Paddlehorn" had changed residences. It is hard to describe the mixed feelings of peace and expectation you experience when glassing the great plains from the bed of a pickup, the clean smell of dry grass blowing gently against your face. Jagged pink peaks rose a thousand feet to our front and left, making me feel tiny in these immense surroundings. Right then, there was no other place in the world I would rather have been!

Shortly, Dale picked up the first small group of pronghorns about a thousand yards away and set up the spotting scope for closer scrutiny of the horns. Rising heat waves made it difficult to get an exact idea, but to my inexperienced eyes they looked black, long, and heavy, certainly bigger than anything I had seen before. Dale didn't need a second look to discard the lead buck as unsatisfactory:

"Under fifteen inches long and not enough mass," he said. "This is a trophy hunt."

Shortly after 10 AM we met Mauricio and his guide Andy, and from the way he beamed, I knew he had connected. He jumped out of the truck to hold the head of a fine sixteen-incher with excellent mass and acceptable prongs. Apparently it had taken quite a fusillade, but the buck was on the ground. I have yet to see a prouder hunter!

The heat of midday caused us to pause for a welcome rest in the shade of a stand of oaks. After a sandwich and a Coke, Dale and I both nodded off in the quiet solitude.

It was going on three when we resumed our efforts for Old Paddlehorn. Two "backup" bucks with good horn length, but one considerably heavier than the other, allowed us to look them over. We decided to try for Paddlehorn once more the next morning and, if that failed, lower our standards to No. 2.

Back in camp, three-fourths of the hunters had scored on excellent bucks in the 80-point Boone & Crockett range. Randall, my other hunting buddy, proudly displayed a long-horned buck that he had managed to put on the ground after considerable shooting. Like Mauricio, he was as happy as the cat that had eaten the rat.

At dawn of the second and last day of antelope season, Dale and I again were waiting for shooting light in the cold cabin of the pickup. As

a magnificent sunrise tinged the eastern horizon in pink and gold, we scurried among the oaks and cedars with a cold wind on our faces. Old Paddlehorn, however, seemed determined to make it through the 1995 hunting season unscathed.

By 8 AM we decided that Paddlehorn might not be so big after all and fell back to Plan B. Now all we needed to do was find No. 2 and have him cooperate. Using our pickup as a portable stand, we first located No. 3 with some does, grazing contentedly among a group of Herefords. But we were not yet ready to lower our standards that much!

After another half-hour of glassing we located No. 2 in the middle of a featureless flat with very little cover. Dale indicated that a stalk would probably be fruitless, but we decided to give it a try anyway.

First we walked, then we stooped or "duck-walked," and in the end we crawled, slowly closing the distance. I think we were spotted at about four hundred yards but managed to keep the band from spooking by freezing every time they gazed at us. At a little over two hundred and fifty yards, the buck raised his head and pinpointed our position. We both ducked down in the brush, holding our breath, not daring to look up. After several minutes, I cautiously sneaked a peek and could see the band nervously milling around.

"The jig is up," Dale whispered as he removed the spotting scope from the tripod so I could use the tripod as a rest. The underlying brush made the use of the Harris bipod impractical.

"Wait until he clears those bushes, and for God's sake, don't shoot a doe. Take your time—but hurry!"

Trouble was, the relatively small antelope appeared and disappeared in the tall sagebrush like rabbits in ragged grass. As I peered through the lens of my Swarovski, set at nine power, I saw the first doe walk across the tiny clearing. Then the two others walked briskly across. As my adrenaline level peaked, the horns of No. 2 floated above the rabbit brush, headed in the same direction. I held my breath as the beautiful buck came clear, although the lower half of his body was still obscured by underbrush. I held a bit high and touched off a 160-grain Nosler Partition from my custom 7mm Remington Magnum. The buck dropped and was swallowed by the sagebrush ocean.

Before I could recover from the rifle's recoil, Dale was slapping me on the back for the instantaneous one-shot kill. The bullet had gone high through the base of the neck, expanding somewhat messily.

Back in camp, the horns green-scored 80⅜ Boone & Crockett points, just two inches below the record-book minimum. And even if I had to lower my standards, I ended up well ahead, thanks to having gone first class.

Oh, and by the way, I got a beautiful black bear just two days later, but that is another story.

uscovy duck (Cairina moschata) *hunting used to be great in Costa Rica. They are protected now. Note e license plate in my Lada jeep, which later went up in flames. Guanacaste province, circa 1983.*

It's extremely rare to find a mountain lion without the aid of hounds, and I do not favor knocking o out of a tree. Guanacaste mountain range, Costa Rica.

This was the best mountain caribou (right) we could find as the migration had not yet started. was my fifth animal on the hunt. British Columbia, 15 September 1978.

This was the bull elk I had to settle for after blowing my chance on a big one. My guide wasn't hap with me and took a lousy picture. British Columbia, 16 September 1978.

y western Canadian moose was stripping its velvet when I shot him. The trophy head now graces my
replace. British Columbia, 8 September 1978.

This grizzly sow was shot with my 7mm Remington Magnum in British Columbia. We had an extr
Columbia, 8 September 1978.

hard time finding it in the thick brush. British

It was getting dark when we reached my Rocky Mountain goat. I was still scared from the boulder that almost got me. British Columbia, 7 September 1978.

Fall in British Columbia is nothing short of spectacular. My Indian guide Amos Achla is in the foregroun

he packhorse is carrying my caribou antlers. British Columbia, 1978.

shot this large ocelot in Guanacaste province in northern Costa Rica using a Sako .222. My bon vife is the pretty one in this picture, circa 1975.

My South Texas whitetail had big, spindly antlers and only one eye, which is probably why I got hi Near San Angelo, 13 December 1981.

he Lazarus buck has thick bases but few points. The picture was taken at my house on my thirtieth rthday. Puntarenas province, Costa Rica, 5 October 1972.

I took this record-class Grant gazelle w a Sako Deluxe in .308. Maralal, Kenya, January 1977.

We had to travel to the desert every day for this gerenuk because the area was overrun with bandits, a we couldn't camp overnight. Turkanaland, February 1977.

s not a very big leopard, but I was extremely proud of it. My professional hunter, Peter Faull, is all
niles. My safari was one of the last hunts in Kenya. Maralal, 31 January 1977.

Mozambique was teeming with buffaloes when I hunted there. I had to borrow a .375 to collect my bu
August 1969

My nyala sported 29-inch horns and was No. 17 in the Rowland Ward record book when I collected it. Mozambique, August 1969.

I didn't realize at the time how lucky I wa in collecting this fine sable antelope. I don remember the trophy fee, but it was probably le than half that of a lion license.

ook my lion in 1969 with a .308, when a license in
ozambique cost $51. Mozambique, August 1969.

I stalked my bushbuck on foot on the last day of the safari. The camp staff is on either side of me. Mozambique, August 1969

hen you shoot an elephant, you climb aboard and take a stroll. Mine carried fifty-pound tusks. The ense cost $111. Mozambique, August 1969.

This nice six-pointer is also from San Lucas Island. The buck's right ear was damaged by ticks, whi infested the island. Puntarenas province, Costa Rica, 20 June 1981.

n Lucas was a deer hunter's paradise, but, unfortunately, when they dismantled the prison camp, achers wiped out the deer population. Poachers sold the meat, hide, and antlers for a pittance. I und this six-pointer on the island. Puntarenas province, Costa Rica, circa 1981.

Note the neck flesh wound from my previous encounter on this good seven-pointer from San Lucas Island. Puntarenas province, Costa Rica, 25 July 1981.

I took this tropical white-tailed buck on the prison island of San Lucas in the Pacific Ocean. My s Ricardo Jr. was about fifteen at the time. Puntarenas province, Costa Rica, 1985.

is croc measured 4 meters, 40 cm (14 feet, 5 $^{15}/_{64}$ inches) and was as big as its African counterpart. We d to hire a tractor to pull it out of the water! Puntarenas province, Costa Rica.

ocodylus acutus *grow very large in Costa Rica; however, shooting one is about as much fun as* *oting a log. Puntarenas province, Costa Rica.*

While Odocoileus virginianus truei *are not very big, they are very challenging to hunt. This one w*
taken near the city of Puntarenas, on the Chapernal Ranch. The rifle is a Sako .308. Puntare
province, Costa Rica, 26 May 1989.

had to track deep into the Mexican jungles of Campeche to get my first jaguar, a female. Manuel Queb on the left. Campeche, Mexico.

Arturo Munguía, my guide, was as happy as I with this trophy whitetail. My outfitter was Jorge Cam
León from Sonora, México, 4 December, 1995.

The Argentine pampas was a flood plain when I collected my blackbuck. The estancia's game warde
Jesús Godoy, is in the foreground. La Pampa province, Argentina, 20 April 1993.

got this nice fallow deer in the pouring rain. It's been my experience that fallow deer don't present challenge. Buenos Aires province, Argentina, 20 April 1993.

The was an exploratory trip prior to my jaguar hunt, and we went deep into the tropical rain fores Nicaragua. The previous week, two peccary hunters died from snake bite in the same area; fer-de-lar is the main culprit. My son Ricardo is holding a shotgun. Río Indio, Nicaragua.

The rain had finally subsided when I took this jaguar in a jungle clearing. Río Indio, Nicaragua.

ere I am with the same jaguar and flanked by my two Nicaraguan guides. Manuel is the one kneeling.
ío Indio, Nicaragua.

My Argentinian boar was of pure European strain. It surprised me to learn that nobody knew how cape it for a shoulder mount. La Pampa province, Argentina, 18 April 2000.

My soaked, fearless tracker—with my bulletproof jaguar—earned every cent of his tip. Limón provinc Costa Rica.

ollected this red brocket deer (Mazama americana) *with dogs. It is almost impossible to determine he animal has horns when being chased by hounds, which is why I don't particularly favor hunting th dogs. Limón province, Costa Rica, circa 2000.*

vould rather eat paca than lobster. I collected ese two from a boat on the Indian River in caragua, circa 2005.

I got this ocelot with a .22 rifle. Ocelots will come readily to bait if you make a drag where you find their tracks. Indian River, Nicaragua.

If you look hard, you will notice the Texas heart shot on my excellent blackbuck, shot in the immen
Argentinian pampas, circa 2001.

› third jaguar was a female. I was wet from perspiration—it hadn't rained that night. The rifle is a ›tom .308 made by the Answer Products Company. Limón province, Costa Rica.

I like a machan to be around 8 or 9 meters (26–29½ feet) high. This one is in the early stages in building and still needs to be camouflaged. Limón province, Costa Rica

My axis deer, which I shot on an Argentinian estancia, *was very nice but the hunt wasn't very challengi*
Buenos Aires Province, 28 April 2000.

I survived for ten days in the Pantanal Hilton. There was no floor, no water, no electricity, and no toile
El Beni, Bolivia, September 2003.

*ıe capybara (*Hydrochoerus hydrochaeris*) is the world's largest rat. The Indians wouldn't touch the eat, I suppose due to its similarity to the rat family, but I later learned the meat is excellent. El Beni, olivia, 22 September 2003.*

enjamín Cordero, my guide, sits with his dogs among jaguar skins. Note the missing ears on the dog n the left. Cordero regularly cuts off a dog's ears if it demonstrates a fear of jaguars. This one showed fear of jaguars three times! El Beni, Bolivia, 18 September 2003.

Cracids abound near waterways. 1 collected a couple to mount, but they also were good eating a provided a change in diet. San Joaquín River, El Beni, Bolivia, 20 September 2003.

How Not to Go Bare on Bear

Chapter 18

Although I had always wanted a black bear, a hunt for some antlered critter would always get in the way come autumn. The way to overcome the dilemma, of course, was to book a hunt for antlered game and bear. Only problem was that the bear would be the secondary animal, and invariably I ended up bear-less. That is, until I found Mick Chapel out of Quemado, New Mexico.

After finishing a successful two-day trophy antelope hunt with Mick on 30 September 1995, I dedicated all my efforts to *Ursus americanus.* Although the North American black bear has the largest population of any bear in the world, finding a large one in five days was another story.

Talking to the guides made me skeptical about finding one, especially since it is illegal to bait for them in New Mexico. Mick, however, was confident that I would score.

Monday morning found my guide, Dale Kalberg, and I driving toward a mountain named Del Buey Vista, which translates to English as, of all things, "view of the oxen." We were to look for tracks around acorn patches and water tanks dug for cattle. If a big track was located, we would still-hunt in the early morning and late afternoon and sit near the water through the heat of the day. All we needed was for the dry weather to continue so the bears would remain concentrated around the water.

I was awed by the beauty of the parklike forest as we drove along a gravel road lined with huge Ponderosa pines interspersed with junipers and cedars. For a change, I wasn't freezing. Although it was quite cold at down, the temperature soon rose to the midsixties, the warm sun dappling the forest floor. The sky was a brilliant, cloudless blue.

When the going got too rough for the pickup, Dale unloaded a Honda ATV. I held on for dear life as he dodged branches and rocks among gaping crevices. The fresh smell of pine needles in my nostrils reminded me of Christmases when I was a child. We checked a couple of water tanks that held big, if old, tracks. We did locate several oak patches but few with acorns.

While returning to camp, we came upon several mule deer and cow elk, plus a tremendous bull that gave us an excellent view of his huge 6x6 antlers, which Dale estimated at over 360 Boone & Crockett points. Come next year, I would be hunting elk with Mick.

Back in camp, Mauricio Vargas, one of my two hunting companions from Costa Rica, raised my hopes by reporting he'd seen a huge black bear, which apparently had been too fast for him.

Dale's reasoning was that if the tracks at the water tanks were old, the owner was overdue to return. Thus our best bet would be to hang around a water tank with old sign. So on Tuesday midday, after the usual routine of scouting the acorn patches, we settled down behind a huge fallen Ponderosa pine, taking care to cut and position a couple of saplings that would partly obscure our view from the water. Dale jokingly suggested that we would have a bear by three.

A sandwich washed down with Gatorade, along with the sun shining on our backs in the warm afternoon, didn't do much for our alertness. Presently we were both trying to keep our eyes open and decided to take turns watching. At 3:15 I told Dale he was a lousy guide—the bear had not yet made his appearance.

I leaned my rifle against the fork of a tree, removed my eyeglasses, and leaned back on the sloping terrain, passing the vigil to Dale. The only disruptions of the calm afternoon were the scamperings of a gray squirrel.

I was dozing a half-hour later when Dale grabbed my hair and pulled me up, gesturing excitedly. My immediate reaction was to go for my eyeglasses and scan the water tank and opposite hill—then I grabbed my 7mm magnum. Dale let go of my hair and grabbed my shirt at the shoulder, pulling me to a standing position. As he let go, I followed his frantic hand to a big patch of jet-black fur moving cautiously through an oak stand not fifty yards away. Dale, too, must have dozed, for the bear had already watered and was on his way out, with the sway and swagger of a big boar.

I'd had the foresight to turn my scope to five power; otherwise I probably wouldn't have found the bear in the eyepiece. I frantically searched for an opening in the maze of branches and leaves as the bear moved relentlessly toward the all-concealing forest. I saw the massive head pass through an opening of about the same size, and as the right shoulder came into view, I slapped the trigger as one would that of a

shotgun. At the deafening roar of my muzzle-braked magnum, the bear disappeared behind a fold in the ground. Thrashing sounds made me leap out of our hide and cut the distance in half, where I fired two more shots at the spinning mass.

I was shaking as I pumped Dale's hand and said, "You might be a lousy psychic, but you're a hell of a guide!"

The bear was in prime condition and wore a beautiful coat, but there wasn't an ounce of fat on him. We had the devil's own time loading him on the ATV and an even bigger problem getting him on the bed of the truck. Back in camp, the hulk tipped the scale at exactly 319 pounds. Mick estimated that the skull would score right around 20 Boone & Crockett points.

As I said, it always pays to go first class, especially if you don't have to lower your standards to avoid returning home empty-handed.

A Lady's Shot

Chapter 19

"I have taken two five-by-six bull elk," I informed Don Miller. "I definitely want to hold out for a big six-by-six, but what may I reasonably expect?"

This was my second hunt with Mick Chapel out of Quemado, New Mexico. Having failed to obtain an elk license two years before, I had hunted for pronghorn antelope and black bear, and scored on both. Every day I had seen elk, and figured that collecting one would be a matter of drawing a license. Consequently, my expectations were pretty high. I had asked Mick to get me the best guide and to make sure he pre-scouted the area. Don had been champion elk-caller for the state of Arizona, and we struck up a friendship right away.

"The big herd bull I saw last week near an abandoned sawmill should score right around 360 B&C points," Don replied to my question. "He was with fifty or sixty cows. We should be at that basin well before daylight. We'll need to get above him.

"Remember," Don added, "tomorrow is our best bet: After opening day the big bulls hole up and you'll probably have to lower your standards."

There is nothing like a hunter's expectation on the night before opening day! As I closed my eyes in the coziness of my tent, I could hear the wilderness around me. A gentle breeze sighed through the towering pines and golden aspens. A lone coyote howled at the sliver of moon above, and a spike bull gave a shrill whistle that sent shivers down my spine. I love classical music but must admit that this wilderness symphony in the frosty night of the Rocky Mountains kindled in me an ecstasy that I doubt Mozart could ever accomplish.

It was still pitch-dark when Don awakened me. I dressed in a hurry, and a face-washing in icy water brought me fully awake. Bill, the camp cook, had a fire going and ham and eggs sizzling. I washed everything down with a Coke—I don't like coffee—and we were off in a heartbeat. Nobody was going to beat me to my bull.

With all due respect, my long legs didn't fit comfortably in Don's instrument of torture manufactured by the Jeep corporation. I held on for dear life as he sped along the rocky, winding road at sixty miles per hour. Fifty minutes later we came to a screeching halt in a cloud of dust. I crawled out of the crowded compartment, thankful to be alive.

"You're in for a walk," Don told me. "Don't dress too warm."

The sky was still studded with stars as we began our morning walk. Not long into it, the shrill whistle of a spike bull broke the stillness. Then the braying bugle of an old-timer sent shivers down my spine.

"Listen—they're moving out," Don said. "We've got to cut them off."

We hurried along in the first gray light of dawn. I was carrying my custom 7mm magnum stoked with Federal 160-grain Nosler Partition bullets.

"Don't shoot for the shoulder—your rifle isn't heavy enough," Don warned. "When and if the opportunity presents itself, slip the bullet in the engine room right behind the shoulder."

We soon left the golden-brown pasture where the elk had been grazing on frost-cured grass. My sins, my years, and my office-spoiled legs weighed heavily upon me as I labored in the thin air up the steep ridge. I cursed myself for not having exercised harder and longer before the hunt. It comforted me to see Don's chest heaving and sweat streaming down his face and neck. I recalled a pithy quite: "Malady of many, comfort of fools." At least my guide was also having a hard time!

As we topped the first ridge, a long-necked tan-and-brown cow crossed an open grove surrounded by gnarled and ancient alligator junipers. Ahead we saw the rumps of the rest of the herd as they disappeared, swallowed up by the hump of the slope.

"We're too late," Don whispered. "We'll have to cut them off again before they disappear into the high timber."

We scrambled down a rockslide and crawled laboriously up a narrow game trail to the next ridge. The sun was rising into a brilliant blue, cloudless sky. I pushed myself to the limit, knowing all too well that opportunity rarely knocks twice on the same door.

It's always my bad luck to find a barbed-wire fence between myself and the game I'm after. I made it through this one, but my awkward backpack and new Cabela's pants didn't. But there was no time to fuss about such details. Don was frantically urging me to hurry and I was giving it all I had. As the saddle leveled out, I was able to catch up to him.

"Freeze," he ordered quietly. I followed his gaze to the stretched-out neck of a cow that had pinpointed our location. If anything, our forced rest served to emphasize my strenuous breathing. The ridge in front was about three hundred yards away. We watched attentively as the elk paraded up it.

"Darn!" Don hissed. "I think the big bull already crossed."

The old cow, apparently convinced we were harmless, lowered her head and began grazing as she walked. We began moving as quietly as possible among the stunted oaks, which gave the impression of a neglected orchard. The wind blowing on our faces was harsh and cold. A golden eagle, superb and powerful, hung like the Holy Ghost in the blue sky, seemingly motionless against the invisible wind. Suddenly he banked, turned, and vanished on the rushing stream of air.

A few steps ahead, Don froze in midstride like a bird dog: "That's him, the big bull—take him."

≈ ≈ ≈

I looked frantically for a rest, but there wasn't any, so I sat down, ready to lean my elbows on my knees. No good—vegetation obscured my view. My indecision obviously irritated my guide—he pulled me up by the collar and ordered me to shoot offhand.

"Too far away!" I pleaded.

"It's a lady's shot," Don answered. "He's the size of a barn."

I tried to steady the rifle with the sling, resigned to shoot. Between the bull's walking and my rifle's wavering, the cross hairs were all over his body. I followed and waited for the cross hairs to settle, already applying pressure on the trigger. But before I could finish my squeeze, the bull disappeared among a clump of junipers.

"He's going over the ridge, and this time we'll never be able to cut him off," Don said, among other expressions I pretended not to understand.

I guess St. Hubert or somebody felt sorry for me: About eight paces away a dead branch stuck out of a lone pine. Standing, I moved ahead and rested my rifle on the limb, hoping the bull would follow the cows across a small clearing. As the seconds ticked by, the empty feeling in my stomach grew.

Suddenly, to the left of the clearing, a pair of magnificent antlers appeared above the stunted oaks. Then they disappeared as the huge bull resumed

feeding. My prize was on its way! I braced myself for the shot and prayed I wouldn't blow it.

Then the bull broke cover, quartering slightly away, sleek in his pelage of tan and brown, his great, ivory-tipped antlers laid along his back. The cross hairs of my Swarovski settled black and sharp against the bull's broad back. *I can't miss,* I assured myself—*he IS the size of a barn!*

The big muzzle-braked seven roared and the huge bull took off at a dead run. As I began frantically to work the bolt, I heard the reassuring sound of the bullet plunking flesh.

"Shoot him again!" Don ordered as the bull reentered the bush. But it wasn't necessary. As the huge animal entered the oaks and turned, I saw him somersault and then heard him crash down the steep slope.

They say you experience mixed feelings upon seeing your mother-in-law going over a cliff in your new Mercedes Benz. In like manner, upon reaching my royal quarry, I discovered that his left horn had broken off at the whale-tail. I was indeed dismayed—priceless porcelain shattered to pieces! Frantically we retraced the crimson trail the bull had left. And we found the broken horn, firmly stuck in the ground. The Mercedes Benz was salvageable!

We measured the unbroken horn and multiplied its score by two. It came to 363 Boone & Crockett points. Don sure knows his way around record-class bulls!

It Could Have Been Worse

Chapter 20

Upon entering the bar, the man was informed by his friends that the sexy blonde who lived near his office had been found by her jealous husband with another man, whereupon he had lost his head and shot them both, killed their two children, and blew his own brains out.

"It could have been worse," the man told his friends nonchalantly.

"How could it have been worse if nobody survived?" his friends retorted.

"Had he found her yesterday, I would be dead," he answered.

It was 5 PM on Friday the thirteenth when the phone rang in my office. I was in the middle of informing my secretary that I would have to work on Saturday to finish a brief before the Supreme Court. Immediately I recognized the voice of Johel Jara on the line. He informed me that the jaguar had taken another cow.

"We need to be at El Gaspar Ranch early in the morning," he said. I hesitated for a moment: I really had to finish the appeal, but decided to work late to get it done and leave at daybreak. I got home at ten and didn't finish eating and packing until almost midnight.

I was tired next morning and didn't make it to Johel's restaurant in the tiny town of La Rita until eleven. On the way, of course, I had a flat tire and had to stop at a gas station to have it fixed.

During a quick snack, he briefed me on the situation at his brother's ranch. The information about the dead cow was second-hand, he told me—he himself had not been there. He also told me that we would take another, considerably shorter road to the farm. It turned out to be the classic choice between the long, easy way and the short, very hard one. We made it to the farm, all right, but an hour later than if we had taken the other way—and only because a yoke of oxen had pulled us out of the worse quagmire one can imagine.

≈ ≈ ≈

Time was getting short, so we set out immediately to where the cow had been killed, only to find the old pugmarks of a female jaguar with her cub. The kill was now five or six days old, and what had not been eaten by the cats had been finished off by the vultures.

Disheartened, we made it back to the little ranchhouse at dusk.

When I awakened the next morning ready to return to San José, I was informed by Johel that his brother Marvin had arrived at the house about 2 AM and had wasted no time in tying a heifer for bait a couple of miles away.

After a leisurely breakfast—I saw no reason for a jaguar to take a tethered heifer when hundreds of others roamed the ranch—we set out under the burning sun and incredible humidity of Costa Rica's Atlantic Coast. We crossed the Gaspar River over a huge fallen log, and fifteen minutes later I was drenched in perspiration as heat waves danced in front of us.

When we reached the edge of the jungle, it was cooler under the canopy of trees. However, bloodthirsty mosquitoes by the thousands were waiting for us. I was wearing a long-sleeved shirt and had liberally sprayed with insect repellent, but the vicious insects always manage to find an unsprayed part of my anatomy or a place where the cloth was stretched tight against my skin.

It was about 9:30 AM when, to my utter amazement, we came upon the freshly killed and partly eaten remains of the heifer, its tether rope stretched tight where the jaguar had unsuccessfully tried to drag its prey away. It hadn't rained for a few days and the ground around the kill was packed hard. Although I couldn't really tell, it looked like a small jaguar. But what the hell—a jaguar is a jaguar, and they are just too elusive to pass up!

There was no time to drive to the nearest town to make a phone call—my office would have to wait, and my wife would understand. Besides, a good machan takes at least three or four hours of hard work and we had to cut the poles to build it.

Upon sizing up the situation, I realized there were hardly any suitable trees in which to build the machan. Now, I can barely shinny up a tree, so the first thing I look for is two relatively thin parallel trunks on which to build a ladder. At a height of about twenty feet, there need to be enough strong branches on which to tie the horizontal poles to stand on and lean

against. I use rope hammocks and here is why: I've spent many a night in tree stands, and if you have to be silent—essential in jaguar hunting—you need to be comfortable.

The only available trees were in a little glade about thirty-five yards from the bait. They had little foliage, though, and I was afraid the ever-alert cat would spot Marvin and me. The moon was nearly full and was scheduled to set about 3 AM.

About 1 PM we ran out of rope, with the machan—called *tapesco* in Spanish—three-fourths done. So we hiked back to the little ranchhouse for more rope and a bite to eat. There I prepared for the possible long vigil. I fetched my custom .308, built on a Remington action by Answer Products Company, into which I slipped five Federal 165-grain Nosler Partition rounds. Then I gathered my two-headed lantern—one section for searching and the other for shooting, and which clamps to my helmet—two hammocks and safety belts, insect repellent, Gore-Tex jacket, two bottles of Gatorade, and a few sandwiches.

We were back at the site by 3:30 PM and finished the machan an hour later—not a minute too early, for I like to be in the tree by four. I wasn't too happy about the finished product: It was quite visible from the ground, even though we cut a few branches to camouflage it. I could only hope the jaguar wouldn't look up!

Comfortable in my perch, I informed Marvin that we would have our cat before nightfall—more to convince myself than Marvin. However, the more I looked at the glade in front of me, the more I realized the setup was far from ideal. For one thing, the machan was too big, and right in front of the jungle from which we expected the jaguar to come was a patch of *gamalote* grass about thirty yards wide. Unlike other animals, jaguars often look up to watch for monkeys, one of their favorite foods. This cat, if he came, would not have to lift his head much to see the two of us. I felt as naked as Adam!

But the place was notable for its wild beauty, and the sun was already setting and we had no time to look for a better spot.

As the sun began to set to our front, its beams broke through the clouds in various tones of orange, yellow, and red. Troops of howler monkeys bid adieu to the vanquished day with roars reminiscent of the jaguar's, and whippoorwills added to the racket, causing me to worry about being able to hear the cat when it started eating.

"I don't think we'll even have to use the spotlight on this one," I informed Marvin. "It will be here any moment."

Half an hour later I couldn't see my own hands and the jaguar had not yet materialized.

"Crafty critter," I whispered in Marvin's ear. "He's waiting for absolute darkness. Nudge me at the slightest sound."

Close to midnight the skies opened in a short tropical downpour. It lasted only about fifteen minutes but had the effect of hushing every sound in the jungle. The world stood perfectly still for about a hundred years, and I strained my ears for the slightest sound of crunching bone.

"Don't even breathe—it will surely come now," I told Marvin after nudging him awake—he was beginning to snore. "And don't fall out of the tree or el *tigre* will get you."

But the *tigre* didn't come, and at 6:30 in the morning we both agreed to call it a day, or rather a night. I ejected the shell from the chamber and handed Marvin the rifle. I would climb down first and have my companion lower all the paraphernalia, along with some of the left-over rope used to build the machan. The first thing down was my rifle, which I leaned against a tree some twelve feet away. Then came the headlamps, hammock, and the rest of the stuff, which I began to accommodate in a canvas bag as Marvin dragged his wet and sorry-looking self down.

Upon reaching ground level and after relieving himself—a really good idea in view of what was to take place within the next few seconds—he went down a steep bank and jumped the stream separating us from where the heifer bait was on the other side. I remember watching Marvin's head and shoulders out of the corner of my eye (the rest of his body was obscured by a fold of the land). He paced around the half-eaten remains for a few seconds, then for some unknown reason decided to check the edge of the three-foot-high *gamalote* grass bordering the little clearing.

Suddenly I was startled by a series of snarling and spitting sounds and Marvin's screams: *"El tigre, el tigre,* he's going to kill me!"

As if in a slow-motion nightmare, I went for my rifle and bolted a shell into the chamber. But all I could see were Marvin's head and shoulders as he jumped in the air to get clear of the enraged cat, which was clawing for his legs. I raced down the bank, jumped the stream, and scampered up the other side, trying to follow my companion's terrified gaze as the bounding jaguar disappeared in the engulfing *gamalote*. I raised the rifle

to my shoulder and followed the swaying grass, but was too late by a few seconds. The encroaching jungle swallowed up the jaguar.

I then turned to Marvin, who looked like he'd gotten a suntan at the local morgue.

"The only reason that *tigre* didn't eat me was because he was not fully grown," he blurted from a heaving chest. "I never imagined my karate training would save me from an enraged jaguar! My professor would have been proud of my legwork or *'cumchi chagi.'*"

Closer inspection of the trampled surroundings revealed that the jaguar had spent all night guarding his kill from the security of the tall grass. But apparently he would not eat until the two skylined "professional hunters" left their perch. This experience seems to prove that trying to convince yourself that a bad idea is a good idea is a bad idea!

Well, it could have been worse: Nobody got hurt.

Business Buck

Chapter 21

The one-week trip to Buenos Aires, Argentina, was strictly for business. My client was covering all expenses, and I dared not mention the word "hunting" or I would lose all credibility. I would carry my small suitcase and not pack a stitch of hunting garb—no boots or, God forbid, a rifle. Besides, it was late January—summer in the Southern Hemisphere—and probably all seasons were closed.

I was almost packed the night before my trip when my home phone rang. It was Alberto Severo, my long-time friend who would be hosting us in Argentina.

"You will be arriving in Buenos Aires on Tuesday and leaving on Wednesday a week later, right?" Alberto asked. "What would you like to do over the weekend?"

I hesitated. "Maybe you can show me around the city. Or we could take in an opera in the evening," I said.

"Sure," he said, "or organize some kind of hunting for you. And you can go lie to your grandmother—I know you and I know perfectly well what you would prefer do over anything else! And don't forget to bring a good pair of boots and at least one change of hunting clothes."

They say the road to hell is paved with good intentions. I was not going to hunt, certainly not, but I found myself switching suitcases and packing green clothes, my hat, and hunting boots—the bare minimum, given that I probably wouldn't be hunting anyway! Unless my client insisted.

The flight north to Miami and then straight down to Buenos Aires was uneventful except that it took forever. Alberto was there to meet me and got me through customs ahead of everybody on some insidious lie—all the customs agents shook my hand and bowed respectfully.

≈ ≈ ≈

After checking in at the Claridge Hotel and a two-hour rest as I tried to shed jet-lag, the three of us, my client included, met at the restaurant for a business lunch. I couldn't help but notice the mounted heads of

red stag, Axis deer, blackbuck antelope, and Russian boar that decorated the walls.

When my client expressed some mild interest in the mounted heads, Alberto explained that most of the exotic animals had been brought into Argentina by a gentleman by the name of Pedro Luro, right after the turn of the century. I kicked Alberto under the table, and we left it at that.

For some reason, the due-diligence conducted over the telephone did not coincide with the actual situation now in Argentina. We met with the people we were to do business with during the next few days and were informed they would need until Monday to think things over. There was nothing to do over the weekend but wait.

The room at the Claridge was $300 a night. Alberto suggested that we could save money over the weekend by going to Manuel de Anchorena's Estancia La Corona for $150 per person per day, which included all food and drinks. Shooting for ducks and pigeons could be included for a modest fee, and he would provide us with shotguns. We would have a chance to look at the country and decide about our business in a more relaxed atmosphere. Besides, Alberto would drive us over there in his new BMW at the usual relaxed speed of a hundred miles per hour.

I hadn't opened my mouth when my client announced that he loved to shoot birds and was ready to go!

Now, I love to shoot birds, but this I can do at home. I had hunted on La Corona before and knew it was teeming with completely free-ranging blackbuck antelope brought in from Pakistan about ninety years ago. Given the choice, I will always hunt big game. Alberto knew this, of course, and told me he would provide me with his scoped Mauser .308.

It was indeed pleasing to find that Mr. Anchorena and his Irish wife Ann readily remembered me, and more pleasing yet to confirm that he had not raised his $250 trophy fee per animal. Along with the buck, a female could be collected at no additional charge, although I wasn't interested because the does are hornless. In no time at all I changed from my city clothes into hunting garb.

It was 23 January and the mercury hovered right around 90 F day and night. My guide of four years earlier was away for the weekend, and we were assigned a young guide by the name of Darío Arbizu. He picked us up at around ten, shortly after we arrived. The estancia provided a

brand-new Toyota double-cabin pickup, in which we headed toward some marshes where we would first do some bird shooting.

As we approached the shimmering edge of the water, thousands of ducks took flight, along with a few Magellan geese, stunning in their snow-white plumage with red beaks and feet. But we were to shoot the big Turkish pigeons that inhabit the Argentinian pampas in pest proportions and are about the size of a domestic pigeon.

I was using a nice Franchi semiautomatic shotgun that, for some unknown reason, was choked extra-full. The birds were coming in rather low among the trees, and I think all I hurt was their feelings. If it were up to me, I would ban all chokes tighter than modified or, better yet, execute all who manufacture them.

After accumulating few birds and lots of frustration, I was relieved to see the pickup appear on the featureless plain. As it turned out, Alberto and my client had done quite well and were all smiles as we headed back to the estancia for a gaucho-type barbecue of Argentinian beef, pork, and chicken, washed down with our choice of red or white Chilean wine. We had a full staff of waiters, maids, cook, and butler and were treated like royalty.

The long trip, the food, and the wine all contributed to make me drowsy, and I just had to take an afternoon siesta. It was too hot to hunt anyway. At 3 PM I was still dead to the world when Darío, the guide, knocked on my door. I awoke covered with sweat from the sultry heat. After washing my face and arms in the lukewarm water of the lavatory and drinking a frigid Coke, I was ready for another taste of Argentinian hunting.

I'm fidgety about hunting with someone else's guns, and this trip was no exception. After dropping off my client with a bird-boy at a designated flyway, we left him enthralled in his bird shooting. We rounded a bend and Alberto pulled out his trusty Mauser from its soft case. After handing me his pride and joy, he opened his briefcase and pulled out a plastic bag holding the widest assortment of .308 ammunition you can imagine! There were pointed and blunt-nose bullets, Remingtons, Winchesters, and Federals. Some looked new and others as if they had been in the Falklands war. I looked at Alberto in disbelief and asked him which ammo the rifle was sighted in for. I should have known better.

"All of it," came his answer as he stepped out of the pickup with his shotgun and bird-boy. "I never miss with that rifle, and neither did my father." Then he walked away.

I could have kicked myself—first the full-choke shotgun and now the Fuehrer's rifle! And, to add insult to injury, Heinz ammunition—all fifty-seven varieties! But, as they say in my country, one has to till the soil with the available oxen.

I opened the plastic bag and selected five pointed rounds that looked similar. I tucked them in my pocket and glanced at the rifle. It looked to be in fairly good condition and sported a fixed six-power Karl Kaps scope with the typical German posts for shooting in dim light. It also had a set trigger. I tried it and found it set to where it would trip if a flea breathed on it. I then tried the regular trigger and, as is usual with double triggers, which I avoid like the plague, found it needed about fifteen pounds of pressure to go off, completely impractical for the task at hand.

But I would have to make-do and set out to try my shooting iron. As Darío and I rolled along the endless plain, a big hare bolted in front of our pickup and zigzagged away at lightning speed. About seventy yards away it stopped and froze, only its head and long ears showing above the stunted grass. I asked Darío to stop the vehicle and fed five rounds into the magazine. I worked the bolt, set the trigger, and took careful aim. There was a loud click and no explosion. I kept the rifle pointed in a safe direction for a few seconds, sure of a misfire. Ever so carefully, I proceeded to open the bolt and found the chamber empty. I worked the bolt again, only to find the bullet wouldn't chamber. I cursed, released the magazine catch, and allowed the rounds to drop into my hand. I put one into the barrel and tried to close the bolt. Unfortunately, Mauser actions don't close unless the bullet is fed from the magazine. And now, of course, the bullet got stuck in the chamber. I considered breaking the rifle in two to extricate the round, but, just in time, Darío produced a straight wire that accomplished the job. After additional cursing and fingernail-breaking, I managed to get a round seated in the chamber, while the hare, undoubtedly amused by my imprecations, patiently waited. I leaned the rifle on the open door and set the rear trigger. Set triggers, slow as they are, which is the reason I loathe them, make for some pretty accurate shooting when used with a solid rest. I touched the bullet off, and the accommodating hare disappeared, shot just under the eye. At least the rifle shot straight!

With a little less effort than the first time, I managed to introduce another of the pointed bullets into the chamber, using all my strength to set the safety on.

It was getting late, and Darío insisted that we hunt from the vehicle. I didn't like that idea much at first, but then considered I had enough handicap with the loaned rifle. Besides, when in Rome, do as the Romans do, and I had learned long ago not to argue with your guide.

The cool evening brought a flurry of activity among the antelope, and we came upon several herds that sensed us and took off at supersonic speed. There is dimorphism among the sexes of this species, the bucks having strikingly beautiful black-and-white coats while the females, in their tawny coats with white underbellies, reminded me of the Thompson gazelles of East Africa. Small flocks of rheas, South American ostriches, raced along with the antelope. Although they, too, attained great speed, they were invariably left behind by the swifter quadrupeds.

But seeing the world's third-fastest land animal (right behind the cheetah and the American pronghorn) and having a mature male stand still long enough for a shot were two very different deals. So for hours we cruised around in what seemed like a fruitless exercise. But the blackbuck, like most animals, has an Achilles heel: It has excellent eyes, ears, and nose and is not curious like a white-tailed deer. And once spooked, it won't stop for that last look. Like the pronghorn, it won't jump a fence but instead will go under it—always at the same place!

Now, La Corona is huge and doesn't have many fences, but there are a few. And of course Darío knew where the crossings were. As a herd about thirty strong streaked past us a good two hundred yards away, headed toward a fence, Darío slammed on the breaks and hissed, "Get ready, the second buck to the left."

As the herd began to quickly filter between the same two fence posts, its two bucks milled nervously around, awaiting their turn to cross.

I boiled out of the vehicle, rested the rifle against the door frame, and tried to move the safety to the off position. But for the life of me, I couldn't move the devilish contraption. I lowered the rifle and used both my thumbs. Finally, there was a loud snap. As I again raised my rifle, my intended quarry was on the other side of the fence, making good time toward Brazil!

I got back in the pickup as big drops from the season's first rain began to pelt the windshield. I would have no choice but to continue my hunt with a round in the chamber and the safety in the off position. Oh, yes, and the light would have to hold long enough for us to find another herd of the skittish antelope.

It wasn't my gun and it wasn't my fault that the big one had gotten away. And besides, it was the sort of "gift hunt" that I wasn't even supposed to take seriously. And for a change, if I came home empty-handed, I would have an excuse that would satisfy me. But as the vehicle spun and swerved in the quagmire of the newly drenched pampa, that empty feeling of frustration set in. I needed another *Antilope cervicapra* like I needed to breathe!

Darío was having a hell of a time controlling the supposedly all-terrain vehicle, which seemed to have acquired a mind of its own. He would turn left and the pickup would swerve right. It would have been a lot of fun on the table-flat pampa, except that we were quickly running out of time.

But Darío knew not only his business but also how to earn an extra tip. Like the automatic pilot of a boat locked on the nearest port, Darío's Loran was locked on the next antelope crossing, and he steered the seemingly floating truck in that direction. I prayed for the light to hold as bolts of lightning lit up ominous cumulonimbus clouds closing in from the south.

≈ ≈ ≈

I suppose the season's first rain to hit the thirsty ground or the thunderclaps, or both, had the effect of stirring up every animal on the endless plain. Hares bolted erratically in front of our vehicle while rheas and antelope raced in the distance, spraying water as they fled. Flocks of ducks filled the leaden sky and flared at the sight of our clumsy vehicle. Relentlessly we pushed on, determined not to blow the slim chance that I hoped fate would grant me.

As if in answer to my prayers, the tall grass in front of us suddenly parted like the Red Sea, revealing a sight that shall forever remain etched in my mind. The setting sun had slipped under the blanket of clouds but was shining directly on a herd of some twenty antelope about a hundred and fifty yards away. The black-and-white markings of the bucks contrasted brilliantly in the ethereal light, and their long and twisted horns glinted sharply against the iridescence of the shining water.

Darío slammed on the brakes, but the vehicle took forever to stop, gliding as if on skates and finally halting sideways to the antelope. As if in a queue, the animals started to slip under the fence in a flowing

motion while the lead buck raced nervously up and down, awaiting his turn to cross.

I set the hair trigger and waited for the buck to settle down for a moment. After a sudden twenty-yard burst of speed to my right, the animal stopped in its tracks for an instant and turned to face me. Although its chest presented a tiny target at that distance, the snow-white hide contrasted sharply against the coarse black post of my telescope. The moment it settled, I didn't worry about trigger squeeze and just touched the bullet off. The little buck disappeared, hit at the base of the throat.

I guess the Fuehrer was right after all—at least about the accuracy of Teutonic rifles!

José María's Tormented Soul

Chapter 22

The night before the first day of a hunt is always exciting—especially if the place happens to be an exotic one and the game sought is on the most-wanted list! Problem is, intense emotions, even positive ones, provide the perfect setting for the nightmares to which I'm prone and which sometimes involve screaming.

After nine hours of flying from San José, Costa Rica, to Buenos Aires, Argentina, I was picked up at Ezeiza International Airport by Néstor Brandoli—Brando to his friends—and whisked through customs without a hitch. As usual, there were no problems with my rifle or ammo. Not even a visa was required! What I hadn't realized was that it would be another nine hours of steady driving to the Estancia La Criolla, located in the province of La Pampa. Through my long-time Argentinian friend Alberto Severo, I had contracted for a seven-day red stag hunt.

I cannot sleep in a car, and when we got there I was so tired I could hardly stand up. Due to the rest stops on the way and having taken a wrong turn, we arrived late in the afternoon. I unpacked and would have gone straight to bed, except they had a welcome dinner—Argentinian-style with wine and all the trimmings. I'm still not sure whether the special dinner was for me or for the visiting relatives of the owners of the *estancia*. Anyway, the visitors consisted of a husband and wife, their young child, and the recently widowed mother-in-law.

It was close to 9 PM when dinner was served, and I gorged myself on three or four kinds of barbecued meat, which I washed down generously with the ever-present red wine. A rum-marinated pudding completed the recipe for a first-class nightmare.

Unknown to me, the recent widow was assigned the room next to mine, a thin sliding door separating them.

I was asleep the moment I hit the pillow. The next thing I knew, I was sitting up in my bed, breathless in a pitch-black room, having been awakened by my own anguished screams. In my dream I had either been abducted by aliens or gored by a world-record red stag. I must have

hurt one of the aliens, I thought, because even more hysterical cries were coming from off to my left. Either I'd had the good sense to sit tight in my semiconsciousness or I was too petrified with fear to do anything. The next second brought sobbing cries of the widow calling her daughter, and then all hell broke loose: Light switches were flicked on, dogs barked outside, people tripped on furniture. Fully awake now, I had the good sense to sit tight and listen.

"Jose María was here, Ana!" the widow revealed to her daughter. "His soul is in torment in Purgatory. He came here to plead for my help. He is being submitted to indescribable torture or he wouldn't have uttered the agonizing screams I heard. I always knew the rumors about his having an affair with his secretary were true, and now he is paying for his sins. We must offer masses and rosaries to purify his soul or he will never come out of punishment!"

When I got up before dawn the next morning to begin my hunt, the visitors were already packed and moving out. They wouldn't even say good-bye. Something about being early to church. Funny, since it was only Monday!

But I guess Jose María's soul didn't think it was funny because in the seven days that followed, I never laid eyes on a decent red stag!

A Shot in the Dark

Chapter 23

When I saw the mounted head of the wild boar in the small curio shop in Segovia, Spain, where my wife and I had taken refuge from a sudden downpour, I knew then and there that I wanted one. I had hunted wild pigs in both Florida and Georgia, but this animal was a far cry from the domestic animals from which those pigs were descended. For one thing, its coarse hair was much longer and thicker, it had a distinctive hump on its back, and its tusks were much bigger. Its overall appearance was vastly different—it really looked like a wild animal.

The friendly shopkeeper noticed my interest and explained how he had waited for this particular animal during several nights in an uncomfortable blind and shot it by moonlight with a 9.3x74R rifle. He claimed the boars were incredibly tough and prone to attack if wounded. He went on to explain how I would be sure to get a Spanish red stag, a fallow deer, or a mouflon if I stayed at it long enough. But with *el jabalí* (the boar) it was never a sure thing.

Little did I know at the time that the handling of my deceased uncle's estate would provide the funds for a trip to the Province of La Pampa in Argentina, where these animals had been introduced by famous Argentinian hunter Pedro Luro in 1908. It is commonly hunters who introduce a great game animal to a foreign country. In this case, the boar had adapted remarkably well, populating not only most of Argentina from the pampas to the Andes but neighboring Uruguay as well.

As it turned out, I ended up at the Estancia La Criolla, about five hundred miles southwest of Buenos Aires. The owner, Emilio Lorda, welcomed me almost as a family member to his quaint but comfortable country home.

Since I had driven all night from Buenos Aires, I slept throughout the morning, to be awakened in early afternoon to a wonderful Argentinian barbecue. The meat and the ever-present wine led me to relax again in an easy chair, after which Emilio drove my guide, Carlos Zocchio, and me to an *apostadero* or tree-blind near a watering hole that attracted *padrillos*

or boars. During the ride in Emilio's battered pickup truck, flocks of rheas (South American ostriches) scampered in the distance at incredible speed. Emilio offered to let me shoot one, but I declined the honor. I wouldn't have known what to do with the bird, and besides, I never take an animal's life if I don't have a good reason to do so.

The blind was built in a caldene tree—very similar to a mesquite in appearance—about sixty yards from the water hole. No artificial light was to be used: There was a full moon and I would be shooting by moonlight. The blind was very cramped, and Emilio warned me about bumping anything with the rifle barrel; he said this would send the pigs scampering for cover. He also left two heavy woolen blankets, pointing out that the temperature would surely drop below freezing shortly after the sun sank behind the western horizon.

Carlos and I sat comfortably in chairs as myriad flocks of doves and noisy, iridescent-green parakeets descended for a last drink before retiring to roost. With nothing better to do, we started a long, whispered conversation about each other's lives. It's amazing how quickly a bond forms between hunters, and it was no different with Carlos. He told me how he had joined the Argentinian army, where he had been a shooting instructor for many years. Then he shared with me how he had been so sick, nervous, and depressed due to an incident the previous year that had nearly cost him his life—not once but twice.

It seems that an organized gang of car robbers had figured out Carlos's schedule for meeting the payroll at his car-battery plant in the outskirts of Buenos Aires. After cashing a check at the local bank, Carlos noticed a car with tinted windows tailing him. Before entering the open parking lot in front of his building, he drove a complete circle around the block. The suspicious car stayed right behind him. He eased into the parking lot, stopped the car, and reached for his Ruger P94 fifteen-shot semiautomatic pistol. Simultaneously he released the catch on his car door and cocked the pistol while pretending to check the odometer. It was January, the middle of summer in Buenos Aires, and Carlos couldn't help but notice that the man getting out of the car to his left was wearing a Rambo-type jacket. The guy left the car door open and looked nervously to his right and left. Then he made a beeline to Carlos's car and reached inside his coat. As the would-be assailant's gun came out, Carlos was ready. In one swift motion he kicked his car door open and, with a two-handed hold, fired three quick shots at his

attacker, who dropped his pistol but was able to make it back to his car. The vehicle came to life and, with wheels screaming, made a U-turn and came for Carlos. The driver's window came down, and a fusillade of shots rang out. But the driver was moving and firing at the same time, and Carlos was quick to duck behind another car. As the car veered away, Carlos opened up with the twelve rounds remaining in his clip. Flying glass littered the pavement as the getaway car disappeared around a corner.

In the meantime, Carlos's employees had called the police and given them a description of the would-be robber's car. It was found about a mile away with no fuel and two or three bullet holes in its gasoline tank. At that point it became known that there were two attacks—the driver had hijacked another car at gunpoint and left his already dead companion in the first car. One of Carlos's shots had taken off the bottom of his heart and the other his left lung. The third one had missed. It's a wonder he even made it back to his car! The driver's seat, steering wheel, and shift stick were covered with blood.

Two days later a man matching the driver's description presented himself at the hospital with a septic gut wound. He pulled through but was given a life sentence for the murder of a well-known doctor from Buenos Aires, shot after resisting the forceful taking of his new Explorer.

But Carlos's problems didn't end there. The Argentinian mafia, it seems, would not be put to shame. Fortunately, Carlos had been forewarned by some of his ex-pupils now on the police force, and he was as cautious as a twelve-point buck coming to water. He had rigged his pistol so that it would fire three shots each time he pressed the trigger, and had Trijicon night sights installed on it. And he never stopped looking out on all sides!

≈ ≈ ≈

One evening he had to work late. As he was locking the gates of his factory, he heard footsteps headed his way and soon saw two heavy-set men crowding each other and decidedly heading toward him. Carlos's army training took over. He smoothly drew his pistol and, trying to keep his cool, focused on the front sight and pressed the trigger not once but twice, right and left. I guess you could say both of his attackers died on the way to the ground.

With four of their members out of action, the "Argentinian Car Jackers Association" decided Carlos wasn't worth the trouble and left it at that. Or so his police friends informed him. Anyway, poor Carlos was a nervous wreck after these incidents and had to undergo psychiatric therapy for several months—until a one-month safari to Namibia and South Africa brought him back to normal.

I was so engrossed with Carlos's story that I forgot I was in a blind and not only raised my voice but bumped my rifle barrel against the cramped surroundings. Immediately there were some hurried hoof-steps to our left as several pigs scattered in all directions. I cursed myself for getting carried away!

As the night wore on, a heavy fog enveloped the pampa, making it impossible to see, despite the full moon. We did hear the splashing of several wild boars as they came to water, but it was impossible to see them, even through Carlos's light-gathering binocular. It was bitter cold as well and I was still tired from the long trip, so we decided to call it a night.

There was no fog on the second night, and we figured it would be only a matter of time before a *padrillo* (mature boar) made its appearance. Thanks to Carlos's coaching, I had already learned to distinguish the males by the distinctive hump on their backs. But it was not to be on this night either—only sows and shoats came to water.

As we climbed into the tree blind on the third night, my last, I remembered the words of the Spanish shopkeeper in Segovia. At about 9 PM a sow and several piglets began noisily splashing the water.

"Don't even breathe," Carlos whispered. "The *padrillo* is probably in the bush waiting to make sure there is no danger—then he will make his appearance."

The minutes dragged slowly by as the young pigs dashed in and out of the water, squealing and grunting. Then a much bigger shape made its appearance, splashing into the water hole. Through my binocular I could see the humped back and muscular body. Carlos grabbed the binoc and took a long look while I checked the animal through my Swarovski riflescope.

After a long pause, he said: "It's not the biggest *padrillo* in the province of La Pampa, but it's for sure the biggest one we've seen. You better take him—this is your last night."

By then dark clouds had moved in and the darned boar was hardly visible. It was so dark I couldn't tell one end of the animal from the other,

and it was harder yet to distinguish the rifle's black duplex cross hairs against the black animal. I raised the rifle against the slaty sky so I could find the cross hairs, then slowly brought it back down to the motionless hulk. Now I knew why the Europeans use bulky scopes with heavy cross hairs. But I still had to wait for the animal to move to determine which end was which.

Carlos was getting restless and urged me to shoot. All I could see was the top of the vertical wire against the water. Then the boar took a couple of steps and I realized he was facing to the right. I was steady as a rock, but for the life of me, I couldn't make out the horizontal cross hair. I moved the rifle to the right and was able to distinguish the hair against the surface of the water. Ever so slowly I moved the rifle to my left again and stopped where I figured the neck joined the shoulder. Before I lost my bearings again, I released the sear.

The bullet was a bit high and to the right of where I thought it would strike, entering right behind the animal's right ear. I guess I cannot say that my trophy boar died on the way to the ground, but it surely died on its way to the water!

I Don't Want a Blackbuck

Chapter 24

They say a wise man is someone who learns from the mistakes of others. A fool learns from his own mistakes. I had read a hundred times that it was a mistake to hunt red stags in Argentina after the rut, which starts around the third week in March and is usually over before the middle of April. But of course I knew better! Problem was I wanted to take advantage of Easter Week in Costa Rica, when everything shuts down anyway. However, Easter Week for the year 2000 was in late April, well after the red stag "roaring" season ended.

Anyway, after I'd collected my European boar on the Estancia La Criolla, Carlos Zocchio drove me the two hundred or so miles to Los Corrales, where I would hunt the red stag, the main animal that had brought me to Argentina. Though I hunted long and hard during six days, however, I never came upon a royal stag, which at the moment topped my most-wanted list. For whatever reason, only the hinds and young remained on the ranch; the big bulls had moved out.

I did see one decent stag: On the second day, my guide of German descent, Ariel Hoven, spotted a nice stag, but since it had only ten points, he wouldn't let me shoot it. The Argentinian game laws do not allow the taking of immature stags on a trophy hunt, imposing an eleven-point minimum.

Since the huge field surrounding the ranchhouse here was planted with alfalfa, every night scores of deer would come to feed on it, only to disappear long before daylight. So in desperation, on the last day of the hunt we decided to collect one of the bigger-looking animals by moonlight. Unfortunately, the moon had been waning every night and wasn't so bright anymore.

On that particular day, we waited until about midnight before walking out into the field. As we left the coziness of the house it was bitter cold, even though I was wearing everything I had brought. Through Ariel's large Zeiss binocular (I had only brought my compacts) we were able to locate the herd bull. He was standing broadside about a hundred and

thirty yards away, and I could make out big antlers, though how big or heavy they were we could not determine. But it was my only chance and I wasn't going to turn it down.

Now, in most circumstances a 130-yard shot from a steady rest like a fencepost is a pushover, but with half a moon to see by, it's a whole different ball game! I cursed myself for not having a scope with coarser cross hairs, but as they say in my country, I had only these oxen to till the ground. I would have to make do.

I went through the procedure (the same one I'd used on the boar) of aiming at the bright sky and then slowly lowering the rifle to my intended target, where I slowly squeezed the trigger. But I must have forgotten to offer a prayer to St. Hubertus, patron saint of hunters, for the only thing that hit the ground was my dignity!

The good news was that I wouldn't have to pay the thousand-dollar trophy fee, which would leave some extra cash for an unexpected expense. What might that be? Well, the Estancia La Corona was on the way back to Buenos Aires, and I didn't have a really good blackbuck antelope.

My long-time Argentinian friend Alberto Severo was due to pick me up next morning, and when he arrived, I told him about my failure to get a stag.

"The next best thing to playing and winning," he said, "is playing and losing. And you have played."

It was a long drive to Buenos Aires, even at 110 miles per hour. All the way, Alberto insisted that I try for a bigger antelope.

"We have to stop to sleep anyway," he said. "We might as well do it in style at La Corona."

"All right," I said, finally giving in, "but I won't shoot unless I see something much bigger than the three antelope I already have."

"Ricardo," Alberto said philosophically, "there are good hunters and 'poor' hunters. Offer your guide a $100 tip for the best antelope on the estancia and see what happens."

As I've said earlier, I'm a slow learner, but this sure made a lot of sense! After a couple of sundowners at our next stop, I took my guide Jesús Godoy away for a personal chat. Upon hearing my offer, he was all smiles.

"However," he warned, "if we are going to collect the biggest buck on the estancia, we will have to do it from the pickup. Otherwise we just won't be able to cover the necessary ground to find a truly big one."

Although I pictured myself belly-crawling as you would for a pronghorn antelope, I would willingly make the sacrifice for the quality of the trophy.

After breakfast in the estancia's formal dining room, Jesús picked me up as the first golden rays of the sun flooded the endless plain.

It was a glorious fall day in the Southern Hemisphere, and I tingled with anticipation as the crisp morning breeze stung my face. Hordes of South American teal and other ducks filled the air as we worked our way around a huge swamp near which the blackbuck preferred to stay. Two huge southern screamers *(Chauna torquata)* lumbered heavily on the rising currents, their characteristic calls echoing across the pampa. Here and there, South American swans with black necks, red beaks, and white bodies struggled to gain altitude as we intruded on the safety of their haven.

I was in for a shock as we crossed into the endless pastures across from the swamp: Literally thousands of the skittish antelope scampered in the distance at the first sight of the pickup, bunching into huge herds the likes of which I had only experienced in Africa.

But seeing the fleeing critters by the thousands, finding the right one, and getting near enough for a shot were very different things! A hunter pays a guide mainly for his eyes, and the $100 "encouragement" was doing wonders for Jesús's visual acuteness. As the pickup lurched and swerved to avoid the thicker stands of star thistle, Jesús spotted the right antelope and careened to a stop on the dew-covered ground.

"The big one to the right!" he ordered. I frantically tried to get the long barrel of my 7mm Remington Magnum out the window.

The buck hadn't gotten big by being stupid and was making good his reputation as the world's third-fastest land animal (after the cheetah and the pronghorn), swerving and dodging on the way to the nearest fence line. Anticipating a quick shot, I had removed the ocular lens cover but not the front one, which would be easy to flip open. In the excitement of the moment, however, I forgot to remove that final lens cover—and, of course, could see nothing when I peered through the scope. By the time I realized my mistake and flipped open the front lens cover, my intended quarry was over a hundred and fifty yards away, on the other side of the fence and stretching the distance with every leap. I decided the shot was impossible and lowered my rifle. But Jesús wasn't going to let his hundred dollars slip away so easy!

"Shoot, damn it, shoot!" he ordered frantically.

Then it dawned on me that this was in fact the biggest buck on the estancia and that I shouldn't let it get away. By the time I again brought the rifle to bear, the target was over two hundred yards away and showed no intention of slowing down. All I remember now is his white rump bouncing and swerving among the thistle as I tried to find it in my cross hairs. My only advantage was that it was a going-away shot and I didn't have to lead him. When the sight picture looked good, I let fly. The little buck instantly disappeared, and although I thought I heard the bullet strike, I couldn't be sure.

"Did you get him?" came Jesús's frantic inquiry. "If you didn't, you still owe me the hundred dollars, for that was the biggest buck on the estancia!"

An empty feeling settled in my stomach as Jesús drove to the nearest gate to get across the fence.

"Why the hell didn't you shoot when he was under a hundred yards?"

I felt I had already made a big enough fool of myself and refrained from answering.

Eventually we found the gate and crossed into the pasture where my buck had been swallowed by the star thistle. Expertly, Jesús found the place where the herd had crossed and began circling the area. As we covered more and more ground, the knot in my stomach got tighter and tighter. I prayed to St. Hubertus for a miracle as the torture became unbearable. Glancing to my right, I caught a flicker of white movement in the corner of my eye. As the pickup came to a stop in a tiny glade in the star thistle, I stepped out the door to admire my magnificent trophy, measuring more than twenty inches from the base of the horn to its tip on a straight line. I still don't know who was more elated, Jesús with his hundred dollars or me with my spiral-horn miracle!

Rather reluctantly, I suspected, St. Hubertus had directed my bullet to the buck's rump and relieved me of many a sleepless night. What I still don't know is whether Jesús was praying to HIS patron saint for his hundred bucks!

Tuy's Jaguar

Chapter 25

I have always wondered whether hunting is an instinct or a learned activity. And although psychologists have always held that it is an acquired habit, I think I could be evidence against that theory, for I have always been obsessed with wild animals—from moths to mammoths—for as long as I can remember.

My earliest memories, before I could read, take me back to my mother or grandmother sitting on a rocking chair beside my bed and reading the adventures of Tremal Naik and Dharma, his trained tiger, by Emilio Salgari, in the treacherous jungles of India. When I went to sleep, of course, I would dream of man-eating tigers and panthers and the relentless pursuit of India's northern Thugees, among whose members murder was a profession.

Although my father was a rancher at the time, living in the country five days of the week, I often stayed behind in my maternal grandparents' house in downtown San José. My grandfather was an impressive man, revered by all. He had come to Costa Rica as a political refugee from Honduras after his uncle, General Domingo Vázquez, who raised him (he was orphaned at an early age), was overthrown as dictator through a coup d'état. Of European descent, almost six feet tall, and with a militaristic education, brilliant blue eyes, balding blond hair, trimmed moustache, and pointed goatee, my grandfather looked like a Prussian general. Licensed as a Civil Engineer at Columbia University in New York State in the late 1800s, he had been in high demand as a builder of bridges in his country—especially since his uncle decided who was in demand.

To give readers an idea of his way of thinking, he would tell the story of how his uncle, during the campaign to overthrow him, had ordered one of his soldiers to stand guard during the night. The man fell asleep and the enemy crept in, killing several of his men. Next morning General Vázquez held a summary court martial, found the soldier guilty of negligence, and personally ordered his execution by firing squad. Then he went alone to present his condolences to the father and mother of the deceased—who

were his personal friends. I believe my grandfather inherited his character from his uncle, as all who knew him will attest.

Meals at my grandfather's house, especially dinner, were formal affairs. Don Manuel would sit at the head of a long table, elegantly dressed in a dark suit, matching tie, and a fresh white or crimson carnation in the buttonhole of his coat. My grandmother would sit at his left and his eldest son—my uncle—to his right. Then came my unmarried aunts, and my older brother and myself—the only grandsons at the time—would be last. Several maids and other help would serve from the left and withdraw the plates from the right. And if my brother or I happened to spill a glass, we'd be whisked off to the kitchen to eat with the servants.

I loved my grandfather, but I must admit that he liked to brag a bit, especially about his exploits in battle during his uncle's campaign. There was the story about how the cavalry, led by General Vázquez and with Major Vázquez as second in command, had broken the weeks-long siege brought by the General's cousin and arch-enemy, Policarpo Bonilla, to the presidential palace in Tegucigalpa . . . and how my grandfather's horse had been shot out from under him as he crossed the Guascarán River on the border with El Salvador, his enemies in hot pursuit . . . and how he had been captured in that country and held for weeks in a dungeon on bread and water . . . and how, on the night before his execution, he was served his last meal—a la carte—after which it was decided instead to deport him to Costa Rica, where he met my grandmother, the richest girl in the country, and married her, but only after ten years of courting her!

≈ ≈ ≈

But his favorite after-dinner story was how he had stopped the charge of a huge male jaguar in midair as it leaped for his neck like a demon from hell! Here is how that story went:

General Vázquez had commissioned his nephew—my grandfather—to build an iron bridge in a remote part of Honduras. And the whole of that country was pretty remote in the late 1800s! After weeks or months of rice and beans, even a change to beans and rice was welcome.

One evening after work, a flock of Central American turkeys *(Crax rubra)* began to call in the distance as the last rays of the sun bathed the tops of the trees in gold. Anxious for a change in diet, civil engineer

Vázquez grabbed his trusted double-barrel shotgun and began to sneak under the canopy of trees for a chance at the wary birds. But every time he advanced, a member of the flock would spot him, sending the rest of the birds fluttering noisily to the next tree. As he went deeper and deeper into the tropical jungle, it became increasingly difficult to see under the huge, epiphyte-covered trees.

Suddenly the hair on the back of his neck stood on end as a sixth sense warned him of danger. He somehow knew that he had become the hunted instead of the hunter. At the crack of a twig behind him, he turned to face imminent danger in the gloom of the forest, shotgun to his shoulder. Two dazzling, fiery red eyes glared from the undergrowth, steel muscles coiling behind them to launch a relentless attack. The instant the eyes of the two hunters met, the jaguar sprang like a silent streak of lightning, huge white fangs seeking the jugular of its antagonist, powerful hind legs ready to disembowel. But my grandfather's aim was true, catching his vicious adversary between the eyes, whereupon he was knocked down by four hundred pounds of hurtling cat.

≈ ≈ ≈

When my grandfather finished his story, a deep silence born of respect and admiration reigned in the dining room. That is, silence reigned until I broke it with a silly statement:

"Tuy," I said, which was what I called my grandad, "the eyes of animals don't glow in the dark unless you shine a light on them!"

Blasphemy! Heresy! Schism! Reason for excommunication!

"How dare you question the word of your grandfather!" he said. "The eyes of a jaguar glow in the dark like the eyes of all cats. Eat your dessert and respect your grandfather. Children have no esteem for their elders anymore. What will become of this country?"

I was in third or fourth grade at the time, and as soon as I returned from school the next afternoon, I procured a couple of milk trays from the kitchen and placed them under some trees on the back patio. For some reason, literally dozens of alley cats regularly visited my grandfather's house for a scrap of food. Before long a particularly large and striped tabby padded along, unable to resist the temptation of a free dinner. Before he finished lapping the milk, I was back from the kitchen with a pitcher to give him a refill, plus a raw

steak. A few minutes later, I had won the cat's confidence and was petting him. I then picked up my newly found friend and locked him in one of the many bathrooms of the manor house.

The rest of that afternoon I was as nervous as a teenager about to inform her parents that she was *ever-so-slightly* pregnant. Although at the time I had not heard about Galileo, I suspect I would have understood how he must have felt just before announcing to the Holy Inquisition that the earth revolved around the sun and was not itself the center of the universe.

I had always been taught to speak the truth. But those teachers had not mentioned that sometimes it's well to have a fast horse handy. Like Galileo, however, I had gathered enough valor to confront the consequences. Truth would set me free, even if I had to burn at the stake!

≈ ≈ ≈

I waited until everybody was formally seated at the table. Then I announced that I had forgotten to wash my hands and requested permission to do so. I left the dining room, quickly fetched the cat from the bathroom, and returned. With one hand on the light switch, I used the other to toss the cat on the table, then turned the lights off.

"Now," I said, "can you see the eyes in the darkness?"

A deathly silence pervaded the room, although I swear my grandfather's eyes took on a red brilliance of rage in the sepulchral darkness. Even the cat stood poised like a statue, afraid to use up all of his nine lives at the same time. Then somebody turned the light on again.

I was already on my way to the door when Tuy's thunderous voice rang out:

"GET OUT OF MY SIGHT!" he roared. "AND THERE WILL BE NO DINNER FOR YOU TONIGHT!"

"Yes," I acknowledged, but then, paraphrasing Galileo, I said to myself, *but the eyes don't shine.*

Jaguar Express

Chapter 26

It was 2 PM on Sunday, 20 September, when the phone rang. I was on the way to a restaurant with my family and had been hurrying them along for the last half-hour. The caller was an acquaintance of mine—Juan José "Ito" Campos—whose voice I didn't recognize at first. He informed me that a jaguar had taken one of his cows. A typical September downpour was coming down, and I hesitated.

"It's raining cats and dogs here," I told Ito, "and even if I hurry, I won't make it to your place before dark."

"It hasn't rained here for over a week," was his reply, "and if you don't come, I will never call you again because I have worked my butt off making a machan for you to sit in. This jaguar is sure to come. I know what I'm talking about."

My wife gave me an angry look as our eyes met, but it was too late. I told Ito I was on my way.

I gulped down a quick lunch and packed my custom .308, my shooting light, a change of clothing—it always rains in the rain forest—and a few sandwiches. With a guilty conscience, I bade my family good-bye. When I pulled up in front of Ito's house in the tiny town of Buenavista, I didn't have a chance to kill the engine. Ito's nephew jumped on his motorbike and signaled me to follow as he took off in a cloud of dust. At least it wasn't raining in Costa Rica's rain forest.

Fifteen minutes later we stopped at a gate and entered a large pasture. I threw my Nissan Pathfinder into four-wheel-drive low and prayed not to get stuck at the last moment. We made it to the farthest corner of the field, and as I stepped out of the vehicle, Sandro Cuendis showed me where the jaguar had taken the heifer. The drag marks were clearly visible, and blood-stained hairs still clung to the barbed wire under which the hapless prey had been dragged.

≈ ≈ ≈

Outside the comfort of my air-conditioned vehicle, the hot, humid air clung sticky and oppressive, as it generally does in the Atlantic lowlands. The nephew and I hurried across a semi-abandoned banana plantation and descended to a bush-choked stream where Ito had tied the reeking carcass of the heifer to sturdy stakes driven into the ground, a necessary precaution to keep the jaguar from dragging its prey elsewhere as they almost invariably do.

Ito had done a good job with the machan, taking the additional precaution of camouflaging its front with banana leaves. As I climbed to my fifteen-foot perch, I tied my knit hammock to two thick branches for the long vigil. Ito was not there—he cannot sit still in a machan anyway—but his nephew would sit with me. I instructed him to be utterly silent, under threat of being used to replenish the bait!

Maneuvering around to get comfortable, I finally settled down with my back to the trunk of the tree. I bolted a 165-grain Nosler Partition into the chamber of my rifle and eased it up to my shoulder for a trial sight at the heifer through the Swarovski scope. To my utter panic, I could see nothing—the muggy, stifling air had completely fogged my eyeglasses. I wiped them clean with my handkerchief and put them back on, but before I could even bring the rifle to my shoulder, they would fog again. I prayed for the jaguar not to come under such embarrassing circumstances, and after about fifteen or twenty minutes of inactivity, my sweating diminished to where I became satisfied I would see my quarry clearly.

While crossing the cleared ground of the banana plantation earlier, I had examined the pugmarks of my intended trophy, verifying that it was not a very big animal, probably a female. However, the big cats fascinate me and I wasn't going to miss a chance to collect another one of these beautifully spotted animals—large, small, or otherwise.

As the afterglow of sunset slowly darkened to crimson, I took two swallows of water, still cool from my ice chest, and splashed a little on my face, which I immediately wiped dry. Flights of green macaws *(Ara ambigua),* silhouetted against the blood-stained sky, screamed noisily overhead, hurrying from the gigantic tropical almond trees, where they feed, to their roosts before the night creatures took over.

Easing back in the comfort of my hammock, I looked up, the soft panoply of gleaming stars filtering through the leaves and branches of my tree. In the absolute silence and eerie darkness of the jungle, I reviewed all

the details to ensure my success. After all, making mistakes is only normal; being unprepared is stupid. I went again through the drill: Yes, the bait was securely tied, my machan was high enough and concealed, and my tree had enough foliage so I wouldn't be skylined. I had an accurate and powerful enough rifle and a light with Krypton bulbs and two headlamps in case one failed. Nothing could go wrong—except me!

I considered my intended quarry and what it might be up to. As the last rays of the sun filtered through the leafy tangle of the forest, it would stand up, stretching its limbs, yawning lazily, the burnt gold of its pelt camouflaged against the black rosettes. The jaguar is essentially visible only when it moves; when it stops to listen, it disappears, the black spots becoming dry leaves and the golden coat rays of sunlight. But when it moves again, the ever-alert eyes of a troop of spider monkeys just might spot the furtive creature, announcing to all who can hear the presence of an animal whose footsteps cannot be heard, whose coat cannot be seen, and whose apparition can spell agonizing death.

As the sun vanishes behind the western horizon, the lord of the tropical forest greets the hour of *el tigre* with a harsh *"Ao . . . ong,"* which it repeats at five- to ten-second intervals over the span of a couple of minutes. The cry begins and ends abruptly, and all creatures of the jungle remain silent out of fear or respect, or both. The hunt is on, and all the denizens of the forest realize that he who is not alert and cautious enough will pay with his life.

≈ ≈ ≈

Lazy by nature, like all cats, the jaguar follows the path of least resistance—in this instance, the trail between the jungle and the banana plantation, made by the clumsy humans. It is a little afraid of them but knows from experience that if it remains still, it will not be detected, because the awkward two-legged creatures, like most birds, cannot see at night.

Under the canopy of trees the ground is soft and moist, even though it hasn't rained for several days. Ideal hunting conditions! Silent as a shadow, the jaguar is in no hurry, seemingly floating along the sinewy path. Upon reaching the pasture's edge, it suddenly stops and sinks slowly to the ground. On the other side of the fence it can clearly see several

cows with their calves calmly chewing their cud. It slinks under the fence and into the foot-high grass, completely disappearing. It knows it is invisible now and that only a shift in the wind will give it away. The slight breeze holds steady. The cat glides on like a wraith, the muscles in its hindquarters gathering. When the nearest calf looks the other way, the attack is launched.

Before the unlucky heifer or its mother can decide where the pounding footsteps are coming from, a heavy paw sends the young one to the ground with the force of a sledgehammer. Instantly, four long fangs sink into the back of its head, crushing the skull like an eggshell. Whatever dying sounds the calf is able to make are drowned by the gurgling blood that flows in torrents.

The herd of cattle panics and stampedes across the pasture, breaking the rusted barbed-wire fence while the jaguar remains locked to its prey. Now nothing is going to deprive the cat of its hard-earned meal! Long after the prey's heart has stopped beating, el tigre will drag the carcass to a secluded place in the jungle, hidden from the sharp eyes of the ubiquitous turkey buzzards that will begin patrolling the sky at first light.

Unlike leopards, jaguars will not haul their prey up a tree, probably due to the lack of other large predators. They will never, however, eat in the open, taking pains to hide their meat in the jungle.

Although the sky was clear, there was no moon and soon I was engulfed in the inky darkness of the rain forest, the huge trees around obliterating whatever stars might have been present. As usual, droves of mosquitoes tormented me. And I would have to rely entirely on my sense of hearing to detect the presence of my hopefully noisy prey-eater.

There was a lazy stream between the dead calf and myself, and every time a fish splashed the water, I would come to full attention, thinking maybe it was the jaguar fording it. But I vowed to refrain from shining the light until I heard the tell-tale sound of crushing bones.

≈ ≈ ≈

The waiting wouldn't be so bad except for the swarms of mosquitoes, which really push one's endurance to the limit. But then again, if it were easy, everybody would do it! It was five minutes to nine when I pressed the button to light up the dial on my new Casio hunting watch.

I did not hear the cat coming. The first inkling of its presence was the sound of a tiny bone breaking. Then another. This jaguar was good-mannered, avoiding the usual crunching and slurping sounds. Actually, it sounded like a smaller animal—but smaller predators don't break bones!

But it couldn't be the jaguar, I reasoned, because something always goes wrong at the last moment and the cat doesn't show up. In slow motion I began to raise my rifle, holding the tip of the barrel with my left hand to keep it from bumping a limb. Ever so carefully I flipped both lens covers open and moved the safety to off. Then the shooting light stabbed the darkness and painted the spotted head of a jaguar, staring directly into my eyes.

The jaguar was directly facing me, and I hate a face shot. But I would hate much more for the jaguar to get away! It was a Mexican standoff as I stared breathless into the cat's face. If it began to move, I would fire, but the jaguar did not seem afraid but rather curious. It slowly raised its head as its ears pricked up. Somehow I had the presence of mind to hold my fire. As the white, muscular chest became visible, I had most of the pull out of the trigger and finally applied the last ounce of pressure. My .308 has a muzzle brake and goes off with a thundering roar. It doesn't kick much, however, and through the scope I saw the blocky head go down. Then the limp body slid down the creek bank and came to rest in a rumpled heap.

At last I had learned enough from Manuel Queb to bag a jaguar on my own. After savoring the incredible occurrence from my perch, I carefully climbed down and walked to my painted trophy. The entire experience felt like magic!

Bullet-Proof Jaguar

Chapter 27

I was lying on my side in a hospital bed the day after back surgery when the phone rang. As I reached for the earpiece on the night table, a stab of pain reminded me that I had a very tender back indeed! It was Ito Campos informing me that a big jaguar had taken one of his fully mature Brahma cows. With great effort I informed him that under the circumstances I would be useful only if he wanted to replenish the bait with my own carcass! He immediately hung up in disappointment.

One month later I was back in my office on rubbery legs. I couldn't sit for long in the same position, nor could I work all day. As they say in my country, I was "for the tiger," a reference to old and useless horses that are sold to feed the felines in the local zoo. Two weeks later I was better but suffering from insomnia and spells of dizziness. My doctor had warned me about driving long distances, especially over bumpy roads.

At 11 AM on 14 August, on the eve of Mother's Day and exactly six weeks after surgery, Ito called me again. The jaguar had taken another one of his cherished cows and this time I had to go.

"Impossible," I answered. "I cannot walk long distances, I cannot exert myself, and, God forbid, I cannot ride a horse."

But Ito would not so easily relinquish the generous tip he had been offered to guide me to the cow-killer, not to mention the revenge he wanted to exact on the marauding cat:

"You can drive your truck within two hundred yards of the machan I am already building for you," he said, "and I will build handrails on either side of the ladder so you may climb with less effort." I hesitated for a moment, and he closed in with the clincher: "And I guarantee this is a huge cat—it has killed a fully grown cow."

"Let me call my neurosurgeon," I told Ito. "I will call you back in ten minutes."

≈ ≈ ≈

First I had a conversation with my good friend and keen jaguar hunter, Dr. Sergio Bonilla (he has taken six of the spotted cats). He urged me to go but mentioned that if I didn't, I should let him have a crack at the cat; otherwise it would probably get poisoned.

Then I called the neurosurgeon, Dr. Eduardo Huertas, and requested permission to hunt a cattle-lifting jaguar. He went through several stages: At first he didn't understand. Then he didn't believe me. Then he asked if I had bumped my head during one of my dizzy spells.

After explaining that I could drive almost to where the jaguar had killed the cow and that all I would have to do is climb a ladder and sit in a hammock, he agreed to let me go. "But if you exert yourself," he admonished, "I will have you right back in the operating room and then you will really be 'for the tiger'."

As I called Ito to tell him I was on my way, I caught Sergio's eyes glaring at me with envy.

I drove home to change clothing and load my hunting car, cringing at the thought of what my family would say. Luckily, when I got there, my wife and son weren't in and I began to prepare and load up as fast as I could. But I didn't quite make it.

"What the hell do you think you're doing dressed in green and packing your Pathfinder?" said my better half. "You must be out of your mind! Your maniacal quest to collect trophies has gone too far."

I agreed that I was a bit crazy, but added that the doctor had given me permission to go. And before getting into a bigger argument, I got in my truck and took off.

I had never been to Ito's ranch, which was about thirty miles from his home. Now, the roads on the Atlantic side of our country are not marked and it is extremely easy to get lost—which of course I did, arriving at the scene of the kill very close to 5 PM after picking up Ito's cousin at a roadside bar where he had been drinking a couple of beers.

The cow had been killed on the side of an old road in an open glade. I parked my vehicle on the edge of the clearing in about six inches of water. Water is everywhere in the rain forest!

I donned my Cabela's rubber boots, which are both waterproof and comfortable to walk in, and grabbed my .308 rifle, headlamp, hammocks, and other paraphernalia to make my vigil more bearable. It had been raining for the past few days and I was in an immense flood

plain covered with water. The dead cow was at the edge of a drainage ditch, half submerged in the murky water. Inspection of the carcass revealed the cause of death, four ragged holes in the back of the neck where it joins the head. There had been no struggle. This was typical of the work of a mature and experienced jaguar: After an incredible burst of speed, it had almost certainly jumped onto its victim's back and sunk its fangs deep into the vertebrae, paralyzing the prey and inflicting near-instant death.

There were no tracks—the grassy ground was covered with water—and thus no way for me to determine the size of my quarry. But from the size of its prey, I was pretty sure I was looking at the work of a fully mature male.

There was no time to waste. I quickly paced the distance to my machan—exactly thirty-nine long paces. That was a bit farther away than I would have liked, and the tree was less luxuriant than I would have chosen, but it was too late to do anything about it. I only prayed that my shotgun ears would hear the crunching bones and tearing flesh and my Krypton bulb would be bright enough for my bullet to find its mark.

As I climbed into my makeshift perch and put things in final order, I told Ito and two of his cronies to talk loudly as they left, so that in case the jaguar was close by watching its meal, it would think it safe to return. There had been five of us altogether, and, knowing that apes could count only to four, I figured I probably could also fool a jaguar. A local by the name of Tito Brenes would sit with me in the machan, and I made him promise to be as silent as a mouse.

Maybe I shouldn't have told the men to make their departure known to the jaguar—as they walked off in the encroaching darkness, they whooped and hollered, I'm sure partly to dispel their own fear. Upon reaching their motorbikes, they opened the throttles and took off with a deafening roar.

Upon climbing to the machan, Tito tried to bring along his own beat-up single-shot 20-gauge shotgun, plus his headlamp, and it took a lot of arm-twisting on my part to convince him to leave them at the base of the tree. As I settled down in my hammock, I realized we had forgotten to tie down the carcass of the dead cow to keep the jaguar from dragging it away. It was too late now to do anything about it, so

I took comfort in the thought that the bait was too big and heavy to be dragged, even by the biggest of jaguars.

As the shadows lengthened and the sun began to sink behind the line of trees to the west, I busied myself assembling and positioning my headlamp, making sure the beam would be perfectly aligned with my rifle when I took aim. Satisfied that I could see the dead steer clearly through the scope, I made doubly sure there was a 165-grain Nosler Partition in the chamber and flicked the safety on and off a couple of times.

Then Tito and I started whispering to each other. He informed me what a fearless jaguar hunter he was, having taken six or seven of the big cats with his trusted shotgun. My concern about the jaguar seeing or hearing us was quickly dispelled by the thought that he would probably scent us first, given that Tito smelled to high heaven. And it wasn't exactly Chanel No. 9! The thought that some hunters use skunk scent to mask their own odor somewhat comforted me—or perhaps the jaguar would think there was another dead animal rotting away nearby.

As the monotonous droning of the mosquitoes filled the still and clammy atmosphere, I was surprised to hear flocks of green macaws *(Ara ambigua)* busily talking to each other in the moonless night. A few whippoorwills called in the distance, and a gentle breeze caressed my face and, better yet, floated away the odor of the already decomposing dead cow. As dusk gave way to darkness, myriad fireflies scintillated in the glade before me, outlining the trees in the otherwise inky sky. Every time a frog or fish splashed the water, I strained to make out the telltale sounds of tearing flesh or crunching bone, but each time it was a false alarm and I eased back into the comfort of my hammock.

Then it came. First a nearly imperceptible tearing sound. Then a snapping bone. Later some slurping sounds. Tito was under me and poked me in the butt, which wasn't necessary. I knew I would have lots of time before I shined my light. The night had become completely silent now, and I could distinctly hear Tito's heavy breathing under me.

Ito had told me this jaguar had been shot at before and that I had better be quick with my rifle after I put the light on him, for he would hold for only a few seconds. Though I had a rest for the fore-end of my rifle, there had been no time to secure a rest for my right elbow, which I would have liked for a rock-steady position. A puny human always tends to shake a little in the presence of the king of the tropical jungle!

Knowing I would have but a few seconds to make my shot true, I tried to remember the exact location of the dead steer as I sat entombed in blackness, staring blindly in the bait's general direction. My heart did a double somersault when the beam of my light hit what looked like a spotted cow! One second later the crouching cat sat up on its haunches and stared at me in surprise, its tail twitching nervously, ready to bolt. Remembering Ito's words, I centered the cross hairs on the middle of the shoulder and touched the shot off.

≈ ≈ ≈

There is nothing louder than the roar of a high-powered rifle on a still night, and hardly anything more frustrating than the utter nothingness of sound after it. Not only was I unable to see anything, I had not heard the bullet strike or the jaguar splash the water as it jumped away. Searching the empty glade with my beam, I wondered whether the five-second apparition of my rosetted quarry had been real or a trick of my imagination.

Then I looked down at Tito, who surely had heard the bullet hit and seen the jaguar jump away on wobbly legs. But his words were not those of reassurance: "You missed him," came his answer to my querying eyes. "He jumped away unscathed. He was already on his way when you fired. And he was a huge cat."

"You're dead wrong," I answered. "That cat is lying dead no more than thirty yards from the cow. Let's go find him." Was I just comforting myself?

We climbed down from the tree slowly, partly to let the cat bleed to death in case the bullet had not been exactly true, and partly to avoid reality in case I had really missed. As we walked up to the cow, I was surprised to find no blood. I thought that perhaps I had shot the cow, but there was no bullet hole in it. I looked at Tito in disbelief.

"I told you it was a clean miss," he insisted.

I felt as bad as a President caught lying to Congress but retained my composure. "Let's go look for my trophy," I insisted. "It's going to be lying on its belly on the other side of the ditch."

"You can't do that," came Tito's answer. "That ditch is chest-deep, and if you try to cross it, your wound will get infected and we will probably have to use you for jaguar bait."

Good point: Now I had two good health reasons not to look for a wounded jaguar in a brushy swamp in the dead of night.

"So what do we do?" I asked in desperation. "Maybe we can return tomorrow with dogs."

"No," Tito said. "I am not afraid of jaguars, and I will bring this one back myself." He then opened the breech of his ancient single-barrel shotgun, closed it, adjusted the pale beam of his headlamp, and waded chest-deep into the murky water of the drainage ditch. I stood on the bank in sheepish helplessness, feeling as useless as a transplanted appendix.

Tito came out on the other side soaking wet, then followed a game trail and was quickly swallowed by the high grass. After a few minutes, I could tell by his light that he had backtracked and veered to the left. Then he checked some ground to the right while I promised St. Hubert not to miss mass the following Sunday. Twenty or thirty minutes later, Tito reappeared on the far side of the ditch shaking his head. "There's no blood and no other sign of your jaguar. I told you it was a clean miss."

My heart sank deeper than the Titanic, and I barely refrained from jumping into the ditch and conducting the search myself. The sight picture had looked good, and I didn't think I would miss at forty yards. But then again, Tito had said the jaguar was already on his way when the rifle went off. And I had been shaking a bit before and after the shot. Or maybe I just wasn't up to it after my operation. There were too many ifs involved.

Then Tito asked me how much I was going to tip Ito, and it occurred to me that he might require further motivation. As he stood by me wet and muddy, I said, "I will give you twenty thousand colones (about $80) if you find the tigre for me."

Tito's face lit up, and I realized right then and there that my chances of retrieving my cat had increased tenfold. With the determination of Ahab, he plunged into the water after my Moby Cat! Again I could follow his progress to the right and then to the left and then straight away. A few minutes later, a shot shattered the stillness of the night, followed by Tito's scream: "To your left, to your left—it's running to your left!"

Surgery or no surgery, pain or no pain, I was not going to let that cat get away. I did try to stay out of the ditch, though—in places it was indeed too deep. But I ran as fast as my weakened legs would carry me

in the knee-deep water, parallel to the cat's supposed line of escape, desperately asking Tito to direct me. But it was useless. Soon I found myself mired down, with visibility limited to about six feet. As I stood there confounded, undecided about what to do next, Tito's words "I found him!" brought my soul back into my body.

I returned to the dead steer and urged Tito to stop tormenting me and to retrieve my trophy.

"I can't pick it up," he yelled. "It's too heavy!"

"Drag it to the ditch and float it downstream to my truck," I instructed.

Half-walking and half-swimming, his shotgun in one hand and the jaguar's tail in the other, Tito finally made his triumphant appearance. Smell or no smell, I embraced him for having helped me pull the biggest jaguar I have ever laid eyes on to the ditch bank. And he didn't waste any time in asking for his hard-earned twenty thousand colones, which I gladly handed over, plus a new skinning knife as a bonus.

We loaded the entire cat in the back of my truck after a few field pictures, after which I dropped Tito at his house.

To keep the jaguar from spoiling, I drove straight home, where I hung it from a beam to cool off. Next morning I weighed it—exactly 165 pounds on an empty stomach, which is about as big as a jaguar outside of the Brazilian Pantanal will ever get—despite claims by some of my hunting friends that they regularly collect specimens with weights in excess of three hundred pounds. These figures, however, invariably shrink when the taxidermist mounts them, no matter how hard he tries to stretch the skin!

≈ ≈ ≈

After more pictures in the morning sunlight, my taxidermist and I proceeded to carefully skin my most prized of trophies. My bullet had entered through the middle of the right shoulder and exited the left flank through a gaping hole. All the pellets from Tito's shotgun (he said he had taken his shot from about twenty yards) had entered behind the right ear through a single hole. Curious, we proceeded to make an autopsy of the carcass. My bullet had disintegrated one-quarter of the heart and severed another fourth. All the pellets from Tito's

20-gauge were lodged in the brain. It was a good thing I had flunked forensic medicine in law school: Otherwise I would have known the jaguar died when his brain ran out of blood within five or ten seconds of my shot!

But Tito earned every cent of his twenty thousand colones!

Ammotragus Lervia

Chapter 28

The Barbary sheep or aoudad has always fascinated me. For one thing, scientists have never determined whether it's an ovine or a caprine (sheep or goat), adding an element of mystery to its nature. For another, it is a handsome and powerful animal, with adult males weighing in excess of three hundred pounds. It has a uniform fawn-colored coat that is lighter in the underparts. And it possesses two striking characteristics that make it attractive to trophy hunters: First, its massive horns, which curve downward and rearward like those of the Caucasian tur *(Capra cylindricornis),* and second, its sumptuous mane, which covers its throat, breast, and upper part of its front legs.

The aoudad's original range included all of arid North Africa and all the mountain ranges of the Sahara, regions that, alas, I never expect to hunt. But fortunately it has been successfully transplanted to Wyoming, New Mexico, and Texas in the United States, where it has adapted so readily that trophies from America far exceed those from Africa in horn length.

I first tried booking a free-range hunt for this animal in either New Mexico or the Palo Duro Canyon of northern Texas, but mainly for economic reasons I was never able to find the right hunt. Then an American friend of mine residing in Costa Rica referred me to Charlie Bruce, operator of the Sycamore Creek Ranch near the border town of Del Río in west Texas, and things began to fall in place.

Given my previous experience with shooting preserves, I was a bit leery about hunting his ranch. But thanks mainly to his desire to visit my country and requesting my help to do so, plus my need to include a good aoudad in my trophy room, we struck a deal. Besides, the ranch had over fifteen square miles and was heavily wooded. We would use a vehicle only to glass; all actual hunting would be conducted on foot.

Due to work commitments, I arrived in San Antonio on 20 May 2001, a bit late in the season—the oaks and cedars would be wearing their leaves, making the spotting of game that much more difficult. Also, the weather would be turning extremely hot.

I rented a car in San Antonio and drove for about three hours to Del Río, where I was met by Charlie Bruce. After a quick bite, I followed him to a beautiful guest house overlooking Sycamore River and settled down for the night.

Morning dawned crisp and bright, and I was awed by the huge canyon that the river had carved in the limestone over the ages. As I stepped out of the house, flock after flock of white-winged doves zipped above my head. To my front, an endless sea of oak and mesquite extended as far as the eye could see. Charlie was there to meet me, and I couldn't wait to get going as we sipped coffee in his house.

"It's not going to be easy," he said. "It has rained a little and the brush is covered with leaves. And the big rams didn't get big by being stupid."

Soon we were rolling along the ranch's gravel roads in Charlie's dark-green Jeep Cherokee, stopping at different vantage points to glass for game. The ranch was a hunter's paradise—at every turn in the road we would come upon white-tailed deer and exotic game, some of which I had never had the opportunity to view before. Blackbuck antelope were everywhere, and they were not as skittish as those in Argentina. We saw a few fallow deer, but none seemed to have any horns. And of course there were the regal axis deer from India, always keeping to the heaviest cover and ready to bolt at the first sign of danger. Scimitar-horned or white oryx from North Africa gazed at us as we drove by. No wonder they are now extinct in their original range! And there were more barasingha, the shaggy-coated Indian swamp deer, than we could count. They, too, stared at us curious and unafraid from about thirty yards. And they, too, have become scarce in their native range. But not so the aoudad—the few we saw that morning were well on their way before we could size them up. We did get a couple of chances, but Charlie insisted we wait, believing we could do better.

≈ ≈ ≈

The next day was similar to the first, except that I was able to collect a really nice axis buck with symmetrical horns over thirty-one inches long. My 7mm magnum bullet first hit a small branch but nevertheless made it to his left shoulder, and I had my buck after tracking him for a short distance.

At daybreak on day three I missed a going-away 200-yard running shot on a really nice mouflon ram. A couple of hours later, we stopped

to glass from the top of a knoll. The sun was hot on our backs, and drops of sweat collected on my forehead. Then Charlie discovered a small band of aoudad rams scurrying through the brush and motioned me to follow him to see if we could cut them off.

"It's a group of bachelor males and they are all big," he said, motioning me to follow him at a crouch. As we came down from the knoll we lost sight of the rams, but Charlie apparently knew where they were headed, for he never stopped going. Suddenly the horns of the first aoudad appeared above the dwarf oak. We pressed on, desperately looking for a clearing as we tried to stay parallel to the sheep. We didn't find a clearing, but we did find an opening where the brush was lower. It would have to do.

As the band of six to eight rams began to cross the opening single-file, I had the rifle to my shoulder and Charlie had his binocular to his eyes. It would be a tricky shot offhand, and I would have but a couple of seconds to shoot. Four or five rams had passed when Charlie hissed: "That's him, the biggest one—take him!"

I had been following each ram, waiting for the order to shoot, and in my mind I had already figured that I would pass this ram too and move to the next. I brought my rifle forward, frantically looking for an opening before my quarry got swallowed by the engulfing brush. I found it at the last moment as the head and shoulders disappeared behind a stunted mesquite. Afraid to lead the animal for fear of hitting a branch, I frantically aimed at the last rib and let fly. As my rifle came down from recoil, rams were scattering in all directions.

Although the sight picture had looked good, one can never be sure of a hit and much less of a fatal one. And I had not heard the bullet strike. But what I did hear a few seconds later were the kicking sounds of an animal trying to get up. My hurried shot had been a bit high and too far back, but it had nevertheless broken the spine, anchoring the animal. I finished him off with Charlie's .22 magnum, which he carries for just such occasions.

We brought my trophy back to the ranchhouse and put a tape to his thick and massive horns. They went just a tad over thirty-three inches, or about one and a half inches shy of the all-time African world record taken in Chad!

Honeymoon Hunt

Chapter 29

To this day, more than thirty years after my wife and I were married, people harass me for taking my bride on a hunt during our honeymoon. My answer is always the same: It is more than logical to invite the person you love to share in an activity you love. And apparently my way of thinking holds up because many of the friends who criticized me are now divorced and I'm still happily married to the same girl.

Anyway, my wife worked for Taca Airlines at the time and was entitled to two free tickets a year. It was her idea that we visit some cousins of hers in Los Angeles and then head for the exotic Hawaiian Islands. I had not yet obtained my law degree—my thesis wasn't finished—but nevertheless I had been working for over two years as an apprentice lawyer to accumulate enough money for a one-month honeymoon trip. Besides, we would get special rates at all hotels for being in the airline business. What my wife-to-be didn't know was that I had recently read an article in Outdoor Life magazine about a guy who had been lucky enough to hunt a strange and exotic beast called an Axis deer with long six-point antlers. The creature had, in some unknown manner, come to the island of Molokai.

At that time, very few people in Costa Rica had hunted outside the country—certainly nobody I knew—so I was on my own about finding out how to do it. We would be spending two weeks in Hawaii, so there would be plenty of time to figure it out. Now, my wife didn't know at the time how serious my CHD (Chronic Hunting Disease) was, and she was a little surprised when I said we should find either a gun shop or a taxidermy studio that could direct us to an axis deer hunt. In the yellow pages I found the number of the Poo-0-Hoku Ranch on the island of Molokai; the name means "Roof of the Clouds" in the aboriginal Kanako language.

≈ ≈ ≈

Room and board at the Poo-0-Hoku Ranch would be less expensive than the daily rate at our beachfront hotel, making it a win-win situation.

Of course I kept my mouth shut about the guide rate and the trophy fee, which by today's standards were a giveaway.

We flew Aloha Airlines directly to the Poo-0-Hoku and were greeted with a glass of white zinfandel. The people there seemed the friendliest in the world, determined to make our stay an unforgettable experience. And it pleases me to acknowledge that to this very day we cherish every moment of our time there.

After a leisurely lunch and a dip in the cliff-edge swimming pool overlooking the sparkling Pacific Ocean, I was assigned a lanky half-Japanese, half-Kanako guide who answered to the name of Henry Nahoopii. He was in turn assigned a beat-up Willys Jeep, which looked like it had survived the attack on Pearl Harbor almost thirty years before. All it was, essentially, was a platform with two front seats and a back one and a Ford engine. A borrowed 7mm magnum and a box of ammo completed my equipment.

We headed for the hills behind the ranch headquarters in early afternoon, and soon I came to realize why the Jeep was so beat up. The volcanic mountains that formed these islands eons ago rose nearly vertically among jagged lava rocks. There were plateaus on top of the mountains, but all the way up our little Jeep wheezed and puffed in low gear and four-wheel-drive. No, the Jeep didn't have independent suspension or power steering, and the air was conditioned by our raising or lowering the windshield, but it got us to where we were going!

When we reached a huge plateau interspersed with patches of low brush, we had yet to see the first of the strange and exotic beasts that had somehow managed to swim all the way from the mysterious jungles of India. I was ready to keep hunting, but Henry suggested we all take a nap under an appealing tree, out of the scorching sun. I couldn't understand his attitude and attributed it to laziness, until he explained that no self-respecting deer would move around in that heat.

Reluctantly, my wife and I and Henry took shelter under the branches of a stunted guava tree—just like the ones back home—and munched on cold apples brought in a cooler box. As the sun began to set, sending out flashes of gold, rose, and magenta against an otherwise azure sky, Henry stood up, stretched his skinny frame, and asked me if I wanted to take a big buck. Did I want to leave the wedding party to go on my honeymoon?

We came upon a huge canyon gouged in the mountain by a volcanic eruption, and Henry informed me that the deer tunneled through it to

go from their bedding to their feeding areas. He asked me and my wife to sit down and remain absolutely silent: "The deer will soon begin to move," he said.

Before long a lone doe stepped daintily into a clearing about two hundred yards away and, after nervously testing the air, tiptoed away. Then a doe and her fawn followed, their white spots reflecting brilliantly in the setting sun. Soon Jungle Jim Guardia would be able to prove to his young and innocent wife what a great hunter and deadly shot he was.

As the minutes dragged by and the shadows lengthened, a steady procession of deer, the likes of which I had never seen in my native Costa Rica, filed past us. Although most of them were does and spikes, there were a few bucks that, in my innocence, I would have taken in a breeze, but Henry kept holding me back.

I was sitting, resting my rifle with my elbows over my knees, when a particular bush across the canyon began to shake violently. Henry's hand tightened around my shoulder. "Get ready," he whispered. I found the shaking bush in my scope just as the most magnificent buck I didn't know existed stepped into the clearing, its heavy, barrel-shaped antlers towering above a muscular, dark-chestnut body.

≈ ≈ ≈

As I centered the cross hairs on my would-be trophy, they were shaking much more violently than the bush the buck had been attacking a few seconds before. My mouth went dry and my blood pressure must have hit two hundred and I felt as nervous as when I asked my father-in-law for my fiancee's hand in marriage.

Through the scope I saw the buck eying me defiantly while Henry, breathing down my neck, urged me to shoot. The tension was unbearable, and right then "Jungle Richard" lost his nerve! Under the most severe attack of buck fever I have ever experienced, I yanked the trigger to end the agony. Under the circumstances, I likely would have missed the side of the Mauna Kea volcano, and of course I missed that buck, which will remain forever proud and stately, etched in my mind. It wouldn't be the only shot I've missed in my life, but it certainly was one of the most humiliating. Every time Henry or my wife looked at me, I felt as uncomfortable as a nun in a bikini.

Dawn next morning found us huddled in the little Jeep as it wound up a track that looked more like a hardened lava stream. In those innocent years it didn't dawn on me that I had blown Henry's carefully laid-out plan and that I was going to pay dearly for my mistake. I didn't realize it then, and wouldn't for many years to come, but my stock options as regards the size of the deer I would take back home had plummeted. Nothing is more frustrating for a guide than to have his dude blow a good stalk or miss a sure shot.

As the Jeep veered from one side of the track to the other in the loose lava rock, I caught sight of a buck's head popping up among the dwarf bushes on a hill across a canyon about one hundred and fifty yards away. I pointed it out excitedly to Henry, and of course he gave me the nod to take him. I jumped out of the front passenger seat, laid my rifle across the hood, and peered through the scope. All that was visible were the head and upper neck of the deer and a pair of six-point antlers that seemed to reach to the sky. For whatever reason—probably because I had a solid rest—the buck didn't jump up and down in my scope. I took a deep breath, let half the air out, and gently squeezed the trigger.

When I recovered from the recoil (at the time I thought the 7mm magnum was the hardest-kicking rifle in the world), my deer was gone and I wasn't even sure where it had been standing. Henry, however, assured me it had gone down like a piano and that he would direct me to where it lay.

After I crossed the gully separating me from my first international trophy and came upon it, a feeling of immense accomplishment came upon me. I had conquered Mount Everest and swum the Atlantic on the same day! In my bursting elation I gave out a whoop that would have put Tarzan of the Apes to shame.

To be sure, the antlers measured only about eighteen inches in length and were quite spindly, but as if to prove the phrase that beauty is in the eyes of the beholder, nothing could have looked prettier to me at the moment—except the smiling face of my bonnie bride. And to my wife and I, the days spent at "Roof of the Clouds" were the closest we have ever been to Heaven! I can only pity those who have never been there.

Calling the African Lion

Chapter 30

Looking back thirty years, I now realize how incredibly lucky I was to have hunted in Africa when I was only twenty-seven years old. I had been married for about a year and had had my law degree for less time than that, and suddenly I found myself with more work than I could attend to and making more money than the president of the Costa Rican supreme court. In those innocent years I thought of course that this situation would last for the rest of my life, so naturally the first order of the day was to fulfill my life-long dream: a full-fledged African safari! I had no children at the time, and building a house to live in wasn't an immediate priority, especially since my maternal grandmother, whose loving memory I cherish to this day, was generously paying the rent of the house my wife and I occupied.

My local hunting experience in those days was limited to weekend forays for doves and ducks and the occasional tropical whitetail, and my international big-game hunting comprised two modest axis deer taken on a three-day hunt during our honeymoon on the Hawaiian island of Molokai.

My grandmother begged me not to go, fearing I would be tossed, trampled, or eaten by the ferocious and truculent beasts inhabiting the Dark Continent. But in the end, after realizing that her attempts to dissuade me were useless, she gave me—bless her soul—$500. In those days that amount went a long way, considering that a lion license went for a little over $50 and an elephant tag—if my memory serves me well—for $111.

For me at the time, the definition of a big-game rifle was a .308. So shortly before my safari I purchased one at a local gun shop owned by a German by the name of Georg André. Thereafter I officially appointed Georg as my hunting consultant and safari outfitter and let him attend to every detail of my most important trip. To my good fortune, he booked my safari with a company named Cotur, owned and operated by an obscure professional hunter by the name of Adelino Serras Pires, based in Beira, then Portuguese East Africa.

≈ ≈ ≈

As I stepped down from the plane in the beautiful port city of Beira, I was approached by a journalist from the local newspaper who wanted to interview me. I felt as important as Lyndon B. Johnson!

I was assigned a short and stocky professional hunter named Alberto Girao, who proved to be both jovial and good-natured and who, in the days that followed, taught me more about animals and hunting than I thought possible. Due to the relative scarcity of game animals in America and in my native Costa Rica as compared to Africa, I was astonished at the abundance and diversity of game we encountered as the safari progressed.

By the beginning of the third week of my twenty-one day safari I had been lucky enough to collect an elephant with tusks weighing 45 and 55 pounds, respectively, two Cape buffalo, and about twenty assorted other animals including greater kudu, sable, nyala, eland, waterbuck, bushbuck, reedbuck, impala, and warthog.

Our camp for those two weeks was a beautiful permanent setup consisting of comfortable rondavels with thatched roofs. For the final week we moved about three hundred miles west to a spike camp named Nhaluiro, set up beside the Pompue River.

On the second night there, as Alberto and I sat around the campfire chatting about the day's events, the sound of a distant roar brought sudden silence to all. Then it came again, a long, hoarse, drawn-out roar followed by a series of short grunts. As anyone who has seen a Metro-Goldwyn-Mayer movie knows, it was the hunting call of a male lion, but I must tell you it sounds very different on a pitch-black night in the African bush than it does at the local cinema. As the roars reverberated in the distance, Alberto sensed my anticipation and said, "The king of the jungle is hunting. Maybe tomorrow we should provide something to feed his appetite."

I had a hard time falling asleep that night, thinking of the most practical way to convert Africa's No. 1 trophy into a rug for my den. On the other hand, I had read too many books containing horror stories about mauled hunters, and the thought of making a mistake and wounding a lion haunted me. Alberto sensed my apprehension and added fuel to the fire by mentioning that about one hundred and fifty Africans a year were eaten by lions in Mozambique alone. And he was quick to tell the story about one of his trackers who, just the year before, had been calling a lion

at night by roaring through a funnel into a two-gallon tin can holding a couple of inches of water. The call must have sounded realistic because a huge male sneaked up on him undetected, pounced with blinding speed, and carried him away into the bush before he or his client could do anything to prevent the tragedy. Alberto included the grisly details about how, in the ensuing pandemonium, they had followed the lion's progress by the agonized screams of its hapless victim, and finally by the sudden and clearly audible sounds of bones being crunched!

When I woke up next morning, I was appalled by the news that my professional hunter was gone and would be replaced by another one coming in the next day. A Rhodesian by the name of Owen Speight had come to camp to visit Adelino Serras, who by the way wasn't present, and out of the goodness of his heart decided to guide me during the day I had no professional. In my diary I noted the day to be 20 August 1969, and to this day I remember the events as if they had occurred yesterday.

We departed camp somewhat late in the chilly morning—the Jeep had a broken spring that needed changing. We used the dry bed of the Pompue River as a road, and our vehicle advanced with little effort. On the way we came upon a small herd of sable antelope, among which was a bull with magnificent back-sweeping horns well over forty inches in length, a much finer trophy than the thirty-nine-incher I had taken a few days back.

About an hour later, Tobías, the head tracker, signaled for us to stop by tapping on the roof of the vehicle. Clearly outlined on the sandy soil were the tracks of a pride of four or five lions, the biggest of which I could hardly cover with my open hand. Farther on we found the remains of two porcupines. If the lions were hungry enough to eat porcupine, we figured it would be rather easy to attract them to a more succulent meal.

By 4:30 PM my new PH had not yet arrived and I had to again convince Owen to accompany me. In the back of the open Jeep was the hindquarter of the eland I had collected the day before and which was beginning to smell to high heaven. Along the way I connected on a nice warthog with a running shot, and after extracting its tusks and cutting open its belly, we dragged it for a few hundred yards to make a scent trail. At the site where we had seen the lion tracks, Tobías drove a strong stake deep into the sandy riverbed and tied the remains of the warthog and the eland securely to its base. Then we backed the Land Rover into the mouth

of a feeder stream of the Pompue about forty yards from the bait and camouflaged it completely with grass and branches. When we at last sat in the Land Rover for our long vigil, the western sun was casting long shadows across the white sand of the Pompue riverbed. A band of green pigeons, sparkling like emeralds in the last golden rays of the sun, flew overhead. We waited in silence.

As the first star-jewels appeared in the darkening sky, Tobías placed the wide end of the funnel he had brought along for calling purposes into a two-gallon tin can holding about two inches of water. Then he roared into the small end: *RRROOOM, OOOMM, OOOMM, UGH, UGH, UGH.* The sound sent tingles of adrenaline down my spine! Ten or fifteen minutes later, Tobías repeated the procedure while I caressed the pistol grip of my rifle with sweaty hands. As the night wore on, I began to lose faith in Tobías's calling, concluding he had done something wrong, scaring the lions away instead of calling them in.

By 8 PM I was beginning to feel rather silly when an answering roar reverberated in the distance to our left. Almost immediately, another lion roared to our right. And then yet another to our front—we were quite literally surrounded by lions! Suddenly my .308 bolt-action rifle didn't seem so powerful after all, especially without my professional hunter's .375 to back me up. Tobías called softly one more time, then ducked into the back of the Jeep.

≈ ≈ ≈

It was then that I detected the slightest of sounds to my rear and realized that something was terribly wrong. The damned lions were supposed to appear to our front, where the bait was and where their black shadows would be outlined against the yellow bed of the Pompue. I did want a lion, even if I had to risk my life to get one, and I did not want to scare this one away. What I had forgotten at the time was that the back of the Jeep, where we had carried our baits, smelled as strong as the baits themselves, and at least one particular lion was stalking us as his next meal. And I must say that suddenly switching places with the hunted brings with it a very uneasy feeling.

I had instructed Owen not to shine the light until I told him to do so. Then, suffering from a serious lapse of judgment, I stepped out of the Jeep

to get a better view of my surroundings, and asked Owen to shine the light when I stood up on the hood. Fortunately, wise lions seldom eat stupid hunters, for as Owen threw the switch of the spotlight, illuminating a veritable wall of grass, an ominous growl send waves of goose flesh through me as the lion, which I never saw, realized his mistake and bounded away into the swaying grass.

Realizing my mistake and remembering Alberto's story of the night before, I quickly climbed back into the Jeep, thinking that maybe I didn't really need a lion rug after all.

After sitting in the doorless Jeep for a few minutes, gazing fixedly at the white sand surrounding the bait, my heart did a double somersault as I made out two shadows slinking in the moonlight. I softly nudged Owen to alert him, remained silent, and tightened the grip on my rifle. The sounds of crunching bones and tearing flesh almost stupefied me. I raised my rifle, rested my elbows on my knees, and peered through the scope just as Owen's spotlight again parted the African darkness. To my utter astonishment, not two but four lions were feeding on the carcass. I hesitated for a few seconds, looking for the biggest one. The lions gave me a baleful look and slowly started to move away. The last one seemed bigger than the rest and looked to have a fuller mane. As the thick post of the German-made telescope settled on the point of the shoulder, I touched the bullet off. Lions sprang in all directions like scalded cats, apparently unhurt. I kept my eyes on the biggest one as it bounded away, worked the rifle's bolt, and fired again as it disappeared into the tall grass. Then all was still as if nothing had happened!

As I sat there, shaking and dumfounded, it dawned on me that I had a wounded lion on my hands in the middle of the night and with no professional hunter to back me up. It took me a few more minutes to decide that since I had created the situation, it was my responsibility to dispatch the lion. Besides, wasn't this the reason I had come all the way to Africa? Suddenly, I again wanted that lion rug with all my heart.

I climbed out of the Jeep with Tobías, to my left, shining the spotlight. The situation reminded me of going behind the school gymnasium to fight it out with the strongest kid in the classroom, only this time I could come out with something worse than a black eye.

First we went around an island of grass in the middle of the riverbed, expecting the lion to pounce on us at any moment. Then we went into it

to check for blood, but with negative results. It just seemed impossible I could have missed an animal the size of a lion from forty yards. But after going into and around the grassy island a couple of times and not finding a trace of blood or hair, I arrived at the hard conclusion that I had missed. Feelings of agony and frustration, stupidity and clumsiness, crept upon me. I couldn't find words hard enough to punish myself. Fate had granted me the opportunity for the trophy of a lifetime and I had blown it. Perhaps I should go to India and become an untouchable!

I returned to the Jeep and sank down in the seat, replaying a hundred times the sequence of the two shots fired and trying to determine what had gone wrong. Apparently, I simply had not been up to the task.

The night wore on slowly, and the excitement and emotions began to take their toll. I was dozing when the sharp sound of a bone breaking brought my senses to full alert. When Tobías's bony hand clenched my left shoulder to alert me, I almost jumped out of my boots as the thought crossed my mind that maybe another lion had managed to sneak into the truck.

Breathing hard to regain my composure, I slowly lifted the rifle and rested my elbows on my knees. Then I nudged Owen to shine the spotlight. Two reddish-white orbs in a snarling face reflected the light as an ominous warning growl increased slowly in intensity. I held my breath and waited a couple of seconds to be sure of my shot. As the center post came to rest at the base of the lion's neck, the trigger broke. The rifle's blast blinded me for a split second, and I prayed for a positive outcome.

This time my lion lay dead on the spot with a broken neck. If I could express what I felt at that moment, I probably would have quit hunting long ago, but suffice it to say that Heaven itself would not have been an improvement. Tobías patted me on the back and excitedly repeated *"Pondoro!"* which apparently meant lion in his native language. Owen shook my hand enthusiastically. I felt like Stewart Granger stopping the charging man-eating tigress in *Harry Black and the Tiger.*

We had a difficult time loading the nearly four-hundred-pound cat into the vehicle, then headed triumphantly to camp. There we were received as heroes, the whole camp staff dancing around my fallen quarry to the beating of drums.

My story would have happily ended there had it not been for an even bigger surprise the next day. Tobías had taken a French client to the same

place to bait another lion, only to find a fresh blood spoor on the sandy soil. My first lion lay in a heap—stiff, rumpled, and stone-dead about one hundred yards from where I had shot him, hidden by the tall grass. My first shot had entered low in the chest area, nearly parting the heart and lodging behind the skin in the off-side. The second shot, taken as the lion was running, had broken the left hip and lodged in the stomach. The lion had been dead all along, but hadn't had the decency to admit it!

To top it all, during the trip back to camp with my lion, the Frenchman had "crawled the stock" of his .375 H&H Magnum in the process of shooting a warthog. The resulting "fool's cut" on his right eyebrow proved to be so severe that his safari ended right then and there. He was more than happy to recoup his $54 lion license by letting me fill the tag, which is why I have both open-mouth rugs on the wall of my trophy room.

Which seems to prove that one man's poison can definitely be another man's plat du jour!

The World's Most Beautiful Deer

Chapter 31

The first big-game animal I hunted outside my native Costa Rica was an axis buck on the island of Molokai in Hawaii, more than thirty years ago. I found this free-range hunt extremely challenging and exciting, and to this day I keep the two mounted heads I collected on that trip, even though they are not exactly trophy size. I longed to hunt this animal again, but it was not to be for many years. I did take a nice buck on a trip to Argentina, but because it was not a very challenging hunt, it didn't mean too much to me.

As mentioned earlier, my first love is cat hunting, and so far I have managed to collect eight different species. But deer are for me a close second, especially if they have impressive horns and a striking appearance. And the axis fills both requirements perfectly.

A little history on the species is in order: The genus Axis has only two species—the cheetal or spotted deer of India and Sri-Lanka *(Axis axis)* and the hog deer *(Axis porcinus).* A mature buck will weigh around two hundred pounds on the hoof and stand about three feet at the shoulder. They have a beautiful chocolate-brown hide across the back, melding to a reddish brown down the flank with creamy white underparts, white throat bib, and almost white ears. The dark hide is lined with rough rows of white spots. To top all of this, a good buck will carry a six-point, barrel-shaped set of horns that can grow three feet long. Axis deer come into rut in the late spring, which is the best time to hunt them, although, like other tropical deer, they are in hard antler throughout the year. This fact is a great bonus to game ranches, allowing them to stay in business all year long.

In the U.S. axis deer were first released on the Edwards Plateau in Texas in 1932, and their numbers steadily increased to over forty thousand today in this state alone, with a healthy population in Mexico's neighboring states as well.

Almost a decade ago, landowner Charlie Bruce invited me to hunt again on the beautiful Sycamore Creek Ranch near the town of Del Río,

Texas. I arrived on 20 July 2003, and even at night it was hot and sultry. Fortunately, the ranch accommodations were superb, especially with the thermostat set at 70 degrees F. Ah, but at this time of the year the vegetation is luxuriant, substantially reducing visibility, and it had been a good spring with plenty of rain. This was not to be an easy hunt.

Charlie picked me up at daybreak the next morning in his beat-up Willys pickup truck, from which we would glass and with any luck sneak up on a good trophy buck. Charlie had twice seen a real monster of around thirty-five inches, but free-ranging axis bucks can be extremely hard to find. We rode and walked alternatively until the heat truly set in; then we beat a hasty retreat to the ranch. Fortunately, there was a beautiful swimming pool overlooking Sycamore Canyon, and with a Coke and a sandwich in hand, that spot was hard to beat. Life just couldn't have been better!

But the cover was thick and the deer were wary and the days slipped by. It became apparent that getting any deer with antlers over thirty inches—the minimum I had set for myself—wasn't going to be easy.

On the third day of the hunt we came upon a herd of about a dozen animals, among them a beautiful mature buck with lyre-shaped, up-sweeping horns. Apparently the herd was moving to water, and we tried to cut them off on foot to get a shot, playing hide-and-seek among the oaks, mesquites, and ironwoods. But we got only occasional glimpses, and they finally gave us the slip.

At the beginning there was no hurry, but now I sensed that Charlie wanted to wrap the hunt up quickly—apparently, too much time had already been spent on this one animal. On the fourth day I began to get nervous: Time was running out and I had yet to fire a shot. Around midmorning, two splendid bucks stepped into an opening about a hundred yards away, but before I could motion Charlie to stop the vehicle, they were gone. We didn't go to the house for lunch, but rather had a Coke and a sandwich in the field, but the deer weren't moving much in the 100-degree weather.

By 7 PM I was really worried—it looked like this would be the last day Charlie was going to put up with me. After all, he was guiding me out of the goodness of his heart and had to return to his normal routine. That's when two bucks jumped across the road and dashed through a dry creekbed. The second one was undoubtedly the bigger of the two, but somehow I hesitated as it bounded away. Charlie slammed on the brakes

and ordered me to shoot. To be honest, I didn't think the buck was big enough, but if I've learned anything over the years, it's that when you're hunting a species you're not too familiar with, go with the pro's opinion every time. Now I was ready to shoot, but the buck wasn't ready to stop. And the fading light wasn't much help either!

Ah, but success depends not only on your own ability but also on the stupidity of others: Just before it disappeared in the mesquite on the far side of the creek bed, the bigger buck decided to stop for a last look. That's when the 7mm Remington Magnum caught him on his left shoulder, the impact toppling him over.

As we walked over to the animal, the first thing that struck me was the deep chocolate-brown of his coat, set off by the rows of snow-white spots. The horns were beautiful and symmetrical, measuring a tad over thirty-one inches. It was then I realized that I had collected an animal graced not only with extremely impressive head-gear but a spotted hide as well. Its striking looks motivated me to pay for a full body mount, which now graces my trophy room.

is is the buck that caused me so much humiliation. As you can see, he is still baring his teeth at me! nora, México, 14 December 2011.

is is my best Coues deer yet, scoring around 110 B&C points. It was bitterly cold when I took the cture the next morning. Sonora, México, 15 December 2011.

I collected this piping guam when it came to eat the flowers of a piuva tree just outside the house. The .22 magnum proved invaluable for small game (right). El Beni, Bolivia, 24 September 2003.

Riding on mules on the interminable plains when the humidity hovered around 100 percent and the temperature was 100 F was very hard work (below). El Beni, Bolivia, 24 September 2003.

:hough my swamp deer was in velvet, the antlers were pretty hard and did not spoil. El Beni, Bolivia September 2003.

Most people think of the cougar as a North American animal, but its actual range is from the most northern parts of Canada to Argentina and most places in between. Heredia province, Costa Rica.

My desert mule deer from Sonora barely missed making the Boone & Crockett record book. I consic
t one of my best trophies. México, 15 January 2005.

r once it wasn't raining when I traversed the Indian River in Nicaragua with my wife, Irene, circa 200

never miss a chance to collect a cat. Curiosity killed this one. Sonora México, 15 January 2005.

I took my biggest jaguar ever just after I had had back surgery. It tipped the scales at 165 pounds.

món province, Costa Rica.

Charlie Bruce is a good judge of axis deer. I collected this fine trophy on the Sycamore Creek Ranc
Texas, 14 May 2001.

I had my black bear fully mounted as it takes up less wall space. Note the position where the bear fel
Near Quemado, New Mexico, 3 October 1995.

his pronghorn antelope with 80$^{6}/_{8}$ points just missed the Boone & Crockett record book, which I sho
ith Mick Chapel. The rifle is my favorite 7mm Remington Magnum. New Mexico, 1 October 1995

This nice Rocky Mountain mule deer was not heavy, but he had a good spread. I almost had a hear attack packing him out! Idaho, 5 November 1992.

ody-wise, my Idaho whitetail was huge, and he sported nice antlers. I took this buck with a running shot om my 7mm Remington Magnum, custom made by Answer Products Co., Idaho, 2 November 1992

This is my best ever bull elk, which I took with Mick Chapel. It scored 363 Boone & Crockett points af taking into consideration the broken antler. New Mexico, 18 October 1997.

The latest Lamborghini prototype, manufactured Namibia, proved an extremely useful hunting vehic Mount Etjo Lodge, Namibia, September 2004.

I never cease to admire the fall colors in Nortl America. We have nothing like this in Costa Rica New Mexico, September 1995.

credibly, all the animals I shot in Namibia proved trophy class, and my steenbok was no exception aftali wouldn't let me shoot anything else. Mount Etjo Lodge, Namibia, 23 September 2004.

Blesbok aren't very challenging to hunt, but they make an interesting addition to a trophy collectio
Namibia, 12 September 2004.

I took this record-class Cape or red hartebeest with one shot from my custom 7mm Remington Magnum
Namibia, 18 September 2004

iant oryx or gemsbok are very plentiful in Namibia but extremely wary. This one sports 36-inch horns.
Iount Etjo Lodge, Namibia, 21 September 2004.

I looked over dozens of kudu bulls before collecting this one; it carries 55-inch horns. Namibia, 2
September 2004.

ack wildebeest were brought back from the brink of extinction by trophy hunters' fees. They are now ite abundant in South Africa and Namibia. Namibia, 14 September 2004.

anybody tells me klipspringers are easy to hunt; I'll shoot him. The mountain I had to climb is in the ckground, so I was a bit worse for wear by the time this picture was taken; Naftali, however, was fresh a daisy. Namibia, 27 September 2004.

This leopard almost added me to his trophy room. He tipped the scales at 145 pounds. Namibia, September 2004.

I already had a blue wildebeest, but this one was too big to pass up. I let the 7mm perform its one-sh magic. Namibia, 17 September 2004.

artmann mountain zebra are striped all the way down to their hoofs, but their bellies are white. This
ıe made the mistake of climbing down the mountain. Namibia, 26 September 2004.

ʃy aoudad went a tad over 33 inches, which is about 1½ inches smaller than the all-time African record.
ycamore Creek Ranch, Texas, 14 May 2001.

A warthog is usually the first animal collected on a safari. This one sported 9½-inch tusks and was take with a running shot. Namibia, 11 September 2004.

Springboks were abundant at the Mount Etjo Safari Lodge, but taking a good one is always a difficu task. I took this one with a running Texas heart shot. Namibia, 12 September 2004.

Bolivia's Yellow Deer

Chapter 32

I had obsessed about going to Bolivia for many years but had been unable to accomplish it. The main attraction, of course, was *Panthera onça palustris,* the giant jaguar of the swamps, which had evolved into a different subspecies of *Panthera* due to its diet of fish and capybara, the world's largest rodent. Over the years, I had taken four jaguars in Mexico, Nicaragua, and Costa Rica, the biggest weighing 165 pounds. A large swamp jaguar could weigh one hundred pounds more. Close behind on my most-wanted list was the South American swamp deer, *Blastocerus dichotomus,* which to me looks like a cross between a mule deer and a blacktail.

Going to Bolivia presented innumerable problems. To start with, I always like to travel with my own hunting rifle, and Bolivia had banned all rifle calibers except the .22, due, I imagine, to its political instability. That alone made hunting in that country unattractive. If a given country does not welcome international hunters, I might as well hunt somewhere else!

As fate would have it, however, a first cousin of mine married a Bolivian by the name of Luis Fernando Torrelio and we struck up a friendship from the day of their wedding. Although he had worked in the United States for the past several years as an industrial engineer, he still had family and friends back home, not only in the capital city of La Paz but also in the city of Santa Cruz de la Sierra, stepping-off place for the Pantanal, a famous hunting area.

Still I postponed the trip, because of seemingly insurmountable problems involved in obtaining a permit to import a rifle. However, I had an important contact: Gene Harris, a curio dealer from Miami whose daughter had been married to the son of Hugo Banzer, then president of Bolivia and a retired general. To be sure, the general's son had died in an airplane accident a few years before, but the family ties had remained unbroken, thanks mainly to the grandchildren they had in common.

≈ ≈ ≈

Gene phoned the president on my behalf, and the very next day the Bolivian Ambassador to Costa Rica contacted me. We met at an Italian restaurant for lunch. Before I could inform him of the reason for our meeting, he began to lecture me on the incredible business climate and the limitless opportunities in Bolivia. He had been a politician all his life and an ex-congressman in his country, and although I tried several times to interrupt, I was unsuccessful. Finally, after at least half an hour of uninterrupted monologue, he looked me straight in the eye and asked why I wanted to visit his country—a trip so extremely important that the president himself (and ex-dictator!) had asked for the ambassador's personal assistance. With as straight a face as possible, and trying to keep my composure, I informed him that I wanted to go to Bolivia to catch a jaguar. At first he couldn't believe his ears. I tried to explain that I was a hunter and collector, that his country happened to harbor the biggest subspecies of jaguar in the world, and that I wanted to collect one, just like Teddy Roosevelt had about ninety years earlier.

It took a few seconds for the thought to sink in, but then he said he would even accompany me there, to make sure I would have no problem with my rifle.

At last I was on my way to Bolivia—with a diplomatic escort to boot. Ah, but fate has its own way of ruining the best-laid plans of mice and men! Before I departed on my long-delayed journey, I had to make all the necessary plans, including where specifically to go. I contacted my longtime jaguar hunting guru and friend from Mexico, Manuel Queb, who helped me figure out how much the whole trip would cost me. With everything arranged, I called the ambassador again to set a departure date.

To my utter astonishment, he informed me over the telephone how he had nearly died during a recent catheterization! It seems that precisely on Good Friday, when everything shuts down in Costa Rica, and with his family away on vacation, he started to feel faint. He asked his chauffeur to take him to the nearest clinic for a checkup. He could hardly stand up as he staggered into the emergency ward bathed in his own sweat.

"You're having a heart attack," said a young doctor fresh out of medical school, whereupon my friend (and my Bolivian passport) were immediately transferred to the intensive-care unit. Of course, all the more experienced doctors were on vacation for the Easter holidays. Before the ambassador could explain that his problem could be due to an inner-ear

infection, the Sodium Pentothal in his serum took effect and he passed out. The next thing he knew, he was going full speed into a tunnel with a bright light at the end and his entire life seemed to pass through his mind in a few seconds. A sense of serenity overtook him as he floated farther and farther away from his earthly problems. Suddenly his state of peace and serenity switched to sheer panic, after which there was a complete blackout. He came to his senses in the ICU, connected to numerous tubes and monitors and surrounded by doctors and nurses.

As he explained to me later, his inner-ear problem had led the inexperienced young doctor to diagnose a heart attack, whereupon he had opted for the catheterization—with almost-fatal results: The patient's heart stopped beating for several minutes, and only the third electroshock brought the ambassador back to life.

That experience had caused the ambassador to quit his job and travel to the United States for a complete medical checkup before returning to Bolivia. So ended my second try for a Pantanal jaguar!

A couple of years passed before Luis Fernando Torrelio, my "cousin-in-law," again convinced me to go on an exploratory trip to Bolivia. If I was able to arrange a jaguar hunt, fine; if not, I would at least get to visit a different and interesting country and be hosted by his friends and relatives. I wasn't overly enthusiastic, because bringing in my rifle was definitely out. On top of all this, as far as I was able to find out, there were no game laws in Bolivia and I wasn't even sure I could take trophies out of the country, when and if I was successful.

≈ ≈ ≈

After reading *The Jungle Hunter,* Joe Cavanaugh's book on South America, I contacted him in Minnesota, and he gave me the number of one Alfredo Asbún in Santa Cruz, whom he claimed could provide me with an adequate hunting rifle. Word of mouth had it that Bolivian prisons were not five-star facilities, so I contacted the Costa Rican ambassador in Bolivia, attorney Didier Carranza, to pull me out of trouble in case something went awry. It turned out he knew me from a legal matter involving a client of his, and he even invited me to his residence for the celebration of my country's independence on 15 September 2003, the day after my arrival. The very next day Didier was nice enough to call from La Paz to inform me that he

had contacted the president of the Bolivian Hunters Association to assist me. I immediately phoned the gentleman, Roberto Dips Zogbi, who assured me he would help in any way possible. With so many people willing to pitch in, I decided the odds were in my favor and gave myself the go-ahead. Besides, Don Roberto had told me that he had a friend who had a friend in Santa Cruz who could provide me with a .308 rifle.

Upon further investigation, I was informed that it would be extremely difficult to find soft-nose hunting ammunition in .308 caliber in Bolivia. Through a friend in the Costa Rican Civil Aviation Administration, I learned that Bolivia didn't have an X-ray screening system and that arriving baggage was not X-rayed anyway. I packed ten rounds in each of two plastic bags and put them inside my hunting boots, which I then stuffed with socks. Ah, but greed is the downfall of man: I decided to pack another twenty rounds in my duffel bag, figuring there would be so much game to shoot in that jaguar and deer haven that I could run out of ammo!

There was, of course, no problem whatsoever when I boarded the Taca Airlines plane in Costa Rica. After all, I had written the gun laws myself, and made sure there would be no hitch in transporting firearms or ammunition in and out of the country. Upon my arrival in La Paz, Bolivia's capital city—which at more than twelve thousand feet above sea level is the highest capital in Latin America—I was asked whether I had anything to declare. I gave the customs agent an innocent look and answered no, whereupon he gave me an unflinching go-ahead.

A battered taxicab drove me the twenty minutes—straight downhill—to the President Hotel, where Mr. Dips had arranged for a special rate of fifty dollars a night, breakfast included. After a complimentary coca tea, which is perfectly legal in Bolivia and which had absolutely no effect on me, I passed out in the comfort of a heated room.

Don Roberto Dips picked me up early the next morning and drove me again to the airport, where I met the man in charge of Taca cargo, who assured me there would be no problem in exporting my eventual trophies. That took care of half the problem. Now only the question of obtaining an adequate rifle remained.

We returned to the hotel and Mr. Dips called his friend about the shooting iron. For reasons unknown, the .308 had suddenly become a .222 Remington and there wasn't any ammunition for it. Now, kicking an enraged 300-pound jaguar to death didn't seem like a good option! After

a few minutes of uncontrollable panic, I called Mr. Asbún in Santa Cruz, who assured me he had a Browning Medallion in .308 caliber with a 2½- to 8-power Bushnell scope mounted on it. It was in perfect condition and he would "rent" it to me. The problem solved, I decided to accept Mr. Dips's invitation to dinner at the hunting-club headquarters before my departure next morning to Santa Cruz de la Sierra.

Upon my arrival at the club, I was struck by the antlers of an absolutely outstanding marsh deer with eighteen points and a spread well over twenty inches, with massive bases. There were also several pampas deer *(Ozotoceros bezoarticus)*, brown brocket deer *(Mazama gouazoubira)*, a North Andean huemul *(Hippocamelus antisensis,* also known as Peruvian *guemal* or Andean deer), and a twenty-five-foot-long (I measured it) anaconda *(Eunectes murinus)*. To my utter astonishment, nobody in the club had the slightest idea about what these deer were or where they came from.

≈ ≈ ≈

After a little sightseeing the next day (there is not much to see in La Paz) and shopping for llama and alpaca rugs, I rushed to the airport to catch my midday one-hour flight to Santa Cruz de la Sierra. I checked my baggage and proceeded to the boarding room. I hadn't been there ten minutes when a voice through the loudspeaker requested that a Mr. Ricardo Guardia present himself to the airport military authorities. I froze for a few seconds, thinking what to do and fearing what had happened, when the summons again boomed through the loudspeaker. I stood up and for a moment thought my legs wouldn't hold me. I asked the lady at the counter where the "military authorities" were and headed there. I identified myself, and a five-foot-tall sergeant (who commanded absolutely no respect) with a machine gun with taped magazines (which commanded a lot of respect) ordered me to follow him. We walked the full length of the airport terminal, and all the way I was pondering what I would say upon being presented with the irrefutable evidence of the high-powered rifle ammunition. Right then and there I decided that I had no choice but to play it cool and give them a dumb "I didn't know" look. I wasn't worried about pulling off the dumb look; remaining cool seemed more difficult.

Presently we arrived at the X-ray room, where the rounds outside my boots showed clearly on the screen. The officer in charge asked me what they were.

"Hunting ammunition, of course," I replied. "I'm going to the fair in Santa Cruz to buy cattle, and my host asked me to bring him ammunition for a rifle for which he has a permit. It's only twenty rounds."

I guess I kept my cool and looked either dumb or honest (probably both!)—the officer wished me good luck and, after I filled out a declaration form, sent me on my way. As I hurried to board the departing airplane, I was breathing hard, undoubtedly due to the high altitude.

≈ ≈ ≈

Flying over the Andes is an experience in itself, with the airplane seemingly touching the crests of the looming, snow-covered peaks. It seemed to me a shame that they are practically devoid of game animals, which, if introduced, could produce an additional source of income to one of the poorest countries in Latin America. When I mentioned this to various people I met during my stay, they seemed amazed that wild animals could have such a high value and that people from other countries would come and pay a generous fee for the privilege of collecting them.

After about half an hour, the mighty peaks gradually gave way to immense lowlands that seemed to stretch on forever. Upon landing in Santa Cruz, I had the sensation of being in a different country. The climate was different (about 85 degrees F), the landscape was different, the people were different, and their accent was more similar to the one in my native Costa Rica than to the Spanish spoken in La Paz. On the way to the Caparuch Hotel, I saw the first rheas, or South American ostriches, on the roadside and was impressed by their large size. Upon paying the taxi driver, I realized that everything here was only half as expensive as in my native Costa Rica. The rate at the hotel, for a very ample room overlooking the swimming pool, with air conditioning and an excellent restaurant, was $40 a night with breakfast included.

By midafternoon I was at the bar having a piña colada when Roland Brückner, somehow related to Luis Fernando Torrelio, introduced himself. A likable fellow in his mid-thirties, he informed me that everything was organized for my jaguar safari. After another drink, we went over to Alfredo Asbún's fishing shop to rent a rifle. After so many inconveniences, I was elated to be presented with a Browning Medallion .308 rifle fitted with a Bushnell varipower scope, all in perfect condition. He even had about twenty rounds of ammunition to offer me.

But here the problems started: Asbún was not about to lend me the only available big-game hunting rifle in the province of Santa Cruz out of the goodness of his heart. He knew perfectly well he had me against the wall: The fee to rent the rifle for ten days was $600! I realized the rifle was worth that amount in the U.S., but we weren't in the United States. I accepted and was immediately informed that I would also need to leave a deposit for the full value of the rifle: $1,700! That meant paying three times the rifle's value for using it during ten days. Roland indicated that I would have no problem getting my money back when I returned the rifle. Again having no choice, I had to accept.

I also proceeded to buy a .22 magnum rifle, legal in Bolivia, for about $300, to use during my stay and then present as a gift to Conrad Brückner, owner of the ranch where I would stay, as a token of my gratitude. On this rifle I installed a Burris varipower scope that I had brought from Costa Rica for the purpose. Oh, and my other boots were stuffed with .22 magnum ammunition, which I could have bought in Bolivia anyway, although probably at a much higher price.

Due to the lack of infrastructure and the immensity of the country (over 1,050,000 square kilometers or 405,000 square miles), the only practical means of transportation is by air. The trip from Costa Rica to Santa Cruz had cost me $1,200 (it would have been less had I not stayed overnight in La Paz), and the trip to the town of Trinidad cost me another $100 in a twin-engine commercial carrier.

Upon landing on a dirt strip in Trinidad, I was in for another surprise: Opening the door of the airplane was like opening a furnace. The temperature was easily around 100 degrees F, with the humidity in the nineties. Ten minutes later I was drenched in my own sweat and feeling very uncomfortable. I had flown in with Roland, my two bags, and two rifles, and fortunately had no problem whatsoever.

Trinidad reminded me of a border town—everyone wore cowboy hats and rode around on bicycles and motorcycles. Here I stayed at the Tahibo Hotel, which was quite acceptable and fortunately had air conditioning and a nice swimming pool.

≈ ≈ ≈

I had dinner with the three Brückner brothers, Roland, Conrad, and Johnny. Conrad informed me that he couldn't accompany me to his *estancia*

(ranch) but said I was welcome to stay there for as long as I wanted. He seemed confident I would get a jaguar in no time, since the place was overrun with them. His foreman, Benjamín Cordero, an expert *tigrero*, would be there to assist me at all times.

At about noon the next day I would fly, for $50, on a commercial twin-engine airplane to the town of Baures, where all the passengers would get off but I would continue to the ranch on my own for another $100. Next morning I would buy enough salt and borax to cure the hides of the animals I might collect, plus the necessary provisions for the duration of my stay. Conrad, however, advised me not to buy much of the latter—otherwise I would miss sampling the local food, which was supposed to be excellent. I agreed but would later regret that decision.

When I arrived at the hangar with enough salt and borax to cure the hide of an elephant, the pilot asked what the borax was for. After I explained that I planned to use it with salt to cure my game skins, he laughed and said he had been leery because borax is also used in the preparation of cocaine. He hid the bags and informed me that he would put them in the plane only at the last minute. When I asked him when the plane would leave, he said, "When it is full," meaning that we would have to wait until there were enough passengers to make the trip worthwhile.

We left shortly after noon, landing in Baures and picking up Mamino Paz, manager of the *estancia*, along with a fifty-gallon drum of gasoline for an outboard motor. I only hoped we would not have to make a crash landing—chances were the gasoline would explode.

We landed on a grass strip near the San Joaquín River about a mile from the house and had to carry everything there ourselves. Let me tell you—carrying a heavy bag a mile in hundred-degree weather is no easy task!

≈ ≈ ≈

Estancia can be translated to "mansion" in the Spanish language, and I assure you that word can be misleading: When we arrived at my place of residence for the next ten days, I was confronted with three wooden huts with thatched roofs and dirt floors, no electricity, no running water, and no toilet. I asked if there was at least a fuel-powered refrigerator, which of course there wasn't. The only available water came from a well set among the huts, and it had a distinctive yellowish color. I asked Benjamín's wife,

Marlen, to please boil the drinking water for me as I really didn't want to get sick. One hut was the kitchen, where there was an open fire. Another was the living quarters for Benjamín and his wife, and the third one had been set aside for me. In it was a wooden bed with a foam mattress, one chair, and one small round table.

But all these inconveniences were quickly forgotten when Benjamín showed me the skins of the last four marauding jaguars he had taken. When I asked how he caught them, he introduced me to a pack of mongrels he claimed were the best jaguar hounds in the world. It struck me, however, that most of them had no ears. Why? Benjamín explained that if a hound showed fear of a jaguar, he would cut off half of an ear. If it was again afraid, he would cut the other half off. If the dog was again afraid and had run out of ears, he would shoot it. The biggest and fiercest-looking dog had half of one ear left, and Benjamín claimed that one had completely lost its fear of the spotted cats. I wondered if it had learned to be more afraid of its owner!

I went to sight in my rifles and, to my great satisfaction, found that although the Browning was off about three inches low and to the right, it printed within three-quarters of an inch at 100 yards after the necessary adjustments. And though the .22 magnum was a rather crude Philippine model, it put one bullet on top of the other at 50 yards.

≈ ≈ ≈

Sweat-soaked from the intensive heat, I told my hosts I would go to the San Joaquín River, about two hundred yards away, for a dip in the crystal-clear waters. They suggested otherwise: A black cayman, lurking nearby, had eaten most of their pigs, and the river was infested with piranhas that would occasionally remove the teats from any cows that allowed their udders to touch the water. After a very short conversation with myself, I decided I would be much better off with dirt on my body than with my body in the dirt, and opted for a bucket of water and a sponge for my daily ablutions.

As the sun set, I was in the process of pouring water over my head from a gourd in a roofless wash-up enclosure when a horde of mosquitoes literally attacked me. I had to make a dash for my hut, which fortunately had screening on the windows or they would have sucked me dry. Mamino and Benjamín laughed at the tenderfoot learning the ways of the jungle.

With all the traveling, I had not had a chance to eat lunch, so by 7 PM I was starving. But now it was time for another surprise: Since there was no refrigeration, all the meat had to be salted and converted into jerky or *charque* as it is known locally. It really wasn't all that bad, but it was so bitter you could not eat much of it. To wash it down there was warm grapefruit juice, which would be my main drink over the next days—anything but that murky water! Fortunately there were chickens, and I had eggs for breakfast, lunch, and dinner. Aside from that, the main dish was rice with melted cheese, which didn't seem to combine too well and which I couldn't eat, no matter how hungry. But survival is a good teacher and I soon learned that the place was alive with purple pigeons *(Columba flavirostris)*, along with red-throated piping guans *(Pipile cujubi)* and Muscovy ducks *(Cairina moschata)*, which, by the way, are the largest duck in the world. And you can believe this: Hunger made me a better shot than I ever was!

I wanted to see as much of the country as I could and thought I could accomplish this best while hunting deer from horseback, the way I hunted back home. I asked Mamino to have two steeds ready by daybreak. Nineteen September was my first hunting day, and I was eager to go well before daylight. But I learned from the first day that Mamino and Benjamín were both lazy: Push them as I might, they didn't have the horses ready and we didn't leave until after 6:30. I had to literally bathe in "Off" thanks to millions of mosquitoes and "no-see-ums."

The best hunting grounds were, of course, on the other side of the river, which was quite wide. So it was decided that we would use the motorboat to get partway across, then pole our way as far as we could, at which point Benjamín would meet us with the mules, for apparently they would be better for the long journey. It was beautiful while we motored, but the poling was extremely hard work and everybody had to pitch in—that is, Mamino, his son, and yours truly.

On the way I asked Mamino and his son when the deer shed their antlers, and he proceeded to explain that there were three kinds of marsh deer or *ciervos*, as he called them: those that had no horns, those that had hard horns, and those whose horns were covered with skin and hair. I tried to explain that deer all over the world drop their antlers every year, have them covered with velvet during the antler-growing time, and rub off the velvet at the start of the mating season. They laughed and asked

me how it would be possible for a buck to grow such a big set of antlers in such a short period of time!

Bucks here, Mamino said, grow a small set of horns when they are young and proceed to add two or more points every year. Try as I might, I couldn't convince them otherwise. Even more astonishing, everybody there, hunters and nonhunters alike, had exactly the same opinion.

They were also astounded that I would keep the antlers of the deer I collected; they believed that if I took them into my house, I would attract bad luck for as long as I had them. I tried to explain that I had about a hundred sets of antlers in a special room in my house, and they stared at me in astonishment.

Taking the conversation a little farther, I asked if they hunted these *ciervos* and whether the meat was good. The answer was that they shot them on sight to make lariats, which apparently were very strong. However, the lariats rotted easily during the rainy season, and they would have to shoot more *ciervos* then to make more lariats. They left the meat for the *suchas* or black vultures, claiming it was unfit to eat, which I suspect is a fallacy. And they would also leave the antlers in the bush, for they had no desire to invite bad luck into their lives.

I was able to corroborate this information when I found a magnificent set of antlers bleaching in the sun. It seemed a shame to let them disintegrate out on the immense plain, but to avoid temptation, I didn't even get off my steed. The situation made me think of how some of my hunting buddies back home would take large antlers they had found and proudly display them in their houses dressed in the capes of smaller deer stretched to the limit to accept the bigger skull. Some of those antlers still contained pink and yellow paint from the wall where they had been hanging for years in the barn of some peasant in Guanacaste province, from which the "trophy" had been removed in exchange for a few coins. As I've said before, vanity and honor are not made to live together!

It seemed a great shame that such a magnificent animal would be sacrificed just for a few feet of rope, especially given that nylon would not only be stronger but last longer. Though I didn't condone this practice, however, I better understood it when we arrived at our meeting place and the mules were saddled. Aside from the bit and the stirrups, all the saddlery had been made at the *estancia*. The saddle tree was made of wood and lined with rawhide. The stirrups were tied with a piece of rope, and the

reins were weaved from the mane or tail of a horse. Several raw sheepskins were placed over the saddle, and two rawhide cinches were thrown over them and under the mule's belly to tie everything down. Most amazing was that this crude saddle was extremely comfortable, maybe even more so than the expensive McLellands I had back home!

≈ ≈ ≈

The San Joaquín is a beautiful and pristine river that flows leisurely across the featureless plain and creates numerous lagoons alive with birdlife. Black-bellied tree ducks *(Dendrocygna autumnalis)* arose by the thousands at the drone of the motor, and I was impressed by the abundance of Muscovy ducks—we call them royal ducks in Costa Rica—which flew in flocks larger than any I had ever seen. There were dozens of jabiru storks *(Jabiru mycteria)* and turkey-size southern screamers *(Chauna torquata)*, light gray in color and with red legs. Each time we neared the screamers, which were always in pairs, they would give a strident call and fly clumsily away. Mamino told me they have large spurs on their wings and that if one is killed, the other will die of grief. Also along the river and swamps by the tens of thousands were purple pigeons; enormous flocks flew over our dugout canoe. If I'd had my Merkel side-by-side, I would have had a field day, although I doubt I could have carried enough shells with me.

As we poled down the river among the water hyacinths, parakeets arrowed through the air in strident green flashes and small flocks of beautiful blue-and-orange macaws *(Ara ararauna)* flew gracefully overhead, their harsh calls echoing across the plain and their brilliant colors brightening the landscape. I filled my lungs with the cool morning air and felt sorry for those who ignore the world of hunting.

After a good hour of poling, we entered a small lagoon, where we met up with Benjamín and the two mules on the bank. He unsaddled his steed, threw his riding equipment into the dugout, and coaxed both protesting mules into the water. The water in the lagoon was deep and there were no water hyacinths. Mamino opened the throttle of the outboard, and the two mules, tied to the stern by their halter ropes, snorted and wheezed in panic. Sometimes it looked like they would go under. It is still a wonder to me how they didn't drown, especially since we repeated this procedure on the way back and several days thereafter, but they always

made it safely to the other side. No, Mamino had no interest in trolling for black cayman!

≈ ≈ ≈

Benjamín had never seen a saddle scabbard and thought mine was a great idea. He insisted that I leave it behind when I departed.

We told Mamino that we would be back around noon and trotted away on our steeds at a brisk pace, skirting the patches of forest and swamp, looking for a cooperating marsh deer buck. Every so often we would stop and Benjamín would climb a tree to search the area. Everything was open-range—there were no fences, and the cattle were free to move anywhere. It struck me how the plain was divided into four very different ecosystems: Near the river was the swampy terrain, covered with short grass. Where it dried out, high, dry grass took over. Then came higher brush, which in places was difficult to negotiate. Farther from the river was the impenetrable jungle. I suppose the amount of water in the soil accounted for the four distinct vegetation types, but nobody could give me a valid explanation.

Aside from birds near the water, it surprised me that the huge plain seemed devoid of all other animal life, especially considering we were so far away from the nearest town. I would later learn that during the rainy season, poachers pole the flooded plains and shoot everything in sight; they salt the meat and sell it for a pittance in the nearest town. It was sad to confirm—in spite of all the propaganda to the contrary—that most countries in Latin America, including my own, have little regard for their natural resources. They see them only as a source of cheap food or as a means to make a perishable piece of rope.

During the long morning, we saw only two young does, Benjamín insisting that I shoot the first one because he needed a spare lariat. When I refused, he asked that I give him my rifle so he could shoot it himself. He gave me a sour look when I explained that I was paying him to guide me and not the other way around, and that the deer would disappear if he continued to shoot the does. His answer, of course, was that his grandfather had hunted deer, his father had hunted deer, and he had hunted deer and there were still a few around, which meant they would never disappear. There is nothing worse than preaching to the deaf!

Upon returning to the river, we came upon a small herd of capybaras *(Hydrochoerus hydrochaeris)*, black and sleek and about the size of a domestic pig. These tailless aquatic rodents have little appeal as a game animal, and I refrained from shooting a big male, although I watched it through the riflescope for about a minute. I guess the wind changed, for suddenly they gave an alarm cry and plunged into the San Joaquín River. It is interesting to note that although water is their natural means of defense—they will disappear under its surface at the least disturbance—they never do so when wounded. Why? Because they are more afraid of the red piranhas, which will leave only the bones after a few minutes of frenzied feeding. Like sharks, they are irresistibly attracted to the scent of blood.

Upon rounding a bend we came upon a couple of rheas, or *pillos* as they are locally known, which took off at incredible speed the moment they laid eyes on us. During the rest of my stay I saw at least two more small groups of these flightless birds, always running because they invariably saw us before we saw them. I couldn't have taken one if my life depended on it.

The next day, 20 September, we were up and ready to go before six in the morning. We rode in the 100-degree temperature for thirteen hours in the opposite direction we had taken the first day. Our only break was one hour for lunch, which consisted of the unpalatable *charque* (jerky), hard bread, and juice squeezed out of grapefruits. Besides another small band of capybaras basking in the sun by the river, we saw absolutely no animals, except for the noisy but picturesque *parabas* or macaws flying low overhead. Wherever the ground was moist near the river, I checked for tracks, finding only those of small animals like armadillos, agoutis, and raccoons. I just couldn't understand how such a vast area could be so completely devoid of any forms of life.

As I said in a previous story, if everything fails, lower your standards. Suddenly a capybara didn't seem like such an unworthy creature and decided it would make an interesting addition to my trophy room. Besides, I could use it to tease my friends, telling them that I had shot the biggest *paca (Agouti paca)* in Costa Rica, which had weighed over a hundred pounds. And to my absolute astonishment, when I showed a picture of the capybara to a distant cousin who claims to be a hunter, telling him it was a *tepescuintle (paca)*, he said that he was no fool and could clearly see it was an agouti (which weighs about six pounds) because its hide had no white spots!

For a change of pace and a change of game, next morning found Mamino and I motoring down the river's lazy waters. Of course, when you decide to go after an animal you have seen almost every previous day, it manages to make itself scarce thereafter. Though we covered a lot of ground, or should I say water, we never saw another capybara.

But I was not to be defeated by such an unworthy adversary, and next morning we were on the river again. At least it was easy hunting—I had managed to tie a chair to the boat, and the breeze generated by our boat speed made for a nice change in the unbearable heat. And we were getting to see myriad bird life, plus a few small crocodiles and caymans. At about 9:30 we came upon four capybaras crossing the river with only the tops of their heads above water (their eyes and nostrils are set high on their faces, no doubt an adaptation to their semi-aquatic habitat). I was hoping they would come up on the bank, but instead they dived the moment they saw us, never to be seen again. It seems these creatures have a most annoying habit of coming up among the water hyacinths with only their nostrils above water, where they are, of course, invisible.

Shortly after 11 we came upon a pair of capybaras sunning themselves on the bank. Because we were in front of them, they made the mistake of running toward dry land instead of charging in our direction and diving into the protecting water. I thought they were lost anyway as they plunged into tall grass, but thanks to my good luck or their bad fortune, however you may look at it, the river made a really sharp turn exactly in the direction of their line of escape. Mamino, who knew the river like the palm of his hand, took the turn and headed for the bank. As the boat streaked to the shore, the bigger capybara dashed across an opening in the tall grass about fifty yards to my right front. I couldn't shoot—the rocking boat made it impossible to hold the rifle steady. As the bow sank into the muddy bank, however, I stood up to see the smaller capybara getting ready to cross through the same opening, and it stopped in its tracks the moment it saw me. I immediately sat down, knowing that upon losing sight of me it would follow in the footsteps of its mate. I steadied the rifle on my knees, and as the big tailless rat tiptoed across the open glade, I released a Nosler Partition that caught it through both shoulders.

I cannot say it's the handsomest animal in my trophy room, but I can say it's the biggest rat in the world—aside from a very few people I know and whose names I will not mention!

Having convinced myself that finding a good marsh buck was as difficult as taking the devil to church, I decided that next morning we would go out into the jungle to try for a jaguar with Benjamín's pack of earless hounds. As I was getting up in the pre-dawn blackness, Benjamín informed me that he had heard a jaguar had been killing cattle in an *estancia* across the river. Why he hadn't said so before, I can only attribute to the reclusive nature of Indians.

As I was gobbling my daily ration of eggs, hard bread, and warm grapefruit juice, Marlen, Benjamín's wife, called me to say that a piping guan was feeding on the flowers of a *piuva* tree *(Tecoma heptaphylla)* just outside the house. I sneaked out with my .22 magnum, rested it on one of the fenceposts, and had no problem in collecting it. About the size of a turkey hen, black with a white crest and red legs, it was such a rare and beautiful bird that I decided to skin it out, and it now graces a small diorama in my trophy room.

We then proceeded to first motor and then pole our way down the San Joaquín River until we came upon another *estancia*, the only other one I would see while in Chipene. Yes, we were told, a big jaguar had been depredating the area's cows, but it had apparently disappeared around the day I had arrived in Chipene.

Upon entering the jungle, I was pleasantly surprised to find that it was not so thick, not to mention the fact that a number of trails made the going quite easy, especially since the terrain was table-flat. And we were in the shade, protected from the blazing sun. But though we walked all day, all the curs chased were agoutis and coatimundis. In other words, the fierce and trained jaguar hounds, like all curs, chased whatever four-legged creature crossed their path. After chasing behind the hounds for hours, I seriously considered cutting off other parts of their anatomy in addition to their ears for the misery they had put me through.

Thoroughly exhausted, hungry, and disgusted, we all returned to Chipene at dusk. There we feasted on another dose of scrambled eggs, *charque*, hard bread, and warm juice, with absolutely nothing to show for our gargantuan efforts.

Right then and there I concluded that I was wasting my time and should try to move to another place that at least had a few deer. The only means of communication to the outside world was a radio transmitter that most of the time produced only beeps and whistles, plus a few garbled and unintelligible sounds.

≈ ≈ ≈

During my one-day stay in Trinidad, I had met a veterinarian by the name of Pablo Yapis who claimed he had successfully controlled poaching on his estate, which consequently became overrun with deer. I begged Conrad to ask Dr. Yapis to let me hunt on his *estancia*. But either the radio wouldn't work or Pablo wasn't in or both, so I had to stay for another couple of days in Chipene, where for lack of anything better to do I spent my time trying to find a buck that didn't exist. Finally the good doctor made his appearance and agreed to my plea, whereupon an airplane would pick me up the next morning to take me to the new *estancia* for the modest fee of $300.

The airplane was supposed to pick me up at 8 AM, but before we left for the landing strip, Conrad called to tell me the pilot wouldn't be able to make it until after 9. Believe it or not, 9 AM became 2 PM, and it was miserable to wait under a small tree feeding the mosquitoes and horseflies, which were particularly hungry that day and had us well located.

It took us less than an hour to reach Dr. Yapis's *estancia,* where I discovered that the accommodations were much worse than those at Chipene. I was assigned a small cement-block room with a dirt floor and a tin roof that made it unbearably hot. Everything was covered with droppings from a family of bats that were evidently using it as a personal cave, and the smell wasn't very appealing. Fortunately—given that the bats came in and out of the room freely through cracks in the wall—the bed I would use that night had mosquito netting. No wonder the owner visited his *estancia* only once a year and stayed no more than a week.

The foreman's name here was Franklin Cordero. He had been called by his boss to have horses ready, so we were on our way by 3 PM. Although the saddle was as crude as the first one, it was equally comfortable and at least I was riding a horse instead of a mule, and a pretty good one at that. The country was similar to the first *estancia*, and though we rode until 7 PM, we saw absolutely nothing. At night I was fed fresh meat from a steer slaughtered that day and, as usual, warm grapefruit juice. Believe you me, if you ever want to lose weight, a Bolivian *estancia* is the place to visit!

Franklin told me that the best time to hunt for *ciervos* was during the months of May and June, just after the rainy season, when the plains are flooded and the deer are concentrated in the higher places. Although this may be true, getting around from a high place to a dry place could pose

a serious problem. I guess it was the usual situation of "You should have been here last month"!

The airplane pilot, Serbio Vargas, was a nice guy in his mid-thirties who accommodatingly agreed to wait for me until 3 PM the next day. Otherwise he would have to return for me on a future day and charge me another $350, which I didn't find appealing, especially because game appeared to be equally scarce here.

Franklin had the horses saddled and ready by 5:30 the next morning and we rode out in the dark. A fresh morning breeze blew in our faces, and I felt that maybe, just maybe, our luck would change.

I was enjoying the superb pink sunrise when we met an Indian cowboy herding a few cows. I signaled him to stop, which he did distrustingly, and asked him if he had seen any *ciervos* recently. He acknowledged that he had seen two the day before and one some time back, but I couldn't get him to give me more information (apparently he didn't understand me clearly or didn't want to). But at least he had seen deer, one apparently with antlers, so we pushed on with high hopes.

By 10 AM we had seen nothing except macaws and the mercury was pushing 100 degrees. The ground was as dry as Bolivia's socialist regime, and as our steeds plodded through the burned-out patches, a cloud of fine ash rose and stuck to our sweat-covered arms and faces, adding greatly to our discomfort. The huge plain was treeless, so there was no protection from the sun. Though I was wearing a wide-brimmed hat and dark glasses, the heat was almost unbearable.

I was struggling along behind Franklin when suddenly he reined in his horse and pointed to a speck in the distance. At first I could see nothing, but after much assistance, what looked like a deer appeared in my binocular. The distance was so great that I couldn't determine whether it had horns. We agreed to try to get nearer without dismounting; the deer were supposedly used to seeing cowboys on the open range. I was excited that finally we had come upon a buck—thus far we had only seen does.

I must have done something terribly wrong in my life; if not, why was destiny continuing to punish me? When we closed the distance to some three hundred yards, my binocular confirmed that the animal was another doe. I got off my horse to rest my sore posterior and again peered into my binocular to watch the doe grow horns, only it didn't.

I was swigging lukewarm water from my canteen, thinking that maybe dysentery would put me out of my misery, when Franklin called my attention to another deer that was feeding some three hundred yards to our left. Its head was lowered and I couldn't see antlers, but it was bigger than the other one, so I reasoned that it had to be a buck. Crouching, I began my stalk on the feeding form, determined to collect it if it had horns of any kind! When I had cut the distance in half, I confirmed to my absolute dismay that this creature was the sixth doe we had seen.

We were hours away from the house and the sun was at its apogee. I couldn't refrain from asking Franklin: "How does the devil know that some people sent to hell come from the Bolivian plains?" He gave me a puzzled look, and I added, "Because the first thing they do is ask for a blanket."

Indians have no sense of humor: He gave me a blank look and dug his heels into his horse's flank.

≈ ≈ ≈

Defeated and frustrated, we decided to return to the *estancia*. There wasn't much time before the plane would arrive to pick me up. Serbio, the pilot, was not instrument-rated and so would have to get me out before sunset. Franklin and I headed in the direction of the first doe, which happened to be on the way home anyway. I kept my eyes on the doe to determine at what distance it would bolt, but I occasionally looked to the sides to scout for other deer. At 120 yards (I later paced off the distance), I nearly jumped out of my saddle upon realizing that the doe had suddenly sprouted a magnificent set of horns. It was not a trick of my eyes, either, for Franklin, too, had reined in his horse.

Miracle or not, I piled off my steed and yanked the .308 from its scabbard. The buck was facing me, but his left shoulder showed clearly above the grass. The scope was set to five power, and the rifle didn't seem to waver in my hands as I touched the shot off. The buck lowered its head and began trotting to its right as the doe, just behind him, ran in the opposite direction. I was fairly sure of the shot, but I frantically worked the bolt and fired again at the quartering animal. It wasn't necessary. The animal took two or three more steps and was swallowed by the high grass. Franklin said something to the effect that I was a sharpshooter,

for he had never seen a deer shot at that distance. After everything had been lost, I had managed to get Wellington in my sights!

As we paced the distance to my fallen quarry, a sense of exhilaration and accomplishment washed over me—I had beaten the odds at the last minute. The buck was in hard velvet, and as I lifted the big head, I noticed that the first bullet had entered on the point of the shoulder and had not exited. The second had entered the left hind leg, breaking it and continuing on into the stomach.

I was impressed by how much bigger these deer were in comparison to the little tropical whitetails I hunted in Costa Rica. I estimated its weight at well over two hundred pounds. It had a shaggy coat of sparse yellow hair with black stockings coming up above the knees. The hoofs were widely splayed, undoubtedly an adaptation for traveling on that boggy ground.

But most impressive of all were the big, heavy, symmetrical antlers, which I later measured at twenty inches in spread and twenty inches in height. It had eight very even points with no brow tines. The face was abnormally long for a deer and the ears very large. I was elated to realize that this was a truly rare trophy and I had taken it under the most difficult circumstances. It will surely have its place of honor in my trophy room, and, interestingly, only the most knowledgeable of hunters will be able to identify it.

After a quick photo session, and realizing it would be very difficult to transport the animal whole, we caped it to the skull and fleshed it. This brought considerable protest from my guide, who wanted to leave the carcass behind for the *suchas* or black vultures. It is just not in me to leave an animal in the field, so I insisted on taking the meat, even if it ended up as dog food back at the *estancia*. And, of course, Franklin took the rest of the skin to make lariats!

As we took the long road back to the *estancia* under the merciless sun, I thought what a great shame it was—for the marsh deer themselves and for conservation in general—that these stately animals are killed on sight by vaqueros for the sole purpose of making ropes that would rot out during the coming rainy season. The magnificent antlers would bleach under the tropical sun when a far better option would be to protect the species with hunting regulations and promote it as an international trophy animal, producing income for the few South American countries it inhabits.

This story should end here, but I still had to get to the *estancia* and back to civilization. When we finally arrived at the horse shed, I was suffering

from heat exhaustion and could hardly make it to the nearest hammock. Serbio, the pilot, was a bit worried when he saw me and had the presence of mind to bring me a pail of water with which I washed my face and head. I'm still not sure whether my trembling was due to the heat or to my emotions. Probably it was both!

But I still had to finish caping and salting my precious deer head, and needed to finish the chore with enough light to reach our flight destination. Fortunately, Franklin proved to be much more dexterous with the skinning knife than I will ever be, and, with my guidance, he had the ears and lips turned and the cape fleshed in record time. Then I mixed three parts of salt with one of borax to pre-cure the skin for the taxidermist.

When I finished I was again drenched in sweat—and hadn't had a pail bath in three days. Serbio saw his opportunity and suggested that we fly directly to Santa Cruz, where I could return to the Caparuch Hotel with its electricity, hot and cold running water, air conditioning, and swimming pool (and no *charque* on the restaurant menu). Besides, I would feel strange boarding a commercial flight carrying a big set of deer antlers plus a dripping deer cape. As I drooled at the thought of an ice-cold Coke, Serbio closed in: He would fly me there for the modest sum of $600. As they say, I had no choice but to sit back in the plane and enjoy it!

The flight was uneventful, except that we landed in Santa Cruz de la Sierra in the last minute of legal flying time for Serbio—the last slit of sun was sinking behind the western horizon, and a few clouds were glowing like molten gold in the fiery rays.

The chef at the Caparuch Hotel was more than mildly shocked when I asked him to boil the skull of my marsh buck in a solution of sodium bicarbonate to remove the flesh. But after I explained that I didn't intend to eat it—and after I offered him a tip—he agreed. The people in the restaurant seemed at least as astounded as I dodged the elegantly displayed tables in my dirty hunting clothes and boots, holding the horns attached to the skinned-out skull of my hard-won trophy.

Then I climbed a stairway to the door of an extraordinary room that lit up completely with the flick of a switch. Upon touching another switch, a breeze from the Andes Mountains caressed my face and lowered the room temperature to around 70 degrees. Then I spoke into a strange

two-way device and a nice lady brought me two bottles of a dark and sweet sparkling liquid, along with two large glasses with unfamiliar chunks of solidified water. In a small adjacent room was a tiny pool that filled with warm water at the turn of a valve. As I jumped in, Coke in hand, I thanked my lucky stars to have been born in the twentieth century!

Early the next morning, with help from Serbio, I arranged to have my trophies shipped by truck to La Paz, fearing they wouldn't be accepted by Taca Airlines. Then I returned the Browning to Mr. Asbún, who immediately handed me the $1700 deposit.

When I left Santa Cruz de la Sierra, everything was peaceful, but upon my arrival at the airport of El Alto, I noticed unusual military activity. I had been cut off from the outside world for ten days and did not know that a coup was in progress to overthrow Bolivia's then-president, Gonzalo Sánchez de Losada. I was scheduled to leave the next day, but the road to the airport had been blocked by angry rioters who wanted the president ousted from power. I called the ambassador, who instructed me to sit tight in my hotel and wait for the airline service to be restored. Fortunately, control over the airport was regained by the military the next day and the ambassador was nice enough to offer me his diplomatic vehicle for transportation to El Alto, so long as I left well before daylight to avoid the pickets of rioters.

Now that everything was arranged with Taca cargo for the shipping of my trophies to Costa Rica, I was finally able to leave the country with no more delays.

≈ ≈ ≈

In three or four weeks I received my precious trophies, fortunately in perfect condition thanks to the salt and borax—along with about two dozen dog and cat brushes from Brazil. It seems the truck carrying them was overturned by protesters upon entering La Paz, whereupon the truck driver had proceeded to repack everything in a hurry, throwing somebody else's merchandise in my box. I ended up giving most of the brushes to my pet-owning friends, but I still use one of them to wipe the dust off my trophies!

The Penlight Panther

Chapter 33

More than twenty years after I had last visited the Dark Continent, the opportunity to return presented itself in the form of the legal handling of an estate. This time I had enough money for a twenty-day safari during which I would seek only large animals or take none at all.

After a lot of correspondence and investigation, I decided to hunt in South-West Africa, today's Namibia, with Jan Oelofse. I wanted to collect the various antelope species this country has to offer, especially a 50-inch-plus greater kudu and a gemsbok or giant oryx. But I couldn't go to Africa without trying for at least one of the Big Five. So when Jan informed me over the phone that my chances of taking a leopard as well as a cheetah would be excellent, I booked a twenty-day safari starting the second week of September 2004.

Upon landing in Windhoek, which means "where the wind turns," I realized I couldn't be farther from home. And I nearly had a heart attack when the driver who volunteered to take me to the Mount Etjo Safari Lodge veered to the left side of the road at eighty miles per hour to avoid an eighteen-wheeler that was also advancing on the wrong side of the road at about the same speed. Upon nearing the lodge, I was treated to the sight of warthogs and steenbok feeding on the roadsides; the animals never bothered even to look up as we passed them not more than thirty yards away.

I must say that the beautiful lodge built in the middle of a huge wilderness was a welcome improvement over the Spartan accommodations I had been treated to on my first two safaris. It even had a swimming pool that elephants occasionally visited to quench their thirst (the water, however, was too cold to venture a dip). And it was no trick to see five or more species of animals at the huge water hole right in front of the dining lounge. Maybe I'm getting softer with age, but it didn't bother me at all to sleep on a soft bed and be able to take a hot shower every morning.

Jan assigned me a professional hunter named Naftali Amoolongo. I informed him that I had been to Africa twice before, and on this hunt

I would take only record-book or near-record-book animals and that I wouldn't mind returning home without some of the animals I sought, so long as all the others were good trophies. Naftali took this literally, and I was not to regret my decision. I had finally matured to where I would prefer no trophy to a poor one.

A big male Panthera pardus was at the top of my most-wanted list, and I had asked Jan to start baiting well before I arrived; I knew from previous experience how difficult and time-consuming this chore tends to be. Naftali informed me that he had two big toms located and one of the baits had already been hit. For the leopard we would sit near a bait in the evenings until around midnight. For the cheetah we would wait at first light near a "toilet tree"—to my great surprise, these cats visit the same tree in a given area to relieve themselves and this is the only productive way to hunt them, aside from bumping into one while hunting other game, which was not very likely.

This schedule proved too much for me; I was getting only about four hours of sleep a night. In addition, the leopard had apparently decided on a change of diet—he refused to touch the warthog baits, which by now were nice and ripe, even though he continued to patrol the dry stream bed near the bait tree. As for the cheetah, he had either become constipated or had changed his hunting grounds.

Eventually, we decided to sit for the leopard first and call it a day, or rather a night, at around 11 PM so as to be able to get up at first light the next morning and hunt for the different antelope. Naftali insisted that we sit even though the bait had not been touched the previous night, whereas it was my opinion that we should sit only after a bait had been partially eaten. From previous experience I knew that the "bait wait" could take up the whole safari, but then, one does not argue with the professional hunter.

≈ ≈ ≈

There are very few or no hyenas in that area, so the bait is not hung high up in the crotch of a tree, as is the custom in East Africa, but rather about three feet off the ground, in the same manner I hang the bait for a jaguar back home. Here, however, the hunter does not sit in a machan in another tree nearby, because this is desert country and few large trees are available. To avoid being detected, you must sit farther from the bait,

usually around fifty yards, in a carefully concealed blind made from the branches of shrubs and small trees and disguised with grass. Because leopards sometimes shy away from a light aimed into their eyes, or so Naftali told me, an incandescent light is also hung from a branch above the bait and a long cord with a dimmer is brought to a car battery in the blind. From what I heard, a transmitter is also sometimes placed at the bait so the professional hunter can listen with headphones for the slightest sound of crunching bones. I thought this was carrying things too far—surely we would hear the crunching and slurping sounds without additional contraptions. To be sure, a Generation III night-vision binocular would have been great, only we didn't have one.

The daily drill was to hunt in the mornings until around midday, come in for lunch, take a one-and-a-half-hour siesta, hunt antelope for a while thereafter, and be in the blind between four and four-thirty. For all our troubles, however, only a couple of badgers and one brown hyena visited our prime bait. Although there were no bugs or mosquitoes to pester us, it got quite cold as soon as the sun set, and even my wool jacket proved insufficient to ward off the biting chill.

Finally, when we decided it was fruitless to sit in the evening for leopard, we would go to bed early so as to be in the blind for the cheetah well before daylight. But try as we might, the two cats managed to make themselves as scarce as honest politicians.

≈ ≈ ≈

On the other hand, the other elements of my safari had gone extremely well: Naftali had guided me to opportunities on about a dozen trophy animals, and so far I had returned the favor by not missing a shot, although the warthog had to be shot twice. I had requested that Jan set up as many baits as possible, because anyone who has hunted leopards knows how difficult it can be to get one to feed. However, only two baits had been set, on the grounds that it would be a cinch to get a spotted cat on a twenty-day safari. Besides, the warthog near the dry riverbed had already been hit, and the leopard would surely return. But apparently, this particular leopard had been shot at before, and although he patrolled the dry water course almost every night after we left our blind, he avoided the bait like the plague.

To be frank, I was getting a bit tired of sitting almost every night in the blind waiting for the leopard to hit the bait. In the process I was freezing my butt off, for it never occurred to me that the temperature would drop below freezing in this neck of Africa. But sitting in the blind wasn't the worst part—that was driving back to camp in a safari car with no windshield or windows for a good hour or so. And to think I'd left my facemask at home, thinking it wouldn't be required!

During the afternoon of the safari's twelfth day, as we were casually driving along looking for an unsuspecting steenbok, we passed the second bait, which Naftali had neglected for several days because it was in an unlikely area. We checked it anyway and found, to our elation, not only that it had been ravenously fed upon but also that the pugmarks in the sandy soil belonged to a fully mature tom—unlike the small female I had managed to collect over twenty years before in Kenya. Problem was it was after 3:30 PM and the lamp and car battery were sitting in the other blind a good hour's ride away. We left Naftali's tracker, Andy, to create a ground blind as my professional hunter tried to convince the made-in-Namibia safari car that it was indeed a Maserati.

We returned to the bait shortly after 5:30 and took advantage of the dimming light to hang the lamp on the bait tree above the rotting carcass. The 150-foot cord barely reached the car battery sitting in the crude blind Andy had made with branches and dry grass to camouflage us. The surrounding ground was quite open, and I hoped the leopard had retreated far enough away so it wouldn't see or hear us and show up only after it was dark. As the late sun melted into a gorgeous sunset, Naftali and I crawled into our blind and made ourselves comfortable in the folding chairs we had brought from the other blind. In a few more minutes it was pitch-dark and only a small sliver of moon showed in the sky.

The leopard was in no hurry. We sat there in silence, straining our ears for the telltale sounds of breaking bone or tearing flesh. Time went by slowly. Only when I turned my face upward could I see the sliver of moon and the glittering stars. It was becoming increasingly cold, but the thought of leaving never crossed my mind; I knew from past experience that the leopard would probably return.

It was going on 10 PM when Naftali nudged me. I had heard nothing. Very slowly and carefully I began to ease the rifle through the port in the blind. I took the time to insert my two ear plugs—my muzzle-braked

7mm Remington Magnum is hideously loud. It seemed like an hour before we both heard the crunch of teeth on bone. Again Naftali nudged me, this time to signal that he was going to shine the light. The hackles on the back of my neck stood on end. I eased the safety off with my thumb and forefinger to avoid the slightest sound and wedged the stock into my shoulder. At that moment I wasn't sure what was greater: My lust for this golden pelt with Stygian spots or the fear of wounding him and putting myself and my professional hunter in the sticky business of digging a wounded leopard out of heavy brush.

If there is one antagonist to fear in the world of hunting, it is a wounded leopard: This animal will often double back and hide in the thickest bit of cover until its intended victim is within a single leap. Then it will exact its revenge, seemingly aware of the uselessness of a firearm at that distance. I was afraid of taking my finger off the trigger or my cheek off the stock as the seconds ticked by . . . still Naftali failed to shine the light as the tearing and slurping sounds became ever more audible. The tension was becoming unbearable. Finally he hissed in my ear that the wind had torn the cables away from the battery and he couldn't find them. A sense of desperation engulfed me. A long, hard stare through the scope revealed nothing besides the color of my fate. I wanted to kill Naftali for fumbling with the cables. Someone had to be responsible!

After half an eternity I realized that maybe the little Scorpion flashlight in my coat pocket could solve the problem. I dug it out and handed it to Naftali with instructions to give me a few seconds to regain my position. As the beam cut a golden wedge in the direction of the ghastly sounds, my first impression was that a tall man in a spotted gown was standing in front of the bait—it was the leopard standing on its hind legs feeding on the hanging meat. However, the moment the light struck the cat, it jumped to the left and disappeared.

The distance was almost too great for the little penlight. I strained my eyes through the scope to catch a glimpse of the immense animal, which had revealed itself for only a couple of seconds. I held my breath and prayed that I would again catch sight of the lithe, beautiful creature. My yearning to take it was overwhelming. Four or five seconds later, curiosity apparently got the better of the cat and it stepped halfway out of the undergrowth. I could hardly make him out because of the dim light and the distance, but regardless of the consequences I was going to

shoot. The leopard was half facing me, seemingly defiant at my having interrupted his dinner.

The flowering grass in front of me appeared to explode at the rifle's roar, immediately followed by the hideous roars of a wounded leopard. I worked the bolt and was ready to fire again, only to find that my vision was completely obliterated by billowy grass raining from the sky. Naftali had the presence of mind to stand up, trying to get the light above the raining debris, and frantically hollered at me to shoot again as the coughing roars came closer. As the flowering grass began to settle, the first things I became aware of were two blazing eyes moving in my direction. The distance had been cut in half, and I fully realized that only my next bullet stood between me and the prospect of being torn to pieces by the savage fury of this most aggressive of all cats. With the scope set at five power, I could see that the leopard's back was broken but that nevertheless he was dragging himself in our direction with his front feet. I held under his chin and touched off another Nosler Partition. The blocky head went down and the cat thrashed a couple of times as I stood up over the again raining grass and bolted a third round into the rifle's chamber. But it was not necessary. I just stood there trembling.

As often occurs during a big-game hunt, the unexpected had at first almost ruined my chance for a most magnificent trophy—and then it had almost ruined my chance to preserve my own skin. This is the stuff of hunting memories, and I cherish these experiences.

Kalkfeld's Crazy Critters

Chapter 34

One animal I had always wanted to collect was a black wildebeest, also called white-tailed gnu *(Connochaetes gnou)*, and when Jan Oelofse informed me that they were plentiful in his concession, I jumped at the opportunity to add one to my collection. Once almost extinct due to overhunting by Boer settlers for their hides and meat, the animals have made a remarkable comeback, thanks to their value for trophy hunters.

Upon seeing the first group of these antelope, I realized how completely different they are from the blue wildebeest I had hunted many years ago in Kenya. And I soon realized they were different not only in appearance but also in character. From a distance they look very much like a Spanish fighting bull: jet-black in color with a powerful, thick neck and shoulders that narrow down to much more slender hindquarters and a set of wicked-looking, downward-sweeping, and upward-pointing horns. The animals are slightly smaller than the common gnu, but their horns are much more impressive, the males carrying a big boss. I also noticed that their long manes, white at the base and black at the tip, stand straight up, their tails have long white hairs, and, to my amazement, they have long white eyelashes!

But what struck me the most about these bovine-like antelope was their attitude—they all appeared to have a serious case of mad-cow disease. Every time we would begin to stalk them with the wind on our faces and taking every precaution to remain undetected, just as we were coming within rifle range—and for no apparent reason—they would suddenly lower their heads, twitch their tails, and take off kicking and bucking until they disappeared in a cloud of dust behind the nearest fold in the land. That usually meant a long walk back to the hunting car and another search for another small herd—hopefully not as mad as the previous one.

The great advantage of hunting in Africa is that there is usually enough game that sooner or later you will get the opportunity to collect the critter you are after. However, as mentioned before, I was set on collecting record-book or near-record-book trophies. Discovering that

the bigger the gnu, the crazier he was, was making it all that much more difficult to herd a big one into my trophy room. As the safari progressed and we hunted other game, if we came up on a herd of black wildebeest, we would drop what we were hunting and go for the gnu. But every time we thought we had them figured out, they would suddenly go berserk and disappear in the distance.

During the afternoon of the fourth day my PH eased the safari car to a stop and peered long and hard through his Swarovski binocular at some distant black spots on a rocky hill. Though the distance was close to a thousand yards, we eased out of the hunting car without closing the doors, to avoid the slightest sound. We dropped into a dry streambed that completely concealed us from the psychotic creatures and proceeded to close the distance, the soft sand muffling our approach. When Naftali Amoolongo figured we had cut the distance to less than half, he motioned me to stay low and carefully raised his head above the bank to take a peek. After a few seconds he lowered his head and whispered, "There are about half a dozen wildebeest in the herd, and the lead bull is the biggest one I have seen in a very long time. Stay right behind me and be ready when I set up the shooting sticks."

When we had cut the distance again in half, we eased up the bank, only to catch a glimpse of the twitching tails of the bucking antelope.

"They could never have smelled us, because the wind is in our favor," said Naftali, "and I don't think they have seen us. They took off because they are insane, but maybe they won't go very far."

As far as I was concerned, they were gone for good, but I hadn't yet seen Naftali and Andy track. At the beginning it was easy, even for me, to see the tracks in the soft sand, but when we hit rocky ground, the going got ever more difficult. But for the tracker and the PH it was like staying on a paved road, moving at a pace I could hardly match. We were taking advantage of every tree and shrub and moving as silently as a cat in tennis shoes. Suddenly Naftali crouched and motioned for me to do the same. He brought up his binocular and took a long, hard look as I tried to maintain my awkward position. Then he motioned me to his side, spread the legs of the shooting sticks far apart, and indicated I should take a kneeling shot.

"The big bull is standing to the left, but right now the smaller one is blocking the shot. Get ready, but don't shoot until he moves off."

I placed my 7mm Remington Magnum in the V of the shooting sticks and prayed for the sanity of my quarry. If only my intended wall mount would stay put and his shield would move. As the seconds ticked by, beads of sweat accumulated on my forehead and mirage slightly distorted my 200-yard target. The small bull was directly facing me and the big one was standing broadside. Then, as if in slow motion, the smaller antelope's head went down and his tail twitched. Almost simultaneously he bucked once and took off. My bull proceeded to follow suit—only he was a second too late. As his head went down, I touched off a Federal Premium 160-grain Nosler Partition. *Whack!* The telltale sound of a high-speed bullet hitting bone reverberated in my ears. My trophy bucked for the last time and fell hard on his side, completely tranquilized after having taken his Valium pill.

Naftali insisted it was the biggest black wildebeest he had ever laid his eyes on and never stopped congratulating me. A quick field measurement revealed a score of 87 inches, placing it among the top ten in the Safari Club International record book. I guess madness is contagious: I was in a haze all the way back to the lodge.

The Kudu Conundrum

Chapter 35

For reasons unknown, at least to me, just one specimen of a certain species of animal will satiate one's hunger for it, whereas other species will always make you want to come back for a bigger trophy. Antlered game, especially white-tailed and mule deer, have that get-a-bigger-one attraction, probably because no two sets of antlers are so similar that they may be confused. Although I do not crave another gemsbok or a bigger Cape hartebeest, just the thought of a big kudu bull will make my heart skip a beat.

For those unfamiliar with this great African game animal, it stands at the top of the "most wanted list" immediately after the Big Five—elephant, rhinoceros, Cape buffalo, lion, and leopard. And for good reason, for it arguably sports the longest horns in the animal kingdom, going all the way up to around seventy inches, although anything over fifty inches is considered exceptional. This animal is called the greater kudu to distinguish him from his smaller cousin, the lesser kudu, which, although very similar, is about half his size. He is also arguably the second largest antelope in Africa after the eland; a big kudu bull weighs in the vicinity of seven hundred pounds. To top all this, he continues to hold his ground very well in most of sub-Saharan Africa.

All the kudu's senses are extremely keen, and once he senses danger and decides to take off, it is best to look for another bull, for it's highly unlikely he'll stop for another look. Old bulls sport a pale gray coat with about six to ten vertical white stripes, which help him blend perfectly with the drab landscape he favors. The kudu is a member of the spiral-horn family, along with the eland, bushbuck, and bongo, and because of his elusive and secretive nature he represents a great challenge to those lucky few who hunt him. His scientific name is Tragelaphus strepsiceros, although there are several different races, the biggest of which is the southern greater kudu, which I would be hunting.

During my first safari to Mozambique several decades before, I had collected a small bull of around forty-five inches, which still hangs in

my trophy room. Knowing that Namibia has some enormous kudu, I informed Naftali that I wouldn't settle for anything under fifty-five inches. I was to question that decision over the next two weeks, especially when my professional hunter refused to let me shoot anything smaller, even though we saw quite a number of bulls that were easily over fifty inches.

There was one particular bull . . . we saw him several times from the hunting car, and he appeared humongous to me. Though Naftali glassed him carefully every time we saw him, saying that the horns would go around fifty-two or fifty-four inches, we always left him for another day. For whatever reason, each time we saw him it was from the hunting car and each time he offered a broadside shot at under one hundred yards. I recall thinking that it would be unfair to take such a magnificent animal under those unsporting conditions.

After I had taken about fifteen of the more common game animals in about as many days, and had not found the kudu of my dreams, Naftali decided it was time to move to another area. We left Jan Oelofse's concession, drove for about an hour on the main road, then turned left to hunt a ranch owned by a German with whom Jan had a special arrangement. In the process, we left behind the flat country and entered huge, rolling hills strewn with tumbled granite boulders and spotted here and there with green thorn trees. The soil here seemed more fertile and the vegetation thicker. There were several dry creek beds fringed with green bushes, which the kudu particularly favored, or so my professional hunter told me. We were able to traverse some of these creek beds in the hunting car, although we had to stalk the narrower ones.

During the second day in this area we were rounding a bend in a winding creek bed when Naftali suddenly slammed on the brakes. I was able to catch but a fleeting glimpse of a humped gray animal with lyre-shaped horns as it disappeared in one jump.

"I didn't get a good look at it," Naftali said as he piled out of the safari car, at the same time ordering Andy to bring along the shooting sticks, "but I'd bet my PH license that bull is just under sixty inches. Come on."

I hate it when the game you are seeking is spooked and you have to make a forced march over rough country and try to keep up with your guide. Up and down the rock-strewn hills I trailed behind Naftali and Andy, trying to make as little noise as possible in the loose rocks and to avoid the wicked thorns that kept clutching at my clothing. Once or

twice Naftali stopped momentarily to set up the shooting sticks as a set of magnificent horns whirled above the green bushes, only to disappear in cover too small to conceal such a big animal. Like bloodhounds on a hot trail, the professional and the tracker stayed on the spoor of the bull, sometimes trotting, sometimes running, while I hauled myself uphill and down for all I was worth.

We were walking up a small hill facing a really big one when Naftali ordered me to crouch and stay behind him. We walked at a steady trot, and then the two sprinters began to run uphill. My chest heaving and sweat running off me, I tried desperately to keep up. Then Naftali spread the legs of the shooting sticks. I followed his gaze to a magnificent kudu bull standing like a statue on the sidehill about three hundred yards away. A surge of adrenaline gave me the extra stamina to cover the six or eight yards to the shooting sticks in two jumps, but I was a second too late. Just as the stock of my rifle touched the shooting sticks, the kudu laid its horns back and took off. I frantically tried to follow the loping antelope in my scope, but it was over the rise in two bounds.

Naftali looked at me as if I had insulted his mother and, without a word, pulled the shooting sticks from under my rifle. I was grateful that he didn't hit me with them—although maybe, even though unconscious, I would have felt better. Without a word, we all dragged ourselves back to the vehicle.

≈ ≈ ≈

When we got back to the hunting car, the fierce sun was high and it was too hot to hunt. Since the leafless trees offered little shade, we all sat in the shade of the vehicle and dozed off. After a couple of hours and a cold lunch, it looked as though Naftali could again stand me and we resumed our hunting, although I avoided his gaze. As we crossed a stretch of open ground, a steenbok erupted from our front left and took off at a speed that would put the fastest deer to shame. It dove into a clump of dry grass a couple of hundred yards away and disappeared. However, the animal forgot to notice that the clump of grass was the only one on a stretch of bare ground.

"Get ready. He may give you a second chance," Naftali said as I jumped out of the hunting car and walked at an angle toward the clump of grass.

Sure enough, as the vehicle passed the clump at about sixty yards, the little antelope's nerves broke and he made a dash for it across the open ground. But since the vehicle had already passed him, after a frantic sprint he felt that maybe we weren't such bad guys after all and stopped for a second look. That's when my 7mm caught him just behind the last rib (I wanted a full-body mount) and he went down as if the ground had been pulled out from under him. The horns went 4¼ inches, definitely record-class, and I regained at least some of Naftali's lost confidence.

But I could tell I had not regained all of Naftali's confidence—because he changed his plan of attack. This time we would camouflage ourselves near a water hole to await developments. The PH even spread out a military-type net to break our outline. I sat on the ground with my back against the trunk of a tree while Naftali spread out the legs of the shooting sticks so that I could fire from a kneeling position. We sat in silence listening to the low, murmuring throb of thousands of doves.

Presently a dainty steenbok walked out of some reeds about a hundred yards away and nervously approached the water. After looking in every direction to make sure it was safe, it lowered its head and began to drink. Naftali fixed the binocular on the little antelope and estimated it at around five inches, bigger than the two heads I had already taken. Suddenly, its ears went up and then its head. The little antelope skirted away as a family of warthogs, a sow with two piglets, wallowed noisily into the water. Then two kudu cows came in gracefully for a drink and remained among the reeds feeding on the lush vegetation.

"Those cows will serve as good decoys for a big *ohorongo*," Naftali whispered. "It won't be long now."

For a half-hour nothing moved. I ate a stale sandwich and drank some tepid water. I was getting drowsy in the warm afternoon sun when Naftali nudged me. About one hundred and fifty yards away, a couple of magnificent kudu bulls were cautiously making their way toward the water, their senses at full alert. I brought the binocular to my eyes and, to my surprise, both bulls looked about the same size. Even Naftali was having a problem deciding which one I was to shoot.

"Don't move until they look away from us. Then take the one in the front—he has a wider spread."

I crawled to the shooting sticks as the bulls lowered their heads and advanced slowly.

"Wait until he turns broadside," Naftali ordered as the knot in my stomach tightened at the sight of not one but two magnificent trophies. "They are both right around fifty-five inches, but the front one looks a bit heavier."

The front bull stood there facing me for about a minute, and I began to shake a bit in the shooting sticks. Then he turned and began walking back the way he had come, parallel to the water. I held right behind the shoulder and touched off a Federal Premium Nosler Partition. A small cloud of dust went up from the bank about fifty yards behind the kudu as he took off at a dead run. Effortlessly he sprang up the bank in a graceful leap and disappeared into a thick clump of green trees, lush because they were near the water. Had I blown an easy 150-yard shot from a rock-steady position? I turned to Naftali in disbelief.

"I think I saw red on its flank," he assured me. "Let's go check."

≈ ≈ ≈

When we arrived at the spot where the kudu had been standing, we found no blood. Even I could follow the spoor where the hoofs had dug deep into the sandy soil of the bank. We climbed eagerly over it and into the clump of trees, where I didn't notice the gray hairs rubbed against the first tree.

"He's hit," the PH announced, "or he never would have run into a tree."

With unfaltering confidence, he and Andy stayed on the trail like beagles. A few yards farther on, Naftali detached a few blood-smeared hairs from a second tree.

"Lower the power on your scope and be ready," he warned.

But it wasn't necessary. Another fifty yards and we came to a magnificent kudu bull lying on its side.

"You will never find a bigger *ohorongo*," Naftali said, smiling, as he extended the steel tape a tad over fifty-five inches. "I told you I don't make mistakes when it comes to size."

Africa's Green Dwarf

Chapter 36

There are so many magnificent large animals in Africa that one tends to forget the smaller ones. These "lesser" animals nevertheless offer incomparable sport to the hunter, often because they can be much more difficult to collect than the more glamorous ones. Such is the case with the klipspringer *(Oreotragus oreotragus),* which stands no more than twenty-two inches at the shoulder and weighs no more than about thirty-five pounds, but lives in the steepest, nastiest, boulder-strewn and thorn-infested mountain country it can find. And believe you me, there are some mountains in Africa worthy of the best alpinists. If you don't believe me, try climbing Mount Etjo, which gives its name to Jan Oelofse's lodge in Namibia.

Contrary to common belief, the klipspringer doesn't spend most of its time with all four legs on the tip of a sharp rock waiting for some dude to collect it. Once the desert sun begins to warm the landscape, klipspringers disappear in the heavy brush of the mountains they call home. Once in the cover, they will tiptoe away at the slightest disturbance without the interloper ever becoming aware of their presence. Like the chamois, the klipspringer is extremely well adapted to its harsh habitat, walking on the tips of its hoofs, which are soft and rubbery, allowing the animal to retain its balance from one tiny foothold to another. The males sport straight, sharp, four- to six-inch horns.

But what I found extraordinary about this little antelope is the color of its coat: The olive-green grayish fur with varying tones of yellow helps the little creature blend perfectly into the dry leaves and twigs of the African landscape. The hair is completely different from that of any other animal in that it's extremely stiff and brittle to the touch and very susceptible to hairslip. Hence a klipspringer must be handled with great care to avoid ruining the coat for the taxidermist.

Klipspringers were not complete strangers to me—I had seen them before in Kenya on a huge rocky escarpment, but they had been too fast for me to get off a shot. Ever since that day I had thought of collecting

one, but since my arrival in Namibia, other options had always gotten in the way. But finally, after collecting every animal on my list except a cheetah, we decided it was time for the klipspringer. And even then, we sat from pre-dawn to a good hour after sunup waiting fruitlessly for the cheetah to come to the "toilet tree."

When we arrived at the base of Mount Etjo, the sun was well up in the sky and beginning to burn, as only those who have been in the African desert can understand. We packed a couple of sandwiches, an apple, and enough water to carry us through the day if need be.

"We still have two more safari days to go," Naftali said, "but we will only hunt for klipspringer today." I didn't realize it then, but the reason was that nobody wants to hunt these elusive animals more than one day.

From a distance the sloping face of Mount Etjo had looked like a cinch to climb, but as we began our ascent, huge boulders the size of a pickup truck made the going extremely difficult. Then there were the loose stones covering the ground, plus the fact that each plant was covered with thorns. It didn't help, either, when Naftali told me to watch where I placed my hands—a particular pit viper happened to favor the same habitat as my intended prey.

We began climbing at around 9 AM, long after the klipspringers had taken refuge from the sun. After a couple of hours of steady climbing, my pants were torn by thorns, my Browning boots showed cuts from sharp stones, my legs were screaming for relief, and I was sweating like a pregnant nun. We were only halfway up the mountain and I was ready to call it a day.

I called for a rest stop and collapsed under the shade of a huge red boulder, with barely enough strength to bite into an apple, which was surprisingly cool and refreshing. Fifteen or twenty minutes later Naftali, who looked fresh as a daisy, urged me to get up and push on. I cringed—not only at the thought of climbing the other half of the mountain but also at what the descent would entail. Relentlessly we pushed on, I with nagging doubt about whether this gargantuan effort was worth the diminutive prize I was after. The higher we climbed, the rougher the going got, and an hour and a half later I again called a halt and drank some more lukewarm water. I was sitting under the pitiful shade of a leafless thorn tree reminiscing about the important things

in life when Naftali walked up to me. I must have looked really spent because he asked if I would give him my rifle so he could go collect the klipspringer. I was indignant at first but conceded that maybe it would be a good idea if he went ahead and scouted for a good trophy while I figured out how they got the water into a coconut.

As I waited in the lonely perch, I could see the safari car in the immense plain below, the tiny image distorted by rising heat waves. A cool breeze began to blow on my face, rustling the wait-a-bits around me. It was a good half-hour before Naftali returned with the news that he had located a good male klipspringer dozing in thick cover. He motioned me to follow as silently as possible. We had only walked about a hundred yards when my guide motioned me to stop. The klipspringer, he said, would be visible from the next boulder, only a few yards away. I lowered my scope to four power, slung the rifle across my back, and crawled to the top of the flat monolith. Naftali slowly raised his hand and pointed in the direction of the thickest bush, about thirty feet away. I hardly dared to breathe, but even at that distance I could see nothing. As my eyes got accustomed to the darker landscape of the heavy brush, however, a horizontal outline suddenly took shape.

It was in a tangle of brush, and there was no way I could make out the head, much less the horns. I couldn't even tell which way it was facing, and I had to trust Naftali that it was indeed a male. All I could do was hold offhand for the middle and pray for the best. As I sent the bullet off, I saw the form come to life in a single leap that took it out of sight.

Quickly but carefully, I climbed down from the flat boulder and came to the spot where my quarry had been standing. There was a tremendous amount of needlelike fur on a flat rock, along with big splotches of bright red blood. Obviously my bullet had hit one or more small branches, opening up before reaching its target. I followed a thick blood trail to my prize, which had managed to run another twenty yards. My quest for the green elf was over.

But the climb down wasn't! Naftali had to cut a sturdy stick for me to use as a cane. Despite its help, I took a rather nasty spill and had to ask Andy to carry my rifle, which I pride myself in having with me always. It took us a couple of hours to climb down, but when I reached the vehicle—with Naftali carrying my prize—a sense of immense

accomplishment washed over me. I had met the elusive quarry on its own turf and, after an immense effort, had succeeded in bagging it.

No, I didn't measure the sharp, straight horns. That would have been disrespectful to a small animal that will always stand at the top of my trophy list for the difficulty involved in bagging it.

Mexican Quest

Chapter 37

Being a slow learner, it took me a long time to find out that the best place to take a really big mule deer was the state of Sonora, México, in an area encompassing the Sonoran coast to around the middle of the state. In fact, I had only a vague idea about the difference between a Rocky Mountain mule deer and a desert mule deer, knowing that the latter is smaller and lighter in color than the former. Pictures of both subspecies made them look darned similar, sporting the big, hairy ears that give them their name, light gray muzzles, an almost black brisket, and the characteristic evenly branched antlers. Both appear steely gray in their thick winter coats. To me they were all *Odocoileus hemionus, hemionus* being the Latin word for mule. Further investigation revealed that there are two races of the desert subspecies, *Odocoileus hemionus canis* and *Odocoileus hemionus eremicus.* This last was the one I wanted—they sport the heaviest and widest antlers, making for spectacular mounts.

Though the two subspecies don't differ greatly in appearance, they do in habits. As their name indicates, the Rocky Mountain subspecies inhabits the mountains and steep canyons and has to drink water regularly, whereas the desert deer gets its moisture from different varieties of water-bearing cactus of the desert and inhabits the desert flats of ironwood, *palo verde, cholla,* and saguaro, where they are difficult to see and to hunt. Because they live farther south and in a warmer climate than their northern cousins, they don't polish their antlers until the beginning of November, and the rutting season doesn't get well under way until around the first week in January. Twice now I'd failed to take a desert mule deer. When I booked my third try, starting 15 January 2005, I vowed that this time I would collect a trophy buro, as they are called in México.

≈ ≈ ≈

I was aware that I probably wouldn't have to shoot across immense canyons, and would likely get a shot at under one hundred yards among

the tangled vegetation that these deer call home. Nevertheless, I brought along my trusted 7mm Remington Magnum that has served me so well on other occasions. For a few long minutes at the airport in Hermosillo, I panicked when my luggage and rifle case didn't arrive, but then was informed that they were in the next terminal for customs inspection. I showed the temporary importation permit that my outfitter had mailed me and was out in the street without a question asked.

A dentist friend by the name of Sergio Bonilla was to be my companion on this trip, during which we would hunt one-on-one. After a drive of about two hours we found ourselves in a small adobe farmhouse with whitewashed walls and Spartan accommodations. After a quick and equally Spartan dinner, we hit the sack with the eager anticipation of the first day of hunting.

I love winter hunting in the desert, where the temperature hovers at around 60 degrees F and where you can walk under an azure sky for hours on flat ground without breaking a sweat, always expecting to see a set of magnificent antlers standing motionless under the shade of a palo verde. As I stole through the more open patches, avoiding the thorns of the *cholla,* the *sabiri*, and the *pitahaya*, I remembered how similar this hunting was to that for the tropical whitetails I hunted back home. These deer, however, were not only much bigger and more spectacular but also much more plentiful, or so I hoped.

But though we were on a remote ranch behind closed gates, we weren't seeing much game, and that included all three of us—Sergio and I, plus a gentleman from Pennsylvania who had come in later the same day. After two days of hard hunting with nothing to show for our efforts, Ron Labrosse, the Pennsylvanian, suggested to our outfitter that we all move to his ranch near Hermosillo, where Ron had hunted previously and which supposedly was teeming with deer.

There was no house on the outfitter's ranch, so we stayed in the best hotel in Hermosillo, the San Sebastián, with huge rooms, hot and cold running water, full air conditioning, and an all-you-can-eat, twenty-four-hour dining room (where the owners surely lost money every day to our ravenous appetites after hard days of hunting). To top it all, it had a really nice warm swimming pool plus a cool bar where we enjoyed a couple of drinks in the evenings. To our amazement, we discovered that the ranch was less than a half-hour drive from the hotel over the main highway and that it was indeed teeming with buros.

After an a-la-carte breakfast, we would get picked up by our respective guides in a pickup truck for the short drive to our hunting destination. We would drive and glass for a while and then walk and glass some more, or find a suitable vantage point—of which there were several on the ranch—and glass from there while trying not to place our butts on a cholla ball. Either way, we were seeing plenty of deer, but as usual, finding the right one was a different story.

Although the rut was well under way, as evidenced by the bucks' swollen necks and their trailing of the does, their gonads hadn't yet overcome their brains, for their instinct to mate never seemed to overcome their instinct to survive. Having taken several Rocky Mountain mule deer before and knowing that I was in one of the world's best places for a trophy-class desert mulie, I swore to hold out for a heavy-horned buck with four points to the side, not counting the eyeguards, and preferably a good spread. Not completely trusting myself to overcome my own excitement and judgment in finding a big animal that might or might not meet the minimum specifications, I instructed my guide, a lanky Mexican cowboy named Vito, not to let me shoot unless the animal qualified as a trophy.

On the hunt's second day we came upon what I regarded as a huge buck standing by himself on a cholla patch some one hundred and fifty yards away. He was facing away from us, carefully munching on a succulent cholla ball without a care in the world—except perhaps for getting thorns in his nose. Every time he raised his head, a magnificent set of antlers with a broad spread was skylined against a magnificent sunrise. But our binoculars revealed it had four points on one side and only three on the other, aside from the fact that Vito considered the antlers not heavy enough. Reluctantly we walked away without disturbing him.

The next day was a repeat performance, with several bucks sighted but passed up. But around five o'clock Vito slammed on the pickup's brakes and pointed in the direction of a bobcat bounding across the desert floor to our left. As mentioned earlier, wild cats, big or small, fascinate me, and I jumped at the opportunity to collect this one—although I'm not sure if I would have fired had I known what my Mexican outfitter was going to charge me for this one. Anyway, curiosity got the better of this cat and he stopped for one last look. My bullet caught him behind the left shoulder, thankfully where there wasn't much bone, which would have caused the bullet to expand and ruin the pelt.

After a short photo session, we headed for the hotel amid a blazing afterglow. We hadn't gone half a mile, though, when Vito eased the pickup to a stop without killing the engine and picked up his binocular. I could see nothing. He urged me out of the vehicle, warning me not to close the door, and we moved to the right behind a screening wall of palo verde trees. As I tiptoed behind Vito in a crouching position, I signaled with my hands to ask him what he had seen.

"Muy grande!" he said and urged me to follow.

Within a few minutes he grabbed my shirt and pointed a bony finger to my left front. I dropped my butt on some cruelly grating rock, which I much prefer to the ubiquitous thorns of untrodden desert. About two hundred yards away, in an opening in the palo verde, I could barely make out the form of a standing deer. Through the Swarovski, set at six power to take maximum advantage of the dimming light, I could make out the horns but not the number of points. However, I had learned to trust Vito and rested my elbows on my knees, frantically trying to stabilize my rifle. Some grass was in the way, but it was too risky to change my position, so I held the cross hairs a little farther back on the body than I would have liked and touched off the bullet. To my utter amazement, nothing happened—the buck still stood petrified in its tracks. I bolted another shell into the chamber, and just as I was about to fire, a jackrabbit dashed in front of the buck, making it bolt in the opposite direction. I regained my feet and ran in the direction of the fleeing deer, and it stopped behind a big ironwood tree, called *palo fierro* by the Mexicans.

"It's hit hard," Vito assured me. "I had the binocular on him when you fired. Only you hit him too far back."

I stopped for a few seconds to reload my rifle with four bullets, then slowly advanced toward the screened buck, knowing that it would probably dash to my right, where there was a stretch of open ground. With my rifle ready and my thumb on the safety, I moved slowly ahead and had cut the distance in half when a magnificent buck with tall and heavy antlers made a furious dash across the open desert. In the dimming light I led him and fired. The buck managed to make it behind the cover of some light bushes, and I fired again. He ran in a semicircle before stopping in the middle of a clearing. As I was about to squeeze off my third round, the front feet of the magnificent creature folded and he sank heavily to the ground.

When I walked up to the fallen monarch, I was awed by the height and thickness of the antlers, and although the spread wasn't wide, long, heavy points more than made up for it.

My Mexican quest was over. But mule deer hunting is addictive, and maybe I will return to look for another one with thick beams, long tines, and a wide spread that will qualify for the Boone & Crockett book. This one barely missed it.

A Score to Settle

Chapter 38

You hunt jaguars on their time schedule, not yours. And the same goes for mountain lions, also known as cougars or pumas. So when the phone rang on 30 December and my then-newfound guide Carlos Gómez informed me in a high state of excitement that a cougar had killed a couple of sheep at a nearby ranch, I packed my gear and took off. In my wake was my wife's admonishment to be back in time for the following day's New Year's Eve celebration.

After a two-hour drive I picked Carlos up at his home and we continued another forty minutes in four-wheel-drive to the scene of the crime. By following tracks on the muddy ground (it's always muddy, muggy, and wet on Costa Rica's Caribbean side), we came upon the remains of a sheep in a patch of thick jungle scarcely two hundred yards from the ranchhouse and adjacent sheep pen.

The building of a machan was the next order of the day, and, being rather clumsy in the art of tree climbing, we cut a dozen or more seven-foot poles to build a ladder, which we completed with the aid of some stout cord. We used the same cord to secure the dead sheep to keep the cat from carrying it away without our knowledge, as had happened to me before. Then, at a height in excess of twenty feet, we tied my two small hammocks. It was getting late—I always try to be in my perch before 4:30 PM—so we climbed in silence to the machan for the long vigil that probably lay ahead.

Carlos was fired up: "The moon comes up shortly after nine," he said. "We should have this cat on the bait before that. He has taken over a dozen sheep and should be a cinch."

I am no newcomer to jungle nights in trees, and I have mixed feelings about it. It's relatively easy; not too much effort is involved, and I'm extremely proud of my small butt hammocks. They sure beat sitting on an uneven and knotty tree branch! And you can take sandwiches and Gatorade and insect repellent and other goodies up there with you. But I'm a fidgeter, and you dare not fidget. And it gets especially uncomfortable

when mosquitoes chew you and tree ants bite you in unreachable places. As the night wears on, your legs cramp and the edge of the hammock bites into your calves. And there is always that uncut branch that pokes into your butt when you lean back and which you dare not cut now for fear of scaring off your quarry. You dare not scratch, cough, or--heaven forbid--sneeze.

The tropical night fell black and sudden upon us. All at once you cannot see the person sitting beside you, and an eerie silence pervades the jungle before the night denizens take over. The crickets are the first to chime in, and then there are the moans of rubbing branches and the occasional crashes of rotten limbs falling on the forest floor. Monkeys bark in the distance, and you try to convince yourself they are announcing the coming of the puma. You strain your ears to make out the little pitters and patters among the rotting leaves, every moment expecting to hear the unmistakable breaking of bones and tearing of flesh that will cause you to shine your light. And you sit in your perch and wait, taut as a guitar string. And you think thoughts like: I'm sixty-five, for heaven's sake—how much longer will I be able to climb trees and clobber unsuspecting critters? And then you wonder how you are going to win that pending law case and collect on the cheapskate who won't pay you after you saved his butt . . . . Then a shift in the wind blows the stench of rotting carcass into your face and brings you back to reality.

As the hours drag by, you begin to nod, only to be suddenly awakened by a deafening clap of thunder as the first drops of an incoming storm patter your cap. I look at my watch and it's nearly midnight. Something went wrong—the cougar never showed up. I have better sense than to sit the rest of the night under the deluge, and we both decide to call it quits.

≈ ≈ ≈

As we come out on the rutted road where I had driven to the ranchhouse, we find the steaming-fresh pugmarks of a large male mountain lion over my car tracks. We follow them scarcely fifty yards into the jungle and come upon the carcass of a freshly killed sheep the lion had been feeding on, a stone's throw from where we had set up.

Wet, cold, and hungry, and certain the daring cat will kill again shortly, I acknowledge my defeat and slink back home.

But the cat didn't kill again shortly. After more than a year I was sure somebody had put an end to his forays, probably with poison, for the killing stopped and his pugmarks disappeared from the muddy car tracks. That is, until 10 March, fifteen months later, when I got a call from the caretaker at the same ranch. He informed me that a jaguar had broken into the pen after tearing down the tin walls, and killed the last three sheep of eighteen in the herd—apparently just for the fun of it, for only one was dragged out and partially devoured.

Three hours later I was again at the site. This time, the sheep had not been dragged to the jungle but rather partially eaten only feet away from the pen where it had been killed. The carcass had been partially covered with brush and grass, which gave me the first indication that it was my old friend the cougar, because jaguars don't cover their kills. Further examination of the sheep pen revealed the unmistakable light brown belly fur of a mountain lion. I was impressed by his formidable strength in pulling off the thick tin plates nailed to the sheep pen. And I was especially glad it was a lion and not a jaguar, given that I have four of the latter and only a small female of the former.

After disposing of the two uneaten sheep, I panicked for a moment upon realizing there were no big trees nearby on which to build a machan. Then I noticed the small tin tool shed that sheltered the generator for the house. It was located about thirty yards from the kill, and would provide a perfect ground blind—the cat was familiar with it and would sense no danger there. The tool shed had no windows, but I turned up a ranch assistant who quickly solved the problem by cutting a small window in the tin siding with a machete. We then placed cardboard along the lower edge of the opening to eliminate any noise I might cause by resting my rifle there for the only shot I would get. Pumas normally return only once to their kills; unlike jaguars and leopards, they will not eat carrion.

We secured the carcass with strong double twine to a nearby tree and a fencepost, to keep it from being dragged away in the darkness.

I'm almost ashamed to admit this, but we then brought into the small shed two chairs and my Igloo cooler containing Cokes and tuna sandwiches. For once I was comfortable, not hanging from a limb afraid I would break my neck. I had food and cold drinks at my disposal, and

I didn't give a damn if it rained cats and dogs—I had a roof over my head! Maybe more important, I could scratch and fidget to my heart's content—only there were no mosquitoes to cause me to scratch and fidget. Incredibly, I was no more than thirty yards from the kill, from the ranchhouse, and from my Nissan Pathfinder.

Knowing that the cat wouldn't return to such a civilized location before nightfall, my assistant and I went back to the vehicle for a bite and a drink. We waited there until 5:30 PM before entering the small shed and closing the door behind us.

It was a moonless night and by 6:45 it was pitch-black. We sat in silence, straining our ears for the slightest sound. At 7:15 I heard a distinct twang and asked my assistant if he had heard it. He said it was a falling branch, but I did not think so. Carefully I took a peek through the night-vision scope I didn't have with me the last time and almost had a fit: The lion was standing broadside to the right of the kill, and through the scope his eyes reflected the infrared light, simulating a car's headlights. As I put the night-vision scope down, all I could say to my companion was, "He's there."

I knew I should wait for the cat to start eating and thus become so interested in his dinner that he would be less aware of life around him. But I had switched to automatic pilot and all I could think about was the shot. I grabbed the pistol grip of my custom .308 with my right hand and the icy-cold steel of the tip of the barrel with my left hand and very, very slowly eased the rifle out of the window cut in the tin wall until the stock's fore-end came to rest on the padded opening. I snugged the butt against my shoulder and the cheekpiece cold against my face. I nudged the helper with my left elbow, and the powerful beam of my Browning flashlight made a brilliant pathway through the blackness to where Felis concolor was standing. For a second the elegant cat glared at the light with great clear yellow eyes and snarled in defiance at the enemy who dared to steal his hard-earned meal. I found the point just behind his shoulder and touched off the shot. When I recovered from the recoil, there was nothing where the lion had been standing. I was so sure of the thirty-yard shot I didn't even bother to bolt in another round—not that there would be another shot if I had missed.

We opened the door and walked out of the shed. I took the flashlight from my helper's hand and walked the thirty yards to the remains of the

sheep. One of the anchor ropes had been broken, which accounted for the twang we had heard, but there was no lion. Panic began to set in as we walked in the direction the lion should have taken. Nothing. With a sinking feeling, we walked in the opposite direction. In one spot my powerful handlight reflected a dazzling light resembling the top of a small tin can. As we moved in closer, the other eye appeared through the short grass. The lion had made it to the fence, thirty yards from the dead sheep. Aside from a broken incisor and worn and yellow teeth, he was in perfect shape and would later tip the scale at over one hundred and twenty-five pounds. That's about as big as a male mountain lion gets in the tropics.

I sat next to him as the adrenaline surge slowly drained from my body and shook a little. It was one of the greatest moments of my hunting life!

The Striptease Buck

Chapter 39

Most desert mule deer *(Odocoileus hemionus eremicus)* hunting in México today is done from a high-rack truck with a combination of cruising dirt roads and glassing. At least, that was the way I had done it three times before, having collected a heavy and tall four-by-four on my second hunt. On my third trip I had tried to hunt the desert on foot, but that didn't last long, thanks to the thick vegetation and because "Even when there are a lot of trophy bucks, there ain't many of them," as John Wootters used to say. So on the second day I switched to the pickup truck. That hunt had been cut short due to delays with my rifle at customs in México City, and although I saw several nice bucks, they didn't give me a chance for a shot.

The one thing I learned on that trip was that if you plan to enter México through México City, you need an additional permit besides the one to transport the rifle in Sonora. I did this on my fourth trip and had no problems—other than having to go through customs, through the police, and through the army, since everything has to be double- and triple-checked, otherwise a lot of people will be out of a job, or so they told me!

On my last trip I was so mad at the Mexican authorities that I swore to myself I would never set foot in the country again. However, in December 2011, when my good friend Jorge Camou León called to offer a really good deal on a hunt on which I could collect one mule deer and two Coues deer, I couldn't resist and booked the hunt. Besides, the Sonora Desert is arguably the best place in the world to collect a giant mule deer, I would be speaking my own language, and I wouldn't be freezing to death (well, at least not to death!), although it was below freezing some mornings.

As usual, I took along my trusted custom-made 7mm Remington Magnum, which would shoot half-inch groups all day, although I was soon to learn the same couldn't be said of the shooter. I would be the first to hunt Jorge's own ranch, about a two-and-a-half-hour drive from

Hermosillo, which had the advantage of harboring both desert mule deer and Coues deer, although not in the numbers present in some other areas. However, I was told the desert Coues deer would be bigger than their Sierra Madre cousins. I hoped they would also be a little less spooky, for they are probably the wariest animals I have hunted.

My two guides would be Martín Valencia and David López, and I would be hunting from my hind legs and not from the comfort of a vehicle. The ranch was neither the high mountains of the Sierra Madre nor the usual flats of the desert, but rather easy rolling hills. Well, sometimes they were not so easy, covered with the usual desert vegetation of *ocotillo, sibiri, nopal, cholla, pitahaya*, saguaro, and of course the ubiquitous mesquite, palo verde, and ironwood runt trees, all of which have thorns impossible to avoid. I mention the names because they become extremely important when you are trying to locate game in that immense terrain and given the incredible camouflage of the creatures that inhabit it. Many times the only way you can locate the quarry is by following your guide's directions, which go something like: "Go down about twenty yards from the ocotillo on the third ridge and another thirty to the right of the palo verde bush" (which is the devil to find because that ridge is certain to have a million palo verde bushes that are hardly distinguishable from the mesquite, especially at four hundred yards). "There you will see an antler sticking out and part of the left shoulder."

It is virtually impossible to find a solid branch in the desert to use as a rifle rest, so after the experience of hunting in Namibia a few years back, I took the precaution of bringing a tripod to use for the long-range shooting I would invariably be subjected to. Ah, but circumstances always seem to wreak havoc with the best-laid plans of mice and men! For one thing, I soon discovered that tripods offer only a one-point hold, which makes them accurate out to about a hundred and fifty yards, especially on a small and camouflaged animal like a Coues deer; for another thing, they can be slow to set up, especially on uneven terrain, as I also was to find out.

Anyway, quite early in the morning of the first day, Sunday, 11 December, Martín spotted a monster Coues buck three hillsides away, at about eight hundred yards. I, of course, could not see it, no matter how hard I tried or how desperate I became, until David asked me to look

through his spotting scope. Even then I had a hard time pinpointing it because of the reflection of the rising sun, but when I finally made the animal out, I almost fell on my butt. The next order of the day was to find a way to get within a reasonable distance for a shot without being detected.

Extended tripod in one hand and rifle in the other, I followed my guides down one hill and up another, then down again and up the second hill, finally humping downhill a third time to where the buck was. With David in front and Martín slightly behind, we began our final approach, sidehilling the ridge where we had last seen the fine buck. We moved slowly and carefully, and as David stepped in front of a *palo verde*, he signaled frantically for me to move up. The buck, standing on the side of the mountain, his wide, heavy, dark rack shining brightly in the morning sun about 125 yards away, was truly magnificent. Even though I really didn't need them, my immediate reaction was to set up the shooting sticks for a sure shot. But the damned things wouldn't stand steady on the uneven and rocky terrain, and before I could get my rifle set on them, the buck decided it had had enough of the nonsense and in two jumps disappeared behind the ridge. Had David looked at the buck the way he looked at me, it would have undoubtedly dropped dead. As we walked back to the truck I had mixed feelings: Should I blame myself and commit suicide, or toss the shooting sticks into the next canyon?

Believe it or not, the next "desert" morning began with a thundering rainstorm. And I don't mean a heavy drizzle but a regular "frog-drowner" that reminded me of the storms on Costa Rica's Atlantic coast. I got up to go hunting, of course, for there are no rainchecks for stormy days and daily rates were not to be forgotten. After breakfast I noticed that the rain had frozen on the windshield of our little Ford pickup truck, and since the rain wasn't tapering off, all that my guides, the cook, and I could do was wait for the storm to let up and swap lies.

Incredibly, it didn't stop pouring the rest of the day, which kept us from leaving the ranchhouse. This was a good thing, because when I got back to my room, I was in time to move my gear to keep it from getting soaked; the roof had innumerable leaks, and because it is so unusual to have heavy rain in the desert, the slope was not steep enough for the water to drain well.

When my alarm clock went off next morning, it was still raining just as hard and, to make matters worse, a regular gale had started to blow. Naturally, I had forgotten to pack a rainsuit, but rain or shine, I was going hunting.

My two guides and I huddled in the battered pickup and headed for the hills, me hoping that my jacket would hold up against the driving rain. The morning was dark and overcast and the rain kept coming down in blustery sheets. Nothing was going to be moving in that miserable weather—and then, of course, it happened. We hadn't topped the first hill in front of the ranchhouse when David slammed on the brakes and the small vehicle careened to a stop. Binoculars went up in a flash, and the next thing I heard was: "Get out of the car and take him!"

I got out of the cab and chambered a round, but for the life of me I could not see "him." We were facing a huge mesquite-covered hill where it would have been hard to see an elephant, let alone a desert mule deer. Among the whispered orders to "Shoot, shoot!" I understood that I was to move ahead to get around an obstruction that was keeping me from seeing my intended quarry, but that was not the case. When I took two or three steps in front of the vehicle, the buck, which was some one hundred yards away, started to walk. The moment I saw him, the thought crossed my mind to return to the pickup to get a rest on the roof, but then I remembered the Coues deer of the first day. Besides, any big-game hunter worth his salt can put a bullet in an eight-inch circle at a hundred yards, let alone the side of an animal twice that size. I followed the buck's progress as he slipped through openings while my two guides begged me to shoot. I was standing in the driving rain when my muzzle-braked rifle went off with a thunderous roar. I counted only two or three pogo-stick jumps of the big ten-pointer as he hightailed it toward the Arizona border.

As the song goes, "I stood alone in the cold gray dawn, knew I'd lost my morning sun." I cursed myself for not taking the rest on the roof of the cab and played and replayed the scenario to figure out what had gone wrong. Yes, I should have used the rest, which had been only a few feet away, but then again, only hindsight is 100 percent certain. The captain of the Titanic shouldn't have been sailing so fast in an ocean littered with icebergs! All I could do was to get back in the vehicle with my tail tucked between my legs like a whipped dog.

Back at the house, I was so wet that David, the older guide, said I looked like a drowned rat. I didn't know which of those last two words he meant more, and really didn't care to find out. Anyway, it was still raining cats and dogs, I was chilled to the bone, and my rifle needed urgent cleaning—undoubtedly the water-clogged barrel was responsible for my miss. So I decided to call it a catastrophe, I mean a day, and relax during the rest of the evening. Jorge showed up that evening to see how things were going, and when he knocked on my door, I had a hard time opening it and facing him.

When I opened my eyes the next day, it was a splendid morning without a cloud in the sky. With Jorge acting as third guide, we would search for the big Coues deer of the first day. Surely we would find him: My jinxed luck had to end sooner or later.

After a hearty breakfast, we left in style in Jorge's brand-new Chevy full-size double-cabin pickup truck. Upon reaching the chain of hills where we had last seen "my" Coues buck, we quietly slid off the vehicle, careful not to slam the doors. A couple of hours of careful glassing from different vantage points revealed nothing besides a few does and a lone coyote. We did a lot of walking and by 9:30 I was sweating heavily in my layered clothing. I asked Jorge and my two guides to stop so that I could slip out of my long underwear, which required removing my shirt, pants, and boots, a process that would take a few minutes. As my companions moved idly away, I was down almost to my birthday suit when I saw Jorge racing toward me with a wild look on his face and gesturing frantically! All I had time to do was slip back into my unlaced boots, grab my rifle and tripod, and follow Jorge in my T-shirt and shorts. Thirty yards away David and Martín were intently glassing a distant hill across a dry riverbed. Shivering in my extra-light underwear, I set up the tripod for the long shot, my binocular hanging from a tree limb with the rest of my clothing.

"On the far-away ridge, about two hundred fifty yards away, there is a big *palo verde* taller than the others," Jorge said. "The big *bura* is facing us. If you look hard under the left side of the tree, you will see one antler, his muzzle, and his chest. Find him through the scope."

Repeat performance! Through the narrower field of view of my Swarovski I couldn't find the damned thing. After much coaching and cursing, I finally spotted the white face with the black nose. And

through an opening in the devilish maze of sticks and bushes, I could finally see the fifteen-inch-wide chest of my prize. The up-and-down movement of my rifle on the tripod was under control, but the cross hairs swayed in and out on both sides of the target as my right elbow was in the air. I begged Martín, who was nearest me, to let me rest my elbow on his shoulder to steady my aim, but he flatly refused—not with a muzzle-braked 7mm. Holding my breath, I touched the shot off, hoping for the best but fearing the worst.

"You missed," came Jorge's vexed comment. "Shoot again—he didn't move."

I frantically worked the bolt and tried for all I was worth to steady my aim. *Ka-boom!* At the rifle's roar I lost my target as the tripod shifted.

"What's wrong with you? You missed again!" roared Jorge, losing his patience. "Shoot again."

I begged St. Hubertus, patron saint of lousy hunters, for assistance as I worked the bolt for the second time. When I found the buck in my scope for the third try, I swear there was a smirk on the animal's face, perhaps a reaction to my faulty shooting, or at least to my ridiculous attire, running around half-naked in the Mexican desert. I resented the sneer and swore to even the score. As the rifled spoke for the third time, the buck reared, took two or three steps to the right, and tipped over, shot exactly through the middle of the chest. I breathed a sigh of relief as my three assistants raced to the downed buck—while I made a beeline to where my clothes hung from a gnarled mesquite.

Upon reaching my buck, I was elated by the size of the antlers, which I had never seen until then, having relied entirely on my guide's good judgment. Actually, they were quite similar to those of the *bura* I had shot a few years back—maybe a bit thinner but taller, and sporting four deep and even points on each side, plus eye guards.

I partly redeemed myself a couple of days later, connecting on a very even 110-point Boone & Crockett Coues buck on my first shot at about the same distance. Only this time I had a bigger target—he was standing broadside.

However, he was not as big or heavy as the buck I saw on my first day, and my *bura* was certainly nowhere near as big as the five-pointer I had missed a few days back. But as they say, I have their numbers. Already I have made plans with Jorge to return next year to try and

connect on a couple of monsters. I don't know if I will, but I will sure have a lot of fun trying, and maybe St. Hubertus won't be so hard on me next time. All I have to figure out now is how to stabilize my right elbow for those long shots.

My Trophy Room

Chapter 40

I guess I was born a collector. Before entering first grade I remember requesting from my maternal grandmother a large wooden box with a sliding glass top, where I kept a sizable collection of butterflies, moths, and beetles preserved in formaldehyde. After my father gave me my first rifle at age eleven, a Winchester .22 semiautomatic, I began collecting different species of birds and small mammals, whose wings and skins I would dry in the shade and preserve either by injecting formaldehyde in the wings or with a mixture of salt and ashes for the hides. I had no knowledge of taxidermy at the time—there were no taxidermists then in Costa Rica—and of course my priceless possessions fell apart after a while.

When I turned eighteen and obtained a driver's license, my father gave me my first car, a Volkswagen beetle, which allowed me the flexibility to visit Guanacaste province in the northern end of my country, where I collected my first tropical white-tailed deer. There was only one taxidermist in the country at the time, if you could call him that; he literally stuffed my first heads with sawdust after curing the skins with, you guessed it, formaldehyde. They looked stiff and unnatural; the eyes were lifeless, and the ears and nose would wrinkle and warp over the years. He was a little hunch-backed man and for some reason was universally known as "Gasoline." Maybe it was because hunters—and/or hunters' wives—wanted to spray the mounted heads with the fuel and put a match to them!

Before getting married at age twenty-six, I kept my priceless heads in my bedroom at my parents' house, and I still remember the pungent smell of formaldehyde given off by the fresh mounts, which would make my eyes water until they dried up (the mounts, that is).

≈ ≈ ≈

Shortly after getting married, I embarked on my first safari to Mozambique, against my family's vehement objections. As soon as I received my mounted heads, plus two open-mouth African lion skins, I started thinking seriously about building a house in which a sizable trophy room was the first consideration—preferable to other modestly necessary amenities like a kitchen, a bathroom, and a dining room.

Thirty years later, after my trophy room filled up, I tore it down except for three existing walls and doubled its size. I worked closely with an architect and took special care not to let anything distract from the display of my trophies. The ceiling, walls, and ceramic floor are all a light ivory color, and there are no beams, chandeliers, or projecting lights. The room has only two small windows, one of which has opaque shades to keep the light from fading my trophies. I installed a sliding ceiling with a garage-type remote control that I open only when I am entertaining. The room has approximately fifteen hundred square feet and a twelve-foot-high ceiling. There are more than a hundred indirect lights with dimmers embedded in the ceiling to create the right atmosphere.

After seeking inspiration from the rooms depicted in the *Great Hunters* volumes published by Safari Press, I designed, along with my architect, two large dioramas for my full-body mounts, plus four small dioramas for my gamebirds. The room now houses approximately 240 game animals, including a few gamebirds, of approximately 90 species. To tell the truth, it's beginning to look a bit crowded and there is a limit to how much I can enlarge it again (about eight feet on its south end), but at least the trophies now look better and don't smell of formaldehyde! See the photo section of this book for pictures of my trophy room.

SAFARI PRESS

SAFARI PRESS